Sybil Marshall was only nineteen when at the end of these memoirs she left the fen, in the years of the agricultural depression, to take up her first job as an unqualified, uncertificated teacher. Afterwards, she became trained, and qualified at the age of thirty-five. She won an Extra-Mural Board Bursary to Cambridge University and thereby achieved her ambition to read English there, going up to New Hall when she was forty-eight. Her first book, *An Experiment in Education* (1963), secured for her an international reputation as an educationist. She is known to thousands of primary teachers and literally millions of children who enjoyed 'Picture Box' on television, which she created and for which she supplied the Teacher's Notes. *A Pride of Tigers* is her third book about the fens she loves so much, and to which she has now returned.

A PRIDE OF TIGERS

Sybil Marshall was born in 1913 in one of the lowest and most isolated of the black fens in what was then Huntingdonshire. All her antecedents, except one, can be traced to within a few miles of Ramsey, back at least to the beginning of the 18th century. Sybil can claim to be a genuine fen tiger, one of the few still left. She writes about her clannish, warm, hospitable, gifted and laughter-loving family, her 'kin', and the friends and neighbours who shared a life-style dictated by the environment and the isolation. Work, dress, food, fashions, customs — everything from a mouth-watering recipe for onion dumplings to the advent of the wireless is recorded.

Books by Sybil Marshall
Published by The House of Ulverscroft:

A NEST OF MAGPIES

SYBIL MARSHALL

A PRIDE
OF TIGERS

A FEN FAMILY AND ITS FORTUNES

Complete and Unabridged

CHARNWOOD
Leicester

First published in Great Britain in 1992 by
The Boydell Press
Suffolk

First Charnwood Edition
published 2001
by arrangement with
Boydell & Brewer Limited
Suffolk

British Library CIP Data

Marshall, Sybil, *1913 –*
    A pride of tigers: A fen family and its fortunes
    —Large print ed.—
    Charnwood library series
    1. Marshall, Sybil, *1913–*
    2. Fens—England 3. Large type books
    4. Fens, The (England)—Social life and customs
    5. Fens, The (England)—Biography
    I. Title
    942.6′54′082′092

    ISBN 0–7089–9235–8

Published by
F. A. Thorpe (Publishing)
Anstey, Leicestershire

Set by Words & Graphics Ltd.
Anstey, Leicestershire
Printed and bound in Great Britain by
T. J. International Ltd., Padstow, Cornwall

This book is printed on acid-free paper

FOR
my family, past and present
FOR
my Edwards and Papworth kin
AND FOR
those dear friends of my childhood
and schooldays
who are still alive and have
so happily agreed to let me use their
real names
in the telling of this story:
Marjorie Whitwell, neé Allpress
Joyce Longland, neé Summers
Jessica Pack, neé Pickard
Christiana Spring, neé Wilmer
Ellen Cooper, neé Canham
and dear 'Mu',
Mrs Juno Muriel Edwards,
who brought song into my life.

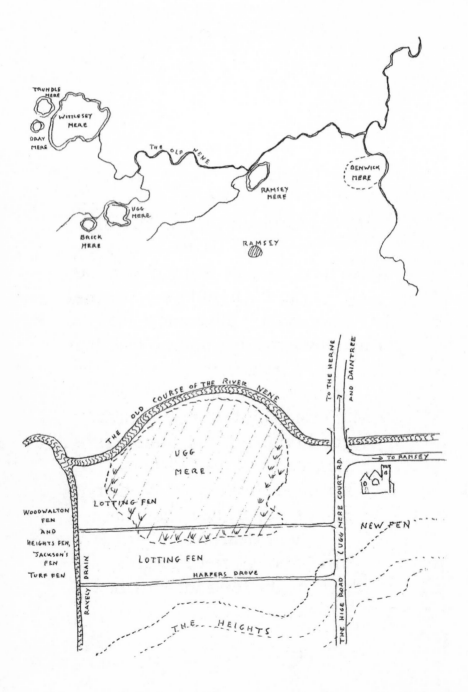

Author's Foreword

This book is quite different from what I intended when I began it. It had been suggested that I write a 'self portrait of the fen' in which I was born before the outbreak of the Great War in 1914. I did not expect any difficulty in finding material, for I knew that my old friends still living would willingly and happily supply me with detail to corroborate my own experience, as well as a lot that I, personally, did not know or remember. This they have done, in measure overflowing, for the fen breeds good talkers and wonderful raconteurs. It is all there ready and waiting, for me to get it on to paper.

So how, and why, did I get side-tracked into writing something that has turned out to be almost a personal memoir?

I had to start somewhere. Both my grandfathers' families can be traced back to the Ramsey area long before my particular fen was habitable, my paternal great-grandfather, being one of the very first to buy land and build within the confines of the half-drained Lotting Fen. So why not start with them?

Then one day, I was reading (yet again) the *Thanksgiving* of Thomas Traherne, a man-of-God who lived and wrote in the seventeenth century. There is one among them in which he gives thanks for being himself, that he is

A living Inhabitant
Of the Great World
And the centre of it.

Well, of course! Is not every one of us the centre of his own world! Where should I start but with myself, and then work backwards?

Once I had put pen to paper, it seemed that I was somehow coerced into supplying what several other readers had asked for . . . more about myself and my immediate family. All the 'Tiger-Talk' that my dear old friends have supplied has got crowded out of this volume; but I have already started on another which they shall have to themselves, more or less, in their own voices. I just hope, as Old Henry would have said, that I am 'spore' to complete it.

Gravestones do not stand long in St Mary's churchyard, where most of my family lie buried. The soft peat simply refuse to hold gravestones up for more than a few years. But who cares about what happens to the cold hard, heavy headstones? It is 'the loving memory' engraved on so many of them that matters, and which is the real memorial.

It has been my joy, as well as my duty, to commit much of that loving memory to paper in this book; and as an old gnomic saying has it,

Monuments made of paper last the longest.
Ely, 1992

1

The Awakening

I remember being in my cradle.

If you do not believe me, you will not be the first. I made the mistake of telling Grandmother so, one day when I was about seven.

Grandmother was Dad's mother, and I her youngest but one grandchild; but between us there was a great gulf fixed, full of all sorts of problems besides that of age.

She was, at the time of my revelation to her about my earliest memory, a formidable old lady, well over seventy.

She was, as she always had been, a Wesleyan Methodist of strict and uncompromising character, and a stickler for The Truth. (Please excuse the capital letters. They carry with them the emphasis that Grandmother's presence and mien always impressed upon me when I was alone with her, which wasn't very often.)

Because of her dedication to The Truth, all fiction was to her Abomination. Into the category of fiction she lumped everything from the novels of Mrs Henry Wood (which she Suspected her married daughters of reading behind her back) to the innocent prattling of children whom she Suspected of Romancing.

If a spoken word was not The Truth, then it was a Lie. There was no half-way house between.

1

Her own truths were those that were manifestly unassailable, such as the Existence of God, the rules laid down by His Word as written in The Bible, and Life after Death (this last confirmed because of the prevalence of departed spirits she claimed to have encountered personally as ghosts or apparitions).

My memory of being in my cradle could not be accepted as The Truth. Therefore it must be A Lie.

Grandmother told me what happened to children who told Lies. When they died, as they assuredly would in the course of time, they Fell into the Bottomless Pit filled with Flames of Fire, and there they Burned Everlastingly until The Day of Judgement, when The Lord would Come Again and separate The Good from The Evil. Such children as I, being Evil, would be sent forthwith to their Eternal Abode in HELL.

As I say, there were no half-measures about Grandmother! She sat, large and upright in her high-backed chair, her knitting-needles clicking against the mutton-bone sheath tucked into her waistband, never missing their rhythm although her rather small, deepset eyes under her mob-cap never for an instant wavered from their hold upon my own.

Even while trembling inwardly at the prospect of my doom as she pronounced it, I could not help thrilling to the sound and grandeur of the majestic words she was uttering. I had already become addicted to words and relished them even as I writhed in my dilemma. And I was in a dilemma, because I knew very well that I had not told any lie at all — but I could hardly expect God to believe me when He had Grandmother's word against mine. *Nobody* contradicted Grandmother. Later on, of course, I read *Jane Eyre*, and how I sympathised with Jane when she was placed in exactly the same situation! But I did not have at my disposal even the one escape route that Jane saw before her — that she must keep in good health, and not die. I was not in good health, and it seemed that my demise was already noted as a Forthcoming Event.

Until we moved from the house where I was born, in Lotting Fen, to the house we now lived in on the farm in New Fen, I had been as fat, tunky and healthy a toddler as ever the fen had produced; but I had 'gone into a decline' as our female neighbours put it, and had turned into a thin, pale, weak and weary child too feeble to go to school, too listless to play, and who, to put it bluntly, was nothing but a grizzling little misery to everybody. Looking back, it seems to me that I was deficient in everything except understanding but as, at seven, I still had not been to school, most folks seemed to think I was a bit short in that department, too. In consequence, they never bothered to mince their words about me in my presence.

I was used to hearing Grandmother, Aunt Harriet, and such of our female neighbours as took it upon themselves to act as Job's Comforters to my despairing mother, telling her that she could not expect to 'rear' me beyond the age of seven, and that now that I had passed my seventh birthday, she must expect to 'lose' me soon. They whispered, behind hands held to their mouths to prevent Mam from lip-reading (because she had been deaf from childhood), the dreaded word 'consumption', which had in those days the same sort of thrill of horror as 'Aids' has now. They took it for granted that a child with the Hand of Death already laid upon her would not comprehend their words.

I understood quite well all that Grandmother said, and her prediction of my Impending Fate had me worried, in addition to being weak and wan and above all, weary. She frightened me. I think I must have confided this to Dad, who stood out like a safe and sunny harbour in my weary waste of listlessness, because somewhere in a shadowy corner of my memory-box is the sound of my own voice saying earnestly to him, 'It ain't them flames as I'm frit of. It's the falling for ever and ever amen.'

Just to be with Dad was comfort enough. Like all the rest of Granmother's children, he had been brought up a Wesleyan Methodist, and was a staunch pillar of our local chapel; but he was not of the same variety of believers as Grandmother and Aunt Harriet. The rantings of our more pessimistic local preachers were more inclined to make him laugh than to quake. He looked beyond the pulpit in which they stood to the wall behind it, where, framed by an ugly scroll, were the words GOD IS LOVE.

I am sure that Dad would have declared it nonsense to believe that such a god would have wanted anybody *scared* to death — and I hope he said so, though I wonder. Even he was very

4

much in awe of Grandmother.

He was, though, very concerned about the physical welfare of his own 'little sweetling' — too much so, I guess, to rush out to meet more trouble by torturing himself about the eventual destination of my immortal soul.

Comforted I may have been, but I was not reassured. I could not but believe myself in danger, on the grounds that I was now seven years old.

Our neighbours — or, at any rate, the female half of them, talked over my head in a way they believed to be far above the level of my understanding. It was their unalterable belief that this loving God of theirs had arranged for human life to be meted out in parcels of seven years. They were convinced that he had allotted to me only one seven-year life span. I heard them say this so many times that I was more or less forced to believe it.

Now my seven years was up. Besides, Grandmother was never wrong.

All the same . . . I had reached the age at which modern child psychologists agree that a child reaches 'the age of reason'. Something began to tell me that Grandmother's logic must be at fault here and there. How, I asked myself, could I (or anybody else, for that matter) manage to reach 'the end of the road' while travelling by a route that had no end, or finish up in Hell via a pit that had no bottom to it? Why were the flames of Hell any worse than those of the Bottomless Pit? And if one fell *for ever and ever* down the pit, when and where did Eternity start? It didn't make sense — though I was, of course, only too well acquainted with the indubitable fact that 'with God, nothing is impossible'. Well, if that was so, God didn't have to cut off my little life just because I'd used up one of His seven-year parcels, did He? In spite of Grandmother, there was still some hope left.

Mam, never at her best with Dad's family or Grandmother's circle, put her faith in my recovery more in our local doctor than in God. Not, perhaps, in this particular instance, a very wise choice.

My mother was a very complex character, a sort of living paradox; but she was, like all the rest of us, the product of nature shaped by experience. She was, at the time of my crisis, coming to her fortieth birthday, very handsome, but very deaf. Dad's transmogrification from labourer to farmer had provided her with status and the means to indulge her rather extravagant ideas in dress, and housekeeping, and the like. She made the most of it, which set a barrier between her and a lot of the other fen women — made worse by her deafness, because, like most deaf people, she continually 'heard' disparaging remarks that were, in fact, never uttered. Her defence was a sharp tongue, which grew worse as she reached old age. It caused us all a good deal of suffering later, but that is part of another story. At the time I am dealing with, it was only a weapon of defence and not needed for attack.

On the other hand, she radiated womanly charm, overflowed with kindness and sympathy, possessed a wealth of philosophical stoicism but was still easily embarrassed. She could be belligerent, like a ruffled old hen, even while displaying a diffidence that signalled that if she lost one more feather she would retire squawking and run for the shelter of Dad's presence. Best of all was her rumbustious sense of humour and her gift of terse and witty comments. (They never failed to delight Dad, and have become aphorisms to the rest of us. No doubt some of them, in context, will surface as I ramble on.)

She was, of course, her father's daughter, which may account for a lot. She was also what a sad and difficult childhood had made her, to say nothing of other events that happened in her teens and perhaps accounted for the vague air of regret and of criticism that we were aware of, but didn't understand. She seemed to us, as to others who saw only the 'outside' face of her, to be bouncing through life in an enviable style of ease, plenty, happiness and success, able to turn on the charm as simply and as rapidly as one wrong word could turn it off again.

Other women (particularly Grandmother and her chapel circle) hated Mam's guts as much as they envied her — yet she could subdue even them with her charm. They thought her 'bold' and 'too forward' (especially in the presence of the opposite sex) to the point of 'being indecent'. Yet that very boldness was in reality a defence against her own timidity and diffidence.

Dad, naturally, was the one who bore the brunt of her weathercock moods, but he understood her better than we ever did. He could sail serenely round the rocks we cut ourselves to pieces on, usually ending any argument with a quip that found her funny bone and produced a rejoinder from her that restored the situation and left us all in a glow of relieved amusement.

Only when some sort of external tragedy struck did Dad's strategy fail. Then she would sulk till we were all half-mad with misery. The loss of the submarine. Thetis plunged us all into a despairing gloom as deep as the Thetis lay; the destruction of the R101 and the Hindenburg scorched and shrivelled us because while she grieved, Mam could be civil to nobody. She became a most powerful and extraordinary character in the course of time, creating a love-hate relationship with most of us, even with Dad; but it is with her concealed diffidence that I am concerned at the moment — the difference between the outwardly confident fine woman, and the diffident, embarrassed, easily put down girl inside her. To me, it was literally a matter of life and death.

I have no option but to break into my own story to explain the situation of 'The Doctor' at that time in a community as remote and scattered as ours.

Our GP was centred in Ramsey, around which his practice extended over a radius of about seven miles of mostly sparsely-populated fens. When he had first taken over the practice, he made his journeys on horseback, though he had graduated to a car by the time I was seven, I think. Neither horse nor car was of much good to him in the depths of the fens, so he rode or drove as far as he could, tied his horse to a gate, and proceeded on foot, carrying his black bag, which children were told contained the babies he 'delivered'. Walking down the 'sluddy' path on the edge of a dyke was a precarious business even in daylight. In the dark, it was nothing short of an ordeal, especially to a man not born and bred to it. Before electric torches came in, a doctor needed urgently at the bottom of a drove would be met at the top of it by somebody with a flickering storm lantern, but walking in the uncertain light of a storm-lantern carried by somebody else is an art in its own right! In high summer, particularly if it was a hot one, the journey was made pretty difficult by the clouds of purply-grey dust that rose in a cloud at every step and stuck to sweaty skin or drifted into eyes already half-closed to avoid the attention of a swarm of mosquitoes.

Naturally, these journeys took the doctor a long time, and had to be paid for. In consequence, he was never sent for in time to do much for his patient. It was usually left too late before the hardpressed family sent somebody on foot (or on a cycle, now and then) to fetch him: and when they got to his door, as likely as not it would only be to find that he had already gone five miles in the opposite direction.

Even so, life is precious and there were times when he could be of use.

Cancer has always been prevalent in the fens. In those days, there was little that could be done for it once it was diagnosed, so it was not much good fetching the doctor. The panacea was 'lodmun' (laudenum), taken in larger and larger doses as the pain increased. Once upon a time, it had been home-distilled from the white poppy which grew there but in Mam's young day it was available across the chemist's or even the grocer's counter. When this source of supply was cut off, suffering was increased to little purpose. In spite of the dependence on 'lodmun', there were times when it was too much for the family to see a loved one in such awful pain, and do nothing. There was always hope that the doctor could help, or perform some sort of a miracle. Of course when fetched out to some such hopeless case, it was usually to 'do something to ease the pain', and make sure it never returned again. Gratitude for such acts of mercy helped to build the mystique that surrounded a country doctor.

His bill followed later. If the patient had rallied, the shock of it set him (or her) back again. If the patient had died, the spouse and/or family had already had to face the cost of a funeral. They would beg for time to pay, which was usually granted, till the doctor was needed again — and again — and again, and the debt grew to impossible proportions. Our doctor had his own system about such debts. He had to live, after all, and one cannot hold it against him that when he realised that there was no hope whatsoever of getting money, he offered instead to accept the grandfather clock, or the old pewter tobacco pot that 'Grandad hadn't got no more use for, never' in settlement. I have heard that when one particular doctor died, his house was stuffed to capacity with antiques, most of them obtained that way.

Grammam, Mam's mother, started 'ailing' when Mam was in her teens. Mam herself had not been able to 'go out to service' like other girls, because she suffered from 'green sickness' — probably acute anaemia brought on by near starvation, for the family were poorer than the proverbial church mice — and the everlasting ear-ache which left her so deaf. As Grandad Rattles (Mam's father) wouldn't work, and Mam couldn't, Grammam had to. She went out washing and took in washing, as well as doing any sort of seasonal work in the fields, such as setting potatoes in spring or 'tater-picking' in autumn. She used to say that if only she could see ten shillings a week coming in, she'd feel like a queen. Sometimes, though, Grandad's pride got the better of him, and he forebad her to go to work in the fields where any of his cronies might see her earning the few shillings he was consuming in the pub. His pride had its limits, after all!

Poor Grammam had not been bred to such a life, but she rarely grumbled. She suffered in silence, and her children suffered with her. Mam was the only one left at home when the load of work and starvation diet at last broke Grammam's health, so it was she who bore the brunt of her mother's distress and her father's temper, at finding his ease and comfort disturbed by illness. Grammam had chronic bronchitis, together with dreadful indigestion, for which she swallowed lead shot, as she said, 'to keep her lights from rising.' Some days, she complained of terrible pain 'across her middle' and in those days she lay down on the old sofa as soon as Rattles had gone out, and lay there writhing in agony, with her eye on the clock. This was not to watch the time till Mam could administer the next few drops of 'lodmun', but to make sure she was up and about again before her husband came back from what he called 'work'. As soon as the time for his return drew near, she would get up, feed the pig and the fowls, and then remove her 'hessen-eppen' (hessian apron). After a good wash she would brush her long and jet-black hair, do it into a neat bun, and don her starched white 'afternoon' apron, bibbed and belted like that of a nurse. By the time her scallawag man came in, his supper would be cooking in the pot on the pothook over the peat fire on the hearth. There was always enough for him, though sometimes none for Mam or her mother. She took good care not to let him know she had been, or still was, in pain.

But some days, even her stoicism gave way, and she sent Mam to find somebody to get a message to the doctor. He would come, perhaps next day, in spite of knowing that from this particular household his chances of getting anything in payment was nil. They had no antiques!

His very presence, however, often lifted the patient's dread and fear. He did good just by being willing to call. Grammam's spirits would rally, and for a time things would be a bit better — until the day he called unasked to bring his bill. Then poor Mam had to endure the embarrassment of watching the distress and misery of her beloved mother as she confessed that she couldn't pay him, and begged for time 'till she could get out to work again'. Worse still was when Grandad found the bill, or had to be told about it. Then he would stamp and rage at both of them for getting 'that bee-ing ol' 'oss-doctor' when there was nothing the matter with anybody.

Such scenes on Mam's memory were indelible. For the rest of her life, she never behaved normally when confronted by a doctor. Part of it was because of the mystique which still surrounds any medical man to this day; part was because of his exalted professional status: part was embarrassment at the memory of bills that were never paid: and part to her fear of not hearing what he said, or hearing it wrong. In aggregate, it produced in this usually proud and confident woman a sort of simpering diffidence that when I was grown-up made me, too, squirm with embarrassment.

It was unfortunate for both of us that when I was in need of a medical miracle, the doctor in question was still the same one who had attended her poverty-stricken home twenty-five years earlier. Mam had been 'Mis Will 'en' for nineteen years, and both she and the doctor had changed a great deal. The 'green-sick' girl was now the wife of a farmer, strikingly handsome, well and tastefully dressed, and in no need of fearing the arrival of a bill for his service. He, on the other hand, was growing old and testy. He

13

now drove a car instead of a horse and trap, and in any case we lived on the high-road, and not down a drove. He did not expect to turn out to visit a mere child. Children could be taken to see him in his surgery in Ramsey.

Nothing in Mam's changed circumstances was enough to break down her diffidence towards him. So to Ramsey I was taken for a consultation.

Ramsey was a fairish way to go — four miles or so, or even a bit more, according to whereabouts in the fen you lived. There were trains from St Mary's station three or four times a day, but that wasn't a lot of use if none of them happened to coincide with surgery hours. (From our house in New Fen, it was only one mile to the station; from Lotting Fen, it would have been two, one of them up an unmade drove.) Then at the Ramsey end, the doctor's surgery was well over half a mile from the station. So a trip to see the doctor by train involved (even from New Fen) a walk of three miles or more, and a long wait somewhere for the surgery to open. The hale and hearty thought nothing of such a bit of a walk, of course — but then, the hale and hearty didn't need a doctor. I did!

I had reached a state of such weakness that my legs would not carry me more than a hundred yards at a time, and the walk to the station became a nightmare to me. I was too big for Mam to carry more than a few yards, and when she put me down, I stumbled on for a little way, and then sat down on the side of the road for 'a rest'. (Mam had much in common with her idol

14

Queen Alexandra, being beautiful, very deaf, and always late for everything.) So while I grizzled on the verge, Mam urged impatiently from the road ten yards or so farther on, scanning the horizon for the plume of smoke that would tell her we had missed the train again.

The year was 1921, one of the hottest and driest on record, which didn't help me much. In the end, Dad decided that he would have to drive us to the evening surgery in the 'light' cart, with Ol' Short between the shafts.

As I have previously hinted, I was already in love with words. They tell me that from the moment I began to utter at all, I picked up words with the greatest of ease, especially long words or phrases that had any sort of rhythmical quality, so that I trotted about chanting 'Peterborough Confedral': 'Horrocks's Calico': 'Capital Redemption': 'Allgloriousabove' and the like. Anything in verse or rhythm had me hooked. But although I was so fond of words, I had the same capacity as every other child for misunderstanding them and misinterpreting them. In my state of sickness, this was to cause yet another problem. The constant predictions of our neighbours that Mam must expect to 'lose' me before long convinced me that I was in danger of being mislaid in some strange place where I should eventually die, undiscovered till too late. Naturally, I took my own precautions to avoid such a mishap by gathering into my hand a large fold of Mam's skirt, and refusing to let go — especially once inside the doctor's surgery. Mam, diffident as always because of her deafness, and in awe of the man who held my life in his hands, sat, self-conscious and simpering, on the patient's chair, while the doctor with the funny face, the funny smell, the funny gadgets hanging round his neck and the outlandish name commanded me to step forward towards him. I resisted, tightening my hold on Mam's skirt. She pushed, and the doctor, whose time was precious and whose patience was short, pulled. My strength became the strength of ten, and I held on — till Mam was forced to rise and approach the august being with me (angry at my stupid behaviour, and highly embarrassed into the bargain). But it had unexpected results. Close to him, she could better observe his examination of me, *and* hear the questions he put to us both. As she told Dad on our way home, she just couldn't make it all out. On about the third such occasion, when the doctor had asked her abruptly if my ear-ache had got better or worse, and had peered through yet another gadget into my ears, she plucked up courage to ask him why was he so concerned about them.

Because that was what he was treating me for, wasn't it?

No, said Mam. It was because of my general debility. (I loved that! General Debility — and I'd got it, or him! Something or somebody new to roll off my tongue and to make up stories about — till I remembered Grandmother's horrible warnings about 'lies', and their conse-quences in the Bottomless Pit.)

Dr Llewllyn consulted his records. Consider-ing the plethora of 'Etherdses' in his scattered

16

practice, perhaps he may be forgiven for treating the wrong young Etherds for the wrong complaint: but he took the huff, as if it were all our fault that he'd been wasting our time and his. Changing course hastily, he decided that it was my diet that was at fault (no doubt hoping to cast the blame on Mam. He was, perhaps, more correct than he knew, because for weeks I had not been persuaded to eat enough to keep a kitten alive).

From now on, he said, I was to have nothing that would cause 'acid in the stomach'. (At least, that's what Mam made of it, and told anybody who'd listen.) According to Mam, though it seems a bit queer, this amounted to a complete ban on fresh fruit and green vegetables. I can't say the prospect of going without cabbage made me feel much worse than I already did, but it was strawberry season and Mam had been tempting me in the last day or two with a stawberry cut up between layers of very thin bread and butter. (I still eat my strawberries that way in preference to any other) And I was aggrieved at the thought of not being allowed to try the 'barley-harvester' apples, because I had noticed that on the loaded tree in the garden, the apples were already beginning to show red streaks on their greeny-yellow sides. The year before, I had helped myself to them whenever I wanted, and loved their crisp, sour, tangy taste. I certainly didn't want them then and there, but you know what any sort of prohibition does, especially with regard to food.

So the days and weeks went by, and I ate

nothing (except for a spoonful of Grandmother's arrowroot now and then); and it did look as if the prophets of doom were going to be proved right, and that I was going to be permanently 'lost'.

Enter Aunt Lizzie.

Now I have to declare that in all honesty I cannot claim to remember at first hand what I am about to relate, though a few fragments remain with me like beads from a broken necklace. The string upon which I am now able to reassemble them was provided by both Mam and Dad, separately, in their old age. They were both good talkers, and I a trained listener. Dad had obviously reached the conclusion that I was old and experienced enough to be given the keys of cupboards in which family skeletons lay hidden.

Mam, on the other hand, displayed her usual two-sided-ness, because on any matters concerning sex this paradoxical streak in her nature was at its most pronounced. She seemed till her dying day to have a hang-up about sex, while at the same time being avid for details about other people's sexual activities. She had obviously made up her mind that I was to be kept as innocent as the driven snow — which was a bit of a paradox in itself, seeing that by the time I heard Mam's unedited version of the story, I had been married and divorced, and had produced one living child, one still-born one, and had mis-carried with a third. All this Mam chose to ignore, in order to keep me 'pure'.

I must intrude one example. When the *Lady*

Chatterley trial was in full swing, Mam could hardly wait for the next day's account in *The Daily Mail*. What she read there made her want to read the book itself. One day when Lois was visiting us, Mam enlisted her help to obtain a copy — making a great to-do of whispering her request while I was out of the room. Lois was genuinely puzzled by the pantomime, and asked innocently what the need for such secrecy was.

'I shall read it,' Mam said, 'but I shan't let Sybil. From what I can see of it in the paper, it's hardly fit for her.'

Lois and I, who had both read the silly, repetitive book years before, got a lot of fun out of the incident, especially on the day Lois smuggled it in while I stood watching through a crack in the door, both of us, nearly suffocating with suppressed mirth. Sadly, we never found out what Mam made of it. She was not what one could call 'a reader'. We, on the other hand, took after Dad in regarding print as a sort of fourth member of the Holy Trinity. Mam was 'agin' print in general, because Dad 'always had his nose in a book' and 'read himself silly'. She was jealous of it because it took Dad's attention from her — and perhaps he did overdo it a bit. He read anything and everything that fell into his hands, and spent whatever few shillings he ever expended on himself at the second-hand bookstall on Peterborough Market Hill. If he ran out of fresh reading, he started back again on our set of Dickens, lingering long over *Our Mutual Friend*, which was his great favourite. Next would come the works of W. W. Jacobs, and

Mark Twain. *Huckleberry Finn* was never out of reach of his hand, whatever else he might be reading, and by the time I was ten I knew great chunks of it off by heart, because he couldn't bear not to be sharing it with somebody. We quoted Huck to each other so often that Mam took umbrage, not recognising it for what it was, and, I think, suspecting it to be some sort of a secret code we had invented to exclude her from our conversations.

I shall now have to apologise for digressing, and allowing my pen to lead me on a detour — 'round by Will's Mother's'. I'm afraid it is likely to do so all the time. My pen runneth where it listeth, taking me with it. It is a bit like being in the wide wastes of the fen on a foggy night, not quite knowing where you are, or where you want to go next. My inconsequential memories are all mammygagged together like the layers of a trifle that hasn't quite set. 'Fools' grub', as the old fen men designated such victuals. 'Fools' grub — too thick to drink and not thick enough t'eat.'

As I said, into the drama of my duel with death, Aunt Lizzie appeared on stage — a character whose entrance must, I fear, be prolonged, and the scene set for her role in the action yet to come.

We must return to Grandmother, who lived, as she believed, strictly according to the Ten Commandments.

Take the second of them, for instance, from which she appeared to derive a two-fold satisfaction. It admonishes against the worship of any other god but Jehovah, and then goes on *'for I, the Lord thy God, am a jealous God, visiting the sins of the fathers upon the children, unto the third and fourth generation of them that hate me, and showing mercy unto thousands of them that love me, and keep my commandments'*.

How comforting to know that one was among The Thousands (surely a bit selective?) who had only to hold out an apron to catch the promised shower of blessings! And what joy to feel free to follow in condemnation of the offspring of the wicked! Even unto the third and fourth generation!

In the comfort of such smug rectitude, they could always find a sinner, like the ram caught in the thicket, as a sacrifice to their stinging tongues. It gave them enormous pleasure to castigate the sinner unless, like Potter Proud, for instance, he was prepared to stand before them in the pulpit and publicly declare both his wickedness and his repentance.

The offspring of an unrepentant were condemned, it seemed, whether or not they ever sinned, or, having sinned, repented.

Now this was a bit hard on me, because the Sinner in our midst was my Grandad 'Rattles'. I was only two generations down from him. Therefore I was already doomed and my fate sealed. The Hand of God was against me. Was I not the granddaughter of that irreligious and 'blastpheemious' old rapscallion who lacked all decency, who was always verging upon crime as well as being steeped in sin, and who showed not a hair's breadth of repentance?

21

His very existence was a disgrace to our community, and to Grandmother, he was Anathema.

It was gall and wormwood to her and to her eldest daughter, Aunt Harriet, that having reached the sensible age of thirty, their splendid, god-fearing 'Bill' should have fallen for 'a bit of a schoolgal' who into the bargain happened to be of that old devil's brood.

Moreover, they were thwarted. They could blister their tongues repeating among their friends the shortcomings of Rattles himself, but now that she was Dad's wife, Mam's shortcomings could only be discussed in private. She was a protected species. Not so, however, was her sister Lizzie, younger than Kate by only thirteen months. She was fair game for all bitter and/or slanderous tongues. 'Bad would become of her', they all agreed.

I only know, of course, what I have been told of her childhood and youth, but it all tallies with what I remember at first hand about her.

She had been an 'owdacious' child, as robust and healthy as Mam had been ailing, and always 'too forrard' for her age. She had inherited a far greater slice of her father's rebelliousness, as well as his charm, than Mam had. As she grew up, the difference between the two sisters became more marked. Mam was pretty, but Aunt Lizzie was beautiful, exquisite in form, face, and feature. Mam, already deaf, was shy, diffident and decorous. Aunt Lizzie was extravagant, bold and fun-loving.

Worst of all, in the eyes of such as

Grandmother, she simply oozed sex-appeal. She could have supplied all Grandmother's and her friends' repressed and dun-coloured daughters with what they lacked without noticing it, the hussy! They resented this quality in her, much as they disapproved of it. Vitality such as Mam had never had warmed the air around her. Both girls had inherited Grammam's velvet brown eyes, but though Mam's turned to a glowing red with temper, they were candles to the sun compared to Aunt Lizzie's brilliance. Hers could be as soft and mellow as the harvest moon rising or as twinkingly innocent as the Milky Way; but let a man come into their orbit, and they exploded into stars of mischief like a firework, or sent roguish arrows sidelong from under lowered lids to transfix him where he stood. No man with his full share of male hormones was a match for them, and in pure innocence, though 'just for devilment' she felled them all, from the itinerant tramp at the door to the six-foot-four, dog-collared Wesleyan Minister who when on a round of visits lost his cool and chased her round the table, begging for a kiss.

She could no more help her effect on men than a fire can stop throwing out heat. It was agreed that by the time she was seventeen she was a danger to be feared by all respectable mothers of marriageable sons. It is said that one of Ramsey's wealthiest farmers, verging on the status of the landed gentry, had a son of whom he was very proud. The son caught sight of Aunt Lizzie at Ramsey Fair. So smitten was he that his infuriated father had to pack him off to Canada to prevent the wreck of his social aspirations — but a breath of scandal fans flames of gossip into roaring, destructive infernos. The boy's life was ruined, his father's heart broken, and Aunt Lizzie's reputation damaged, without fault on anybody's part.

She left home soon after this incident, and sought refuge in 'good service'. She went north to a place too far away, and too costly, for her to come home often.

(She must have been home, though, on that Sunday evening when she and Mam went to church and encountered Dad. It was fourteen years since he had watched Mam, aged seven, being christened, and decided she was the only girl for him. If he had not already been so fixed in his mind, I wonder if it might not have been Lizzle instead of Kate who married him at Christmas the same year. As it was, he and Lizzie were always the best of friends, and Dad championed her even when his conscience sometimes rebelled against her unconventional behaviour.)

She was as quick-witted as she was beautiful, and had learned a lot from mixing with 'her betters'. As parlourmaid in a wealthy household, she had been taught refinement as well as the way things were done in higher social circles. She spoke well, knew how to deport herself in company, and stretched her meagre means to indulge an already excellent taste in clothes. The mean old women in the fen dubbed her as 'that dink-me-doll hussy, putting on airs like a lady': but to anyone who did not know her background, she must have been 'that elegant young lady with the roguish eye'.

She had lost nothing of her all-conquering charm. Refinement had only widened its range. What followed is tragedy or triumph, according to which way you look at it.

She couldn't be happy, so far away, because like Mam she was always afraid that in one of his rages, her father would harm Grammam. She changed her job only to be where she could get home and back in a day. The job was as a general maid in the household of a young, aristocratic doctor just setting up a practice in a market town not too far away. There must, I feel sure, have been a more mature abigail as general housekeeper, for the proprieties would have to be observed to the letter if the doctor was going to get the sort of patients he wanted.

But whoever the housekeeper was, she failed utterly to prevent the young medic from falling hopelessly in love with his so-beautiful, so elegant, so tender, so frolicsome, so roguish young beggarmaid: and, of course, she with him.

They must both have known from the very beginning that there was not a vestige of hope for them, that their love for each other was no more than a mirage of what might have been if circumstances has been different. That knowledge did not prevent them from making the most of the situation while it lasted.

Aunt Lizzie's presence in the town had set a lot of other young hearts beating among the men more nearly of her own station in life, or even a bit above it. She could have taken her pick from among tradesmen, artisans and small farmers, and the rivalry among these for even a smile from her served as a useful smoke-screen for a while.

Then the housekeeper left. She probably observed, or at least suspected the truth. Aunt Lizzie became the doctor's 'housekeeper', but malicious tongues began to wag. What could they do? There was simply no way they could continue to live *a deux* without placing his professional career in jeopardy.

I do not know, and shall now never find out, whether the decision to make it a *menage-à-trois* was taken with the full knowledge and consent of the third person involved, or whether in their distress the lovers simply used him. What happened was that Aunt Lizzie exercised her choice among her other swains, married him and imported him in apparent utter respectability into the doctor's household.

The man she chose (thereafter one of my two Uncle Bills) was a very small, exceedingly neat and well-spoken young man who had served a full seven-year apprenticeship as a cabinet maker, and was a very good craftsman. He was highly intelligent, but bitter because his father had not allowed him to take up the scholarship he had won as a child. In these more egalitarian days, he would, I think, have probably become a professor of sociology or politics. As it was, he had educated himself, with somewhat dire consequences. He had taken great care with his diction and vocabulary, resulting in a degree of pomposity that drove everybody into a state of

26

frenzy and, of course, set up the hackles (we always said 'ickles') of Aunt Lizzie's fen connections. Rattles absolutely detested him, and always referred to him as 'the little cock-ant'. (He was married to Aunt Lizzie for well over fifty years, and I knew him extremely well. He was proud of me and loved me, and I have reason to be grateful to him; but I never *liked* him. It is all too possible to love someone without liking what the person is or does. It is my considered opinion that Uncle Bill knew perfectly well what the situation was, whether or not the doctor laid all the cards on the table and offered him a deal. I think it suited his prospects, his purse and his politics to become a willing cuckold.)

The three principals, at any rate, all seem to have been satisfied, and for some time (running into years) perfectly happy with the arrangement. If Mam and Dad knew what was going on, they kept the truth from Dad's family, who could hardly cast aspersions on a woman, however beautiful, who had her own lawful wedded husband living with her at her place of work.

So the great love-affair still continued, until, as always, Fate interfered. Fate must be of a very jealous nature — she rarely leaves a truly happy situation alone for long.

The doctor's titled-lady mother became a widow, and decided that it would be sensible for her to go and live with her bachelor son, and 'keep house' for him, She 'sussed' out the true situation before she had been there a week, and Aunt Lizzie, with her lawful wedded husband,

27

was sent packing. Uncle Bill found work in Peterborough, and the rot in Aunt Lizzie's life set in.

I do not suppose that her story was uncommon, or that the sorrows of the couple were sadder than many a young couple in our sex-obsessed so-called 'permissive' society of today; but it has taken me a whole lifetime to understand fully how that period of true happiness accounted for events still to come.

Aunt Lizzie had in her a tough streak of independence, and a fenland ability to meet trouble philosophically; but in spite of being able to 'set a hard heart against hard sorrow', the romantic Celt in her also gave her the tendency to grieve hard.

For a while, Uncle Bill worked on the railway, and they were given a tiny railway house in a street that gradually went down and down till it was occupied only by outcasts from other working class areas. While she had lived with the doctor, he had found her an apt pupil (medically), and she knew a lot that prevented her poverty-stricken neighbours from sending for a doctor when he wasn't needed, or made her badger them into asking for medical help before it was too late. She possessed also (as her doctor had often told her) the soft, firm, soothing hands of a healer. Nursing 'came natural' to her, and she put that skill at the disposal of her neighbours, however unpleasant the circumstances. To them, she was a sort of approachable angel of light. But the effect on her was — or seemed to Mam and Dad to be, — anything but good. Mam, of course, was concerned with the social disgrace that she felt rubbed off on her, and on us. Dad was, as usual, between the hammer and the anvil. His mother, who knew nothing about the affair with the doctor, only thought Aunt Lizzie had sunk to her proper level, and said so. Dad was troubled for her but even his tolerance had been stretched to its non-conformist limits by what had happened, and he had reservations that resulted in him keeping silence about her, either about her past, or her present gentle slide downwards. In this, neither circumstances nor Uncle Bill helped much. As the twenties teetered towards the Great Depression, and Labour came into power for the first time, Uncle Bill edged further and further to the left until he became as near to being a Communist as made no odds and lost his job. Then abject poverty was also added to Aunt Lizzie's lot.

The depression had not yet hit farming (that came later) and Dad was doing well, so he didn't mind helping; but in 1926, my uncle who had run away from Rattles at the age of fourteen to become a miner, was also in desperate straits. Mam took a trip to see him (before the strike became general, I suppose) and returned with five out of his six children, who were with us for the rest of the summer. She had found them quite literally starving, their Sunday treat being a dose of Scott's Emulsion spread on a slice of dry bread. She simply packed them up and landed them in the midst of our plenty. As with the evacuees in World War II, I don't know which of the guests or the hosts suffered most!

Sympathy with Aunt Lizzie began to wear thin when, in an attempt to stretch their more than slender means, she took in a permanent lodger. He became, as it were, an unwanted member of our family. He was a railway guard whose wife had had mental trouble and had turned violent towards him, so that he was forced to find refuge somewhere. In his defence it has to be said that he was clean and hardworking, and took his responsibility towards his deserted wife very seriously. He visited her every week, and shared his pay packet with her, though he often returned to Aunt Lizzie's care with scratches down his face or his head bashed by a poker. Nevertheless there was something about that man, and Aunt Lizzie's friendliness towards him, that made him absolutely unacceptable to us. We detested him and despised him, the whole boiling of us, from Dad down to me. As he often had days off and could travel free (and no doubt passed our aunt off as his wife) he was usually with her when she paid us her visits to collect eggs, butter, a bit of ham or a joint of pork out of the porkpot. We could not hide our terrible, unreasonable dislike of him, and he was about the only person I ever remember being obviously unwelcome in our house. His skin must have been as thick as that of a rhinoceros, because he kept on coming, even though Aunt Lizzie took the hint (and the huff) and cut her visits down to an absolute minimum.

Maybe she realised that Uncle Bill was also becoming less and less welcome. He talked of nothing but his left-wing politics — a subject Dad resolutely refused to discuss with anybody because it usually lead to unpleasantness. So Uncle lectured, and Mam (foolishly because she knew nothing whatsoever about it) argued, and Dad suffered. I think he suffered much more from Uncle's 'put on' speech than from what he said. His diction was 'refained', his spiel full of long words he had picked up but pronounced in ways we hadn't heard before. He always said 'yewman' for 'human', for instance, and talked with feeling of the 'mass-acres' caused by the 'cap-hit-a-list warmongers' of the 'ante-war period', and so on.

Now Dad, who never spoke anything but his old fen 'twang', knew a lot about words from his endless reading, and the combination of Uncle Bill's politics with his pretentious speech and misuse of language drove Dad, as he said 'to distraction'. He just could not endure it, and would sometimes be rude enough to get up and leave the table to stop himself from exploding — though when Uncle Bill had gone away again, we usually had the pleasure of a good laugh at his expense, especially as Mam was a most excellent mimic, and could 'do' Uncle Bill 'to a T'.

(The only word Dad himself ever had any trouble with, to my knowledge, was 'amalgamate'. He simply could not remember whether it was 'amalgamate' or 'amalmagate' — and as he said, you wouldn't have expected it be a word he

31

had a lot of use for. But somehow or other it was needed every time he had to open his mouth in public, or at a drainage committee meeting, or in conversation with any 'hedicated' man. I heard him trying it both ways so often in my childhood that I still have to think 'amalgam-ate' to get it right myself.)

As things went from bad to worse with poor Aunt Lizzie, her entourage of down-and-outs brought to us for a day's outing and a good meal grew and grew. Outcasts that for all her piety Grandmother would not have allowed to cross her brick doorway were never unwelcome in the way the lodger was, or, for that matter, our dapper little Uncle Bill. Mam's sympathy was roused, for one thing, and her innate hospitality brought into play. It was nothing for Dad to come in starving hungry for his 'dockey' only to find Barmy Bob sitting in his place at table, and the pudding made for his own meal being wolfed down the gullet of 'George Wall-Eye'. Then he would say not a word, except of greeting, go round the table to kiss Aunt Lizzie and sit down next to Mam with a wink as he took from her hand a plate of bread and cheese and pickled onions. If anybody grumbled afterwards, it was Mam — but I wonder now if she felt some guilt that she had such a lot while her sister had so little, and that in her heart she was ashamed of being ashamed of this unconventional relative. Mam was a bunch of contradictions, and her warm heart was at war with her pride. She acknowledged in deed, if not in word, that

Aunt Lizzie was a greater and truer Christian than herself.

While this slide downhill for Aunt Lizzie was accelerating, her erstwhile partner in social misdemeanour had found a slippery slope too. His lady mother took over, and in his unhappiness he allowed her to dominate him completely. She offered him as bait whenever any wealthy county family was fishing in the matrimonial pool for a husband for a daughter who looked as if she might be going to be left on the shelf. In this determination to provide him with a bride, he resisted her doggedly, throwing his heart and soul into his work of healing the sick — with an added patience and loving kindness that made his name beloved among the poor and helpless of that terrible period; but, his long day's work done at last, he went home to his study — and a bottle. Sad company, but solace that he needed.

Just at the crucial moment of my illness, Aunt Lizzie paid us one of her very occasional, unannounced visits, mercifully *alone*.

She was visibly distressed by the plight she found me in and rounded on Mam and Dad in her outspoken way for ever allowing me to get into such a state.

What good, she asked, was it doing anybody to drag me to a money-grubbing old flannel-britches of a quack at Ramsey? He wasn't fit to treat a blue-faced monkey, let alone a child! Compared to 'her' doctor, he was nothing but 'a broken-winded pismire' (the

33

ultimate expression of fenland scorn). Could they not see that I was dying before their very eyes?

Both Mam and Dad bridled a bit — Mam out of self-defence, and Dad because any reference to 'her' doctor made him uncomfortable. Neither of them needed telling that 'her' doctor was not the one on whose panel at Peterborough she was registered.

I can judge, now, what it must have cost Aunt Lizzie to propose what she did, which was that she should take me secretly for a consultation with 'her' doctor.

The meeting was soon set up — I know not how.

So Aunt Lizzie and I set off (with Mam dithering in the background) on another journey involving several wearying changes of train. I can just recall the big, handsome man with the beautiful voice (so different from Dr Llewelwyn's monosyllabic commands) who examined me. I remember Aunt Lizzie's silent tears as he told her that my only hope was immediate surgery, to prevent my terribly septic tonsils from poisoning me further. He gave my aunt his word that he would use every bit of influence he possessed to get me priority treatment at Peterborough hospital, and with that, we left.

None of us ever saw him again. He died, of drink, within a year of our visit. I hope seeing Aunt Lizzie again did nothing to hasten his end — but what is life with a hollow place where your heart should be? Perhaps he was the lucky one, because she lived on, childless and unsatisfied, to the age of eighty-nine.

I know, of course, who he was, and where he lived and died, but I shall not disclose anything more about him. I owe it to both of them to let their star-crossed love fade into the mists of history. Perhaps, in some respects, I feel myself to be their child, for it was the two of them together who gave me back the life that was slipping from me.

Her doctor kept his word, and within a week I was half-dragged, half-carried by Mam to our station, en route for Peterborough. There Aunt Lizzie met us and took over, conducting us to the hospital, where I was handed over by a weeping mother to an equally tear-drenched aunt, who unclasped my clinging hands and pushed me through a door into the keeping of a strange, stern, starched, crackly-aproned nurse.

And while Mam and Aunt Lizzie waited outside the door (I am sure well within hearing of my screams) the surgeon in charge decided on the spot that I was too weak to withstand any anaesthetic and proceeded to remove my tonsils there and then, without one. (The less said about that memory, the better.)

Then, limp with terror and pain, I was handed back to Aunt Lizzie through the same door, and transferred from the nurse's shoulder to Aunt Lizzie's, who was given a large pad of gauze to protect her best costume jacket from blood. In spite of it, she was soaked with my blood, her own tears and sweat by the time she had carried me back to the railway station, where, perforce, Mam had to take over. Aunt Lizzie completed her task by going, soaked as she was, to the Post Office, where she sent a telegram to Dad to meet us at our end, to save Mam the struggle of carrying me the mile home.

I realise that there will be many who find it hard to believe what I have just recounted, but I swear that every detail of it is as true as Grandmother would have wished. Perhaps it may serve to put the 'failure' of our modern NHS into perspective. Perhaps little, sickly fen-tiger cubs were expendable, anyway. Perhaps the surgeon felt as many an army surgeon on a battlefield must have felt, that I was doomed anyway.

Be that as it may, the swift if brutal treatment had almost miraculous results. Within forty-eight hours, I was licking an ice-cream cornet — just about *the* most unhygienic food that could have been allowed to slide down a still raw throat, now I come to consider it; for the ice-cream itself was made (I guess in the most primitive of conditions) in the kitchen of an old man named Wade, who then proceeded to hawk it, in a sort of insulated container vaguely resembling a small milk-churn, round the fen in a horse-drawn trap. It did me no harm, anyway, and in another forty-eight hours I was demanding food. My delighted and relieved parents thereafter (as we should say in the vernacular) 'stuffed me both ends', and before many weeks were past I was as fat, as sturdy and as tunky as I had ever been before.

It would be entirely ungrateful to all concerned for me now to complain that from that time to this I have never been anything other than fat, sturdy and tunky! Especially as my rapid return to life brought with it a widow's cruse of energy and a *joie-de-vivre* that so far have never diminished. Maybe my excursion to the very verge of the Bottomless Pit made me appreciate every day out of range of the smell of sulphur as a sort of added bonus.

It seems that without the least bit of conscious intention of doing so, I have made Aunt Lizzie's the first portrait in the gallery of my fen-tigers, so it is right for me to put the last touches to it before returning to my own story.

Some years passed, and both Lois and Gerald, though grown-up, were still at home. I was at school, but growing up fast. The pattern of our lives had changed, particularly as our life expanded and our social circle widened. We saw less and less of Aunt Lizzie, who seemed to us to be letting herself go from bad to worse. To put it bluntly, we were ashamed of her. We kept in touch and saw her very occasionally. The outbreak of the second war cut us off even more, and broke up our home in the fen, forcing Mam and Dad out of it for ever when they came to help me over a very sticky patch in my personal life.

Then, one night in March 1950, Dad suddenly deserted me, for ever — just like that.

It was a very strange experience. I managed to get our doctor to Dad, but he died five

37

minutes later. Mam was in shock, my eight-year-old daughter asleep in the next room. I was alone as I had never been before. The doctor (another medical saint in my calendar) led Mam away, sat down on my bed with her and took her into his arms, pulling her head down on to his shoulder. He indicated that he would stay while I got help. I went out on to the landing and peeped through the crack in the door for my very last look at Dad, bereft, very helpless and forlorn. And then, standing there, I felt, almost like an electric shock as it were, a charge of strength and purpose hit me. I knew that whatever was required of me, I could do it. I no longer felt alone or inadequate. Swiftly and methodically I roused my little girl, carried her to our nearest neighbour's house, knocked them up and asked them to take her in. I phoned Lois, who was, luckily, only eight miles away. Then I set off to fetch 'the women' — the layers-out of the dead. It was midnight in a village without light of any kind other than the stars, and few of them. I had no torch, nor had I stopped to put on a coat. The sisters who undertook the necessary if grisly work for their neighbours lived up a narrow lane, a turning off the country road. I strode along on my errand without a tinge of fear or horror, buoyed up, it seemed, by the presence of another self beside my ordinary one. Then I went home and Lois came. Mam insisted on being taken downstairs. With the doctor's help, we installed her in her own chair, and he then sedated her, waited till she was asleep, and left. Lois sat by her side while I found all that 'the women' needed, calmly ironing a clean pair of Dad's pyjamas for them to put on him. The incredible ability to cope, to make decisions and to defer grief still seemed to be welling up from some strength other than my own. Lois and I, clinging to each other, decided not to ring Gerald, who was farther away, till dawn broke. There was nothing more to be done. The women left and I went into the kitchen to make us a cup of tea.

The telephone was in the hall and as I looked at it I knew that above everything else, at that moment, I wanted Aunt Lizzie.

There was no telephone in the mean street where she still lived, so I rang the Peterborough police and begged their help. Thirty minutes later, they rang back. Aunt Lizzie would be on the first bus from Peterborough to Cambridge next morning.

Dawn broke and Lois telephoned the news to Gerald, who came at once, so utterly heartbroken that I left Lois to deal with him, while Mam still slept, blessedly unconscious of his distress. I knew what I had to to do — catch a bus to Cambridge to be there when Aunt Lizzie arrived. The need of her was by now a physical thing, an ache that was somehow holding off the hurt I knew must come sooner or later. It was part of the uncanny extra force inside me.

As the time for the arrival of her bus drew near, the first doubts began to assail me. What had I done? She was seventy; she had had no warning; she had had no time to prepare in any way for such a journey. Just what sort of old tragmallion, dressed in jumble-sale clothes thrown on in the dark, would step off the bus to greet me? I quailed at the thought, almost wanting to turn away, in spite of my need of her. Then the bus drew in and I saw her — standing on the platform, clinging to the pole, in her eagerness to get to me.

She was clad in smart, immaculate black, with her snow-white hair swept back under a fashionable, neat black hat. She was gloved and at the throat of her white blouse wore a pinchbeck brooch containing a tinted photograph of Grammam. As soon as she stepped on to the pavement, her love for me poured out all round me like a sweetly scented soothingly warm shower, and tears I had not yet shed began to run down my face. As I sobbed on her shoulder, I mumbled out my gratitude to her for coming to my call.

'I was expecting it,' she said. 'I had been warned. I knew the moment it happened, just before twelve. I've been with you all night — every minute since Bill died.'

(Of course! I had forgotten how 'fey' she had always been about such things; or perhaps I had never believed her, till that moment.)

'It is so good of you,' I said.

She drew herself up, as regal a figure as ever Old Queen Mary at her most majestic.

'Good of me?' she said. 'IT IS MY DUTY.'

How glad I am to be able to remember her

like that — a proud woman, still very beautiful and full of dignity. One who knew the meaning of Love in all its many aspects, and was not afraid of any of them.

2

Words: From the Cradle to the Grave

I was glad not to have to find out for myself the truth (or otherwise) of Grandmother's predictions of Life Hereafter. She, on the other hand, soon did. She died in the November of that same year, on Gerald's eighteenth birthday and in the same month that I had my eighth and consequently opened my second seven-year parcel of existence.

Grandmother had just completed her twelfth, being nearly eighty-five — 'mairster to the end' as she said on her deathbed.

Deathbed scenes were related among the women with the same sort of relish as people stood and gazed at the waxwork of the Death of Prince Albert in Madame Tussaud's. I was all ears for the details of the last moments of all my grandparents (except Grammam, and there was a special reason for that. I witnessed it, aged five.)

Grandmother, having had 'a few words' with Aunt Harriet, had taken herself off to live with her youngest daughter, my Aunt Loll. (Her name was actually Flora Mahala, but who could expect a child to get through life burdened with that!) She was the sweetest and kindest of Dad's sisters, with a sense of humour very like Dad's, which the other two sisters lacked entirely — and

42

she had had far more than her fair share of troubles already. Nevertheless, she took Grandmother in, and before long the old lady, no doubt still fretting, took to her bed, and all agreed it was the end. Aunt Eva was sent for from Sheffield and Aunt Harriet (of whom her sisters were in awe) became chief nurse. Curiously and contrary to what one would have expected, she always had been an excellent nurse.

Grandmother, true to her principles, chose to die on a Sunday, thereby ensuring that all the menfolk (except, perhaps, my other Uncle Bill from Sheffield) were also in attendance in the crowded bedroom. Towards evening, the invalid asked for a basin of bread and milk. Aunt Harriet hurried away to prepare it, crumbling the bread small and sweetening it. Grandmother took one sip and waved it away. 'Pap!' she said, scornfully. Aunt Harriet retired, her feelings mortally wounded, to the foot of the bed.

Aunt Loll tried next, with the same unfortunate result.

Now Mam, the outsider, was not among the inner circle around the deathbed, though visible on the outskirts. Grandmother heaved herself up and found Mam within her sight.

'Kate,' she said. 'Do you go and make me a mess o' bread and milk.'

Mam went. She cut the bread into large cubes, salted and peppered it and poured boiling milk on it. Then she added a walnut-sized lump of butter to the top of it and climbed back up the narrow stairs.

To the utter disgust of all three of her daughters, the invalid devoured the lot, down to the last drop of butter-streaked milk, from Mam's hands. (The others afterwards hinted that it was that heavy meal that had hastened 'the end'.)

A few minutes later, Grandmother declared that she was going to get out of bed. Aunt Harriet forbade it: Aunt Loll pleaded.

Grandmother heaved herself up again and surveyed them all grimly.

'I've been mairster in my own house all my life,' she said, 'and I'll be mairster to the end. Kate, do you get me out o' bed.'

Mam did, and got her to the side with her legs hanging down, which was what she seemed to want. And while Mam held her there, having got her own way, Grandmother just sighed and went off to find out The Truth.

She was, for that period, quite a wealthy old woman. Dad 'took charge' of the funeral, but it was Aunt Harriet who made the decisions. Our own churchyard being subject to flooding, so that the coffin was let down into water except in a dry, hot summer, some people had a preference for being buried in the cemetery at Ramsey — which cost a good deal more anyway, so there was a bit of cachet about it, too. I can't think how grandmother could have afforded to have Grandad buried there in 1906, but she had done, so of course her own grave by his side had already been bought and paid for. It was decreed that Grandmother's nearest and dearest should be conveyed behind the

44

hearse in 'proper' mourning coaches, at a walking pace, of course, so that the less fortunate could follow on foot in couples. The grandchildren were to be provided with 'decent suits of solemn black' (at their parents' expense, of course — Aunt Harriet hadn't got any children). Only my cousin Ruby, aged four, and I, aged eight (near enough) were excused. Thus it was that I watched the long solemn procession from the tiny window of our landing, held in the arms of one of the women who had come to prepare the funeral tea. First the hearse — an ornate black contraption with plate-glass sides to show the quality of the coffin and its fittings. The wood of the canopy of the hearse was ornately carved into a sort of parapet round the top, on which rested the 'floral tributes' to the deceased.

Each corner of the carved black parapet boasted a vaguely angel-like figure, from whose black head sprang four black ostrich-plumes. Four black horses, shining as if they had been recently black-leaded, drew the hearse, proudly tossing their wonderful heads as their polished black hooves struck sparks from the cup-sized lumps of granite with which the high-road was made up. The headband of each horse carried a tall decoration of black ostrich plumes.

The mourning coaches, sons of the hearse except that the windows were small and black-curtained (to hide from public gaze the tear-stained faces if the occupants so desired), were drawn by two horses apiece, every horse being be-plumed in the same fashion.

Behind the last of the coaches, the grandchildren headed the long procession (I can recall, as in a photograph, the backs of Gerald and Lois, who were first in order of precedence because of Dad being Grandmother's only son. This caused a lot of ill-feeling, because there were other, older, granddaughters.)

Then came the straggle of friends and neighbours, every woman in her best black, every man in his Sunday black bowler. All very impressive and awe-inspiring to eight-year-old eyes. The undertaker, of course, strode sedately and pompously before the hearse, wearing a black top-hat and wielding a long black wand. The six bearers, also in top-hats, walked three each side of the hearse.

Ordinary folk went to their graves on the shoulders of their neighbours with two sets of bearers to take over from each other if the droves were muddy or the way too long. But that wouldn't have done for Grandmother — or, more likely, for Aunt Harriet. Our neighbours didn't possess top-hats. Mr Swearer, Ramsey's most prestigious if not only undertaker, had been commissioned to supply a full complement of top-hatted carriers.

I suppose the funeral tea must have been held at our house, but if so, I remember nothing at all of it, except a visit from Grandad Rattles, on his way home from some nefarious undertaking no doubt, and perhaps hoping for some funeral baked meats. He had his old cap pulled rakishly over one eye and the usual scarlet 'neck'andkercher' round his throat.

Mam was still wearing her smart new black and standing by the big carved-mahogany chiffonier when Rattles opened the door and skulked inside. One glance told him that Dad had gone out to do the yardwork, so he addressed himself to Mam.

'I see you took th'ol' wise-woman for a bloody j'y-ride,' he said.

There will be times when it is necessary for me to exchange my fen-tiger's skin for my Cambridge University cap and gown. These passages can always be skipped, if the reader feels like it.

If Grandmother had done little else for me, she had taught me a useful lesson — never to expect other people to believe you if you tell the simple truth without embroidery or varnish. Wearing my academic 'hat', I found myself in the USA, working among other academics whose chief concern was the development, psychology and education of the minds of children.

It was at a social gathering of such folk, one sultry, humid evening in the middle of a heat wave in Philadelphia, that I repeated the remark I had so innocently made to Grandmother some fifty years earlier that I remember being in my cradle. The result, I fear, was really much the same. The medical man on my left at the dinner table explained the improbability of such a memory by giving me a breakdown of the development of the infant mind during the first few weeks of life. (O, how our American cousins do adore having something to 'explicate'!) Waiting his turn, the child psychologist on my right then explained to me *why* I believed I could remember such an incredible thing. What I was in fact remembering, he said, was an adult talking in my hearing of some incident that had happened to me in my cradle, thus creating in me a sort of impression that I now interpreted as memory.

It was too hot to argue and the clams were too tough to talk around, so I let them get away with it. In any case, they were both well-known pundits on such matters and nearly as uncontradictable as Grandmother; but I was vastly irritated by them none the less and felt how marvellous it would be if I could dare to seize the horrible 'arty' bit of pottery in the middle of the table and hurl it through the window to let some heat out and some commonsense in. As I chewed my way through the leathery 'specialties', I reflected why it is that 'experts' so often get things wrong. Once they become experts, they know all the answers, so they don't ask questions. They simply reach out, take down the most likely ready-made explanation from the peg and use it, whether it fits the case in point or not. Take my unadorned statement, for example. Neither Grandmother nor The Pundits were interested enough to ask me what I meant. In their different ways, they all implied that I was telling a lie.

Now that, in vulgar fenland parlance, really 'capped my arse'. As it happened, there was a very simple and perfectly straightforward explanation, which, given the chance, I could and would have produced at once.

What I actually remember so vividly was waking up in my cradle.

It was a very important and significant moment, as I now recognise — an Awakening, in every sense of the word.

The cradle in question was a Victorian relic made of wicker. It stood on wooden rockers and had a hood at the head end. From end to end it measured, I guess, about three to three-and-a-half feet and was at least eighteen inches wide without the flat flange that ran all round the sides. It fitted, almost exactly, the alcove on one side of the protruding hearth in the 'house-place' of the cottage where I was born. The hearth itself was wide, designed to burn the 'cesses' of peat still obtainable locally although the turf-digging trade had almost died out by the beginning of the Great War. Being the size it was and so conveniently handy, I was put down in it for my afternoon nap for as long as I needed one, or on any other occasion when tiredness overcame me. So when The Awakening happened, I was not a baby at all, but a toddler going into three.

By deduction and by putting together the details I recall, I think it must have been late August or early September of 1916, when I was a couple of months short of my third birthday. I must have roused from my nap without anyone noticing, so I sat up. I put my hands, one each side, on the flat flange of woven wicker to support myself and sat quite still, taking in the scene before my eyes.

The rest of my immediate family were all at tea, seated around the square table in the middle

49

of the house-place — so it must have been about 4 p.m., at which time of day Dad often nipped home on his bike to have a cup of tea and a wash and brush up before returning to Grandmother's farm to do the yardwork and 'supper-up' the horses. The wall the other side of the table contained the large front window, which was dressed with curtains of white lace caught at sill-height into bands of gold-yellow velvet. Between the curtains was a triangle of intense blue sky.

Mam was in the act of picking up from the hearth a large blue enamel teapot, which showed up against her white 'afternoon' apron and her coal black hair like an object carefully placed for effect in a Dutch interior painting. She had only just begun to put on weight, I think, because that memory is the only one I have of her that closely resembles the photograph of the tall, slender, exceedingly beautiful girl Dad had married fifteen years previously. Dad was sitting in his high-backed Windsor chair, about four feet away from me. (It was one of his peculiarities that he rarely sat square to the side of a table. At home, he usually pulled his chair to the corner of the table, crossed his legs right over left and leaned forward. It never ceased to irritate Mam, but she could never cure him of the habit.)

On this day, though, he had actually pulled his chair right up close to the table leg, so that he had one foot planted each side of it. When my newly-opened eyes photographed him in my mind forever, he was in a most curious position, leaning over to his right and looking downwards over the arm of his chair, while his left arm was raised high in the air; and in that hand he held a fork which had a slice of tomato stuck on one of its prongs. The reason for this curious antic was plain to me at once. One of our everlasting supply of black-and-white kittens had climbed up his trouser leg as far as his knee. Just as I looked at him, he took it by the scruff of its neck and gently detached its clinging claws, so that it hung vertically from his hand for a split second before he dropped it to the floor.

Dad was in his shirt-sleeves, which were rolled up a fraction higher than he wore them (no doubt because he had just had a good wash before sitting down to tea). The lower part of his arms and his hands, were as dark brown as the wicker work on which my own chubby hands rested, but above the normal sleeve-line his skin was abruptly, startlingly, unbelievably smooth and silky white. The demarcation line was as clear and unbroken as if it had been carefully painted on.

I deduce from this that the summer had been a hot one and that the main harvest had been gathered in, or Dad would not have been at home at tea time. The tomato, too, serves to set the time of year, because there was then no fruit of any kind to be had out of season. (Indeed, if it had been available, I think it would have been an unwelcome innovation, because it was an essential quality of Time that its rhythm was marked by what one ate — new potatoes on Whit Sunday, for instance, a duck saved to be killed when new green peas were ready, sprouts as soon

51

as the first frost had been on them and fresh pork again as soon as there was an 'R' in the month.) Dad's shirt, which I could see between the varnished slats of his chairback, was a deep creamy colour with a thin vertical blue stripe. It may have been made of heavy cotton, but it is much more probable that it was of flannel, which men preferred even in scorching weather because it absorbed the sweat. It was collarless and the neckband was undone, exposing to view Dad's very long neck, on which there was the same sudden change of colour as on his arms. His hair stood up in little spikelets, still wet from his sluicing at the sink, and his face in profile was silhouetted against the blue triangle of sky between the curtains.

The rest of the scene is not quite so distinct — a little subdued, as the background of a picture often is. I am vaguely aware of Lois's back by Dad's right side and of Gerald's face across the table, by the side of Mam's empty chair. I cannot swear that I remember the grandfather clock behind Gerald, by the side of the window, though I think I do. But the psychologists may be right about that one detail. The clock continued to stand there until we moved from that house twelve months later to go and take over Grandmother's farm: so that detail may possibly have been added afterwards from knowledge and familiarity. I concede nothing else to them, or their professional spiel about my memory being an echo of what somebody else had said. Who else could have seen what I saw from my peculiar point of view, even if there had been anything whatsoever about it to cause comment? Far less could anybody but me know what tremendously significant revelations were disclosed to me in those few seconds of time.

As I sat upright in my cradle with my fat little fists clutching the sides, I was suddenly, and with amazing clarity, aware of myself as an individual: of my own identity.

Until that instant I had been, as it were, alive but still unborn, still sealed in the womb of my family, like a chicken inside an egg. Now, in a flash, I was ME. A separate Me, who had a body and thoughts, and a will of my own. It was as if Somebody had pressed a button which instantaneously brought into action all my wits. I saw and comprehended, not only that I was a distinct and separate person, but that all the other seated round the table were individuals likewise, with different faces, voices, sexes and personalities. The pundits won't believe me on that last score, but I *know*; and in the fen we all know what 'knowing' means. Our adage is that 'knowing beats thinking's arse off'.

Waking up in my cradle was like a second birth, with a second christening at which my own personality was bestowed on me.

Take, for example, my life-long love of words. The other members of the family were always so amused by my ability to pick up and repeat any words I heard that they went on telling tales about it as long as they lived, so I must bow to the psychologists again and accept that I would not have remembered so much if others had not so constantly spoken of it afterwards. Nevertheless, I *do* remember some incidents in my own right. As a baby, Gerald had been given a rag book with lurid pictures in it. It was still about, and was shown to me again and again 'to amuse the baby'. I do not remember anything of it except one page. I can see the old book, with its 'pinked' edges, lying on the flat flap of my high chair. The picture is of a huge bulldog with either a puppy or a kitten playing between his front paws. I was no more interested in this particular picture than in any of the others, except that Dad, in passing behind me one day, ran his finger along the printed caption and said 'Dignity and Impudence'. What a wonderful phrase to add to 'Horrocks's Calico' which I had already picked up. In the same way, Dad read to me over and over again the verses accompanying Louis Wain's cat drawings. I don't remember the pictures at all, but the words are still available to me, if only in snatches:

Into the fender, head over heels
Just to see how funny it feels!
Into the coal-scuttle — that's no place
For a snow-white kitten with a spotless face

or

Mr Tom Mouser, and Little Miss Mew
Went for a ride all in a canoe
Little Miss Mew in the stern she sat down
And put up her sunshade, in case she got
    brown

54

and the other verses, all complete.

Many are the neighbours who, since I have grown up, have given me a word-picture of an incident that happened in chapel when I was about three. I do retain a vague, uncertain memory of it myself, more concerned with Mam's embarrassment than anything else.

She had continued to sit in the front pew, where Grammam had always sat. It was a sensible arrangement, because Mam was so deaf, but in any case, the 'Etherds' pew behind her was already full with Dad, Aunt Harriet and Uncle John, Aunt Loll and Uncle Jim, when they were all there together — to say nothing of Grandmother in her lifetime and my paralysed cousin Vernon when he was taken in his wheelchair.

Mam and I were thus directly beneath the pulpit, right under the preacher's nose.

On this specific occasion, a well-liked minister who had left our circuit was paying us a visit, so that both the main body of the chapel and the gallery were full to overflowing. We had reached the sermon, with the minister in full flood of words and earnest passion. He put his hands on the front of the pulpit, leaned forward and said 'Ah, my friends! As long as I remember . . . ' but he got no further. I had been sitting, half-asleep, with my head resting on Mam's plump arm. Galvanised into action by the minister's phrase, I leapt up on to the seat, turned to face the whole congregation, and said:

As long as I remember
I never shall forget
To take an um-ber-ella
When it comes on wet

and abruptly sat down again. My audience exploded into a roar of laughter with a comet-like tail of unsuppressable giggling and chuckling, and the minister wisely announced the final hymn.

And for those whose imagination strives to create a visual image of the incident, I can tell them what I was wearing at the time. It was an elegant little coat, fitting at the waist, made of black satin and lined with pale pink silk. My bonnet matched, being made of black satin with ruched pink silk all round my face and tied with pink ribbon bows under my chin. The outfit was completed by a pair of soft black leather boots that laced almost up to my knees.

I adored that coat and bonnet, which may account for my vivid recall of my first-ever nightmare. On our way to chapel, we had to cross 'the planks' over a fairly wide dyke almost opposite our house. The plank, only ten inches wide at the most, dipped towards the middle, especially if there was more than one person crossing it at a time; it also bounded up and down as they trod. Usually, I rode over it on Dad's shoulders and from up there the black water beneath me was quite frightening; but sometimes I insisted on walking the plank myself, aware that it was a challenge I had to meet sometime.

In that first ever, but never to be forgotten nightmare, I crossed the plank in my pretty black-and-pink outfit, reached the bouncy middle and fell off into the water. I screamed and screamed for Dad to get me out, and he did — jumping off the plank and into the water, There, underwater, I reached out to find him, always just out of reach of his arms. But at last he caught me and held me and we rose to the surface together. But the head that broke water was not Dad's. It was, instead, a horrible white and shiny bladder of lard!

(At a pig-killing, the pig's bladder was filled with lard till it was almost as big as a party balloon and when the lard had set, the bladder was hung on a hook from the pantry ceiling. A horrid, horrid sight, with the vestiges of red veins just staining the shiny, greasy whiteness. No doubt it was my dislike of this common sight combined with tales of 'The Hooky Man' and the ordeal of crossing the plank that inspired the nightmare in the first instance, but the memory of it still raises goose-pimples on my arms.)

It was not the much worse, ever-recurring nightmare I first had when I was six and from which I still suffer immeasurable horror and terror. That belongs to another sequence.

I was still no more than three years old. The sound of words intrigued me long before I attached meaning to them; but when I did, I became an avid and nosey listener to conversation. My hearing and my understanding being more acute than many were used to in a child of my age, I was a constant eavesdropper, especially when other women made comments to each about Mam, even in her presence, safe in the knowledge that she would not hear them. They forgot their own oft-repeated warning that 'little pitchers often have big ears'.

I have been everlastingly grateful to the good fairy who gave me this gift at my Awakening. All my life I have been able to distinguish separate voices in a hubbub such, for instance, as one has to endure in that barbarian form of modern entertainment we call a cocktail party. In a crowded restaurant I can (and am afraid still do) listen to and follow the conversations at the three or four adjacent tables while still taking part in that at my own. Railway stations and bus stops provide me with an infinite variety of situations and emotions concerning people I may never set eyes on again. Even waiting in a car park is a pleasure rather than a bore, and as for supermaket check-outs . . . Putting two and two together, I can only suppose that my unfailing interest in people comes from the fact that it was people that I first saw and heard the moment I was aware of my identity. Words, stories, poems, hymns, bible-readings and even Grandmother's strictures all concerned people. So did the books that Dad was forever reading. I began to make out that it was words plus people that made books — and I wanted to be able to make books. By the age of ten, I had decided I wanted to join the ranks of Dickens, Twain, Henry Ainsworth, W. W. Jacobs and Mrs Henry Wood (the only authors of adult books whose names I was aware of). I soaked up books like *Queechy*, *A Peep Behind the Scenes* and *The Girl of the Limberlost*, along with others of the same lachrymose variety that by this time Lois had in her library. Many of our books were rescued by Dad from the truck-loads of 'London Muck' (i.e. the contents of London's dustbins) that Dad bought to spread as fertiliser on the land. They were put into the side-oven of the hearth to 'fumigate' them before we were allowed to read them — and as far as I know, none of us suffered as much as a sneeze from our contact with them. It may make folks in this age of hygiene and paperbacks wince, but it is possible that book-starvation produces more real readers than a surplus of cheap pulp.

Another source of books was our annual prize for attending chapel Sunday School. They were poor fare, but they were books. On prize-giving Sunday you could usually go home with more than the one that had been handed indiscriminately to you. Other children who were not so book-minded could be bribed to part with theirs. To the day of her death at eighty-two, Lois treasured a little book inscribed 'Given to Lois Edwards by Hilda Cook, for a ride on her bicycle'.

Long before this age, though, I had given proof that writing was 'my thing'. From a very early age, I had enjoyed holding a pencil to 'scribble' (literally). This presented a logistical problem. By the time of my late intrusion into

59

the family, Gerald was ten and Lois nearly nine. Patterns had been established — at table, for example. Dad's place was on one corner of the table, Mam's on the other, both near to the hearth. Gerald's 'place' was next to Mam, Lois's next to Dad. When meals had been cleared away, everyone did his own thing in his own 'place'. Dad propped up his book or spliced rope for the weights of the old grandfather clock, or made out drainage-rate demands, in his place: Mam set up her sewing machine in her 'place': Gerald had his meccano or his paints or his *Boys Own Paper* in his: and when Lois wasn't at her beloved piano, she put her dolls in hers — leaving them there to claim her space if she got up to go and play *La ci darem* or *On Wings of Song* just once more.

Sybil-come-lately had no place of her own. Her high chair was plonked down wherever it would be least in the way.

After my Awakening, I began to resent this. I obviously gave it some serious thought. Heaven (of which I seemed to hear a good deal, one way or another) took shape in my mind as an infinitely long mahogany table with D-shaped ends. God sat in His Place at the top end. The other end was too far away to see, but between the two ends were rows of chairs pulled up to the table and on the back of each one was a name. Somewhere there must surely be a place clearly marked for me!

When bedtime came, we were sent into 'the shed' to wash. Lois had the job of slopping a cold wet flannel round my chops when I was a toddler, because there was no hot water anywhere except when the copper was heated for baths on Saturday. Then we got into our nightwear and said our prayers. When I was three, Lois was twelve and Gerald thirteen, so they had been allowed to give up the ritual of kneeling with their heads in Mam's apron and repeating their prayers aloud; but they (and Dad) were expected to attend to the ceremony of the recital of mine.

This consisted of saying 'Gentle Jesus, meek and mild' followed by a long list of 'God-Blesses'. The longer I made the list the longer I put off bedtime. This crafty trick of mine was not very popular with any of the others who couldn't get on with their own concerns till I'd finished. I strung out the list of aunts, uncles, cousins and friends as far as I could and then hit on the idea of including every cat and kitten by name, as well as Rattles's old pony and Grandmother's horses, our own last litter of pigs and every other lamb I could round up. I understand that the chagrin of the rest was modified by their amusement at what I would say next, but all the same Dad often got into trouble afterwards for allowing his gaze to take him back to Fagin's Den or Boffin's Bower before I had finished.

So they were all giving me their accustomed attention one night when I began my prayers very earnestly and came to the last verse of 'Gentle Jesus'.

Fain I would to Thee be brought
Gracious God, forbid it not
In the Kingdom of Thy grace
Give a little child A PLACE-
TO SIT DOWN AND SCRIBBLE AND WRITE!

Never, I think, in the long term has a heart-felt
prayer been more fully and graciously answered.

And here I sit, all these years later, at my desk
in my own study, just casually recalling the
people, places, events, conditions and objects
that Time like an ever-rolling stream, has borne
away. There's a bitter-sweet taste to nostalgia. I
know how Grammam felt when she wrote in her
diary in 1917, on the day of Grandmother's farm
sale, 'Sold our dear old pony. Put it in Mrs
Edwards' sale. Gone but not forgotten, by John
and Mary Papworth.' (The diary is among my
'treasures'.)

I could hardly expect that all the fairies at my
christening would be benevolent ones. The bad
fairy who decreed that my mental map should
forever be upside down so that all my life I have
either been lost or about to become lost, having
no sense of direction whatever, I could have
done very well without. She put a curse on
travelling that has been a bugbear all my
life. Trains I am on get diverted: buses break
down: London taxi-drivers have even been
known to take a wrong turn if I am the
passenger. Ships run into hurricanes, or fog in
the Hudson River that causes it to sound like a
herd of cows blaring for lost calves, while all
other carefully made arrangements collapse like

a row of dominoes. A train from Halifax (Nova Scotia) to Montreal had faulty brakes that threw us all from our bunks to the floor every time they were applied. At Trois Rivières a criminal escaped from gaol jumped from the train and killed himself, necessitating hours of interrogation by Quebec's police. More than twenty-four hours late for an appointment in Montreal, I entered that beautiful city flat on my face in the corridor, the brakes being unavoidably applied again. And so on, and so on. I am obviously not meant to be a traveller! As the driver of a very fast and very powerful car, the jinx has only been applied to sending me the wrong way so that I arrive in Aberystwyth when an audience awaits me in Cardiff. The miles, the hours and the petrol I have wasted does not bear thinking about. But at least this female Jonah has learned one lesson. As far as my bad fairy is concerned, you may all take heart: I DO NOT TRAVEL BY AIR. Never have, and never will.

This complete inability to find my way anywhere (however familiar) has been both an amusement and an irritant to my academic colleagues. Waiting for me at a meeting, someone was bound to report that I had been 'last seen, wandering vaguely' down a corridor in the wrong block of the University. One of my psychologist friends — I did have some — opined that this complete lack of direction might possibly be due to my having been born in the featureless fens where there were no landmarks to help me to orientate myself. I might have believed that if

63

others born within half a mile of me did not set out without a qualm for Vladivostok or Tamenrasset and get there without taking a wrong turn.

American psychologists were less kind. One of them explained his theory that it was brain damage at birth, as a result of prolonged labour. If so, I'm the exception that proves the rule. My mother barely had time to get to the top of the stairs before she dropped me — no doubt on my head, so it may have been brain damage after all — though Aunt Lizzie was there to catch me. There is, of course, a story attached.

The news of my advent had been welcomed by nobody. Mam herself was most put out, especially as she was not sure of her pregnancy until she was 'about four months gone'. We still lived in Fern Cottage, down Harper's Drove, when I was born, in the house Dad had had built years before he was married.

At the time of my birth Grammam was ailing again and Aunt Lizzie had promised to be available. To save trouble, Grammam was installed in our house. The hamlet boasted two midwives who also acted as 'monthly nurses', but though one had been engaged for the actual birth, she had not been asked to stay on because of Aunt Lizzie being available there. The other midwife was a rather nosey, not too clean and foul-mouthed woman whom Mam detested and swore she would not have near her. There was no reason why she should be needed.

However, three days before I was born, Grammam was once more stricken down with pain and the doctor, hastily sent for, pronounced her doom. She could not live, he said, beyond three weeks at the most. She herself was not told, but she must have been the only person in the fen not to know. There are no secrets in a village. Every intimate detail leaks out and is blown from cottage to cottage, seeping in through cracks in windows and doors, like the silk-soot dust in a fen-blow in May. Just as the layers-out of the dead seemed to smell death from afar and always be at the ready when wanted, so did accoucheurs keep their noses to the wind and ears open for any sign of their being needed, booked or not.

Besides these professional interests, our situation intrigued every neighbour because it was a bit unusual. Every day might be Grammam's last. Equally, every day might be my first. All the women were agog at the thought of death and birth coinciding, as in a knitting pattern where you 'make one, knit two together' and end up with the same number of stitches.

They talked themselves into believing that Mam was only waiting to give birth on the day Grammam died and watched for every sign that might predict the day. Grammam rallied. 'Ah,' said the know-alls. 'Tha's a bad sign, that is. They all'us do, yer know, just afore the end.' Mam began to clean her pantry. 'She wou'n't be long now. They're all'us restless, once the baby's 'ead's down.'

If Grammam broke wind, or belched, it was reported all over the fen faster than a voice bounces off a satellite 26,000 miles into space

65

does now and sad heads were shaken for 'poor ol' Polly Pa'per'. If she hummed or sang (as she had done all her life), she was practising to take her place in the choir of angels: if she whistled (she could, and did, whistle like a bird) she was whistling up The Black Dug, portent of Death. Omens of death were amazingly prevalent, it seemed. They came in flocks, darkening the sky like starlings homing to a reed bed.

A pigeon had been seen perching on the ridge of our roof: an owl had swooped low, asking 'Who?' as it flew: a robin hopped up and down the brick doorway, hoping to get over the sill into the house and so deliver his dreaded message: dogs were heard howling at night and a cockerel crowed before midnight. In cottages all over the fen where the occupants were, as far as we knew, no blood kin to us that could actually be traced, clocks stopped without reason: ticking-spiders ticked away the seconds of Grammam's life: candles burned blue and produced sooty 'coffins' on the wick: mirrors and pictures fell from their nails on the walls: a sprig of last year's Christmas holly was discovered still lurking behind a chest of drawers: the wind moaned down drainpipes: a huge bee came out of hibernation and buzzed about a room, denoting the visit from the Stranger (Death): tablecloths and sheets were unfolded to reveal coffin-shaped creases. And when Aunt Harriet dreamed that she had head-lice, there could be no doubt about the outcome. Grammam was doomed.

When such omens appeared simply and, as one might put it, *casually* to a family apparently in perfect health, they caused unease and disquiet — but life went on until they were either proved to be infallible by a child being drowned or a grandfather dying suddenly in his chair, or until in the course of normal routine they were forgotten and the spine-tingling horror gradually faded. But when, as in the present instance, there was a sacrifice immediately to hand and already marked for death, there was no reason at all why the thrill of such portents should not be enjoyed to the hilt — by everybody except us, of course. Everybody at Fern Cottage, I should have said, because it was only in the very middle of this interesting suspense that I first put in my appearance.

Grammam, confounding all the Cassandras, did not die immediately. She got up when she could and indeed was sitting in the rocking chair when Lois and Gerald had their first glimpse of me. But her attacks were too frequent thereafter and she was put to bed 'for the last time' (as everyone thought) the day after I was born. So Mam lay at one end of the upstairs passage with me in a clothes-basket beside her and Grammam lay at the other end of the passage, as Mam believed, dying. On the third day, Mam could stand the separation from her beloved mother no longer. Breaking all the rules, she climbed out of bed, picked up the clothes basket, trotted along the passage and climbed into bed with Grammam. She was going to spend every moment that remained with the mother she adored.

The effect on Grammam was little short of

miraculous. To put it in a nutshell, she resolved not to die — and didn't.

Then another disaster was brought on us. Aunt Lizzie had already overstayed her leave and had to return home, now that Grammam was seemingly out of immediate danger: but Mam's fortnight of lying-in was not yet up and Dad could not manage without a housekeeper of some sort. Ol 'Mis' Harper being engaged elsewhere, it had to be the other one. Let's call her Ol 'Mis' Bladger. She came and took over during the day while Dad was at work, much to Mam's and Grammam's disgust.

During the period Grammam had been with us, Grandad Rattles had been looking after himself at home in 'the carriages'. Grammam worried: Aunt Lizzie said it it wouldn't hurt him: and Mam said it served him right and she hoped he'd starve. There wasn't much chance of that, because he rarely went anywhere without his gun.

In spite of the torture he had inflicted on Grammam since the day he'd married her, there are bits of proof here and there that he did, indeed, have a deeply-rooted affection for her — as well as relying on her, especially in a crisis. When told of her impending death, he made a point of calling to see her every day — always, naturally, at the time Dad was just about to sit down to his tea. Rattles and Ol 'Mis' Bladger were birds of a feather and understood each other very well. She saw to it that there was always plenty for his tea and his bag often provided something to be transferred to hers. If

Dad sometimes went a bit short, 'Mis' Bladger's large family down the drove didn't.

Her ideas about feeding 'hinfalids' like the two upstairs at Fern Cottage were as scanty as what she provided for them. It consisted mostly of a basinful of 'bread sop', sometimes with a drop of milk poured over it and garnished with a spoonful of sugar and a sprinkling of grated nutmeg. More usually it was salted and peppered, with a nob of butter floating on the top.

As Aunt Lizzie had not yet returned, Ol' 'Mis' Bladger stayed on and an evening came when Grandad brought with him a beautiful young but full-grown hare he had shot. 'There', he said, slinging it down. 'Kate's bin a-fancyin' a jugged hare. There'll be plenty for us all for our tea tomorrow.'

When it came to it, there were 'words' between her and Grandad as to where all the best joints had gone. She told him that Dad had had it and Dad that Rattles had. All she'd got left, she said, was enough to make some broth for 'them upstairs'.

The strong-smelling watery gruel that reached them did not send either into ecstasy. Mam, really quite herself again, was ready for a good solid meal and even Grammam was 'peckish'. Their nurse had picked me up and taken me downstairs to be 'topped and tailed', so they had no option but to tackle the hare broth. Grammam took a spoonful while Mam was still summoning up her courage to try it. Next moment, Grammam was forcefully spitting her spoonful back into the basin and 'cagging'. Then she fished about in the horrid mess to find the lump she had just spat out. She thrust the spoon with the offending morsel in it under Mam's nose. 'That' she said 'IS ITS WOWKS'. Mam thrust her basinful aside and they both collapsed back on to their pillows and began to laugh, and laugh, and laugh. Mam averred that it was that good laugh that set her mother back on the road to recovery. She didn't die until I was five years old!

Meanwhile, downstairs Ol' 'Mis' Bladger was attending to me. When she took me back to Mam, she was also carrying a saucer in which reposed a greyish-creamy mess. She put me on the bed while Mam prepared to feed me, and I was, it seems, 'making mouths' in the anticipatory way that babies have. 'Look at 'er' said Ol' 'Mis' Bladger. 'She's a-askin' for a bit o' whatever it wa' as yew fancied while yew were a'carryin'. Jack says it wa' a 'are as yew fancied, all the while.' And before Mam could stop her, she had plugged my mouth with her finger, covered with some of the mess from the saucer, rubbing it all round my gums and palate and especially my lips, in spite of my lusty protests. So, if for the rest of my life I have been less than normally intelligent, as in the matter of finding my way, for example, or if my ideas have seemed to others to be scatty, let it be remembered that the first skerrick of solid food that ever passed my lips was a grimy finger-full of baked hare's brains.

It happened that one evening I was accompanying a senior colleague on a long journey in a

70

car. He was a dedicated teacher, and one whose opinions I respected a great deal, in spite of his being by this time well set into the university mould. We used our time together on the journey to try to construct a programme for the coming year. With pure academic caution and reasoned argument, he demolished every tentative suggestion I offered. After about ten good ideas (as I thought) had been reduced to educational colanders by the number of holes he picked in them, I lost my temper. I sat up, struck the fascia-board of the car with my clenched fist, and said 'O *why* are you such a bloody pessimist?'

(For me to have been reduced to swearing is some indication of the strength of my feeling. Grandmother's strictures still hold.)

My companion took his eyes from the road long enough to look down at me before answering. Then he said *'The trouble with you, Sybil, is that you were breast-fed on demand. You still act on the premise that life will go on treating you like that forever.'*

I have a sneaking feeling that he may have been right. I thought about it very often when enduring the interminable committee meetings which are an inevitable part of a university teacher's lot. I kept myself sane by playing what I call 'The Nightwatchman's Game' (*'Human' natur'* said the nightwatchman *'is a very funny thing; an'* I know, *'cos I've seen a lot of it in my time . . .* ') I watched the behaviour of my colleagues. It occurred to me once that those of them who never appeared to show impatience in the lengthiest of discussions must have been

71

bottle-fed by the clock, and had learned very early in infancy to endure such periods of frustration with passive hopelessness. Moreover, the acerbity with which they squashed any optimistic proposals that might have brought the meeting to an end perhaps indicated that when at last they had been given a bottle, they found that the milk had turned sour with standing.

So perhaps I ought to give the psychologists best, after all, and agree that the traumas of early infancy do have a lasting effect. What a good thing I never related to any of them, as far as I can remember, the story of the hare's brains. What would they have made of that!

There was, as it happens, an incident involving me and a cradle told by adults many times in my hearing, though it has nothing to do with my memory. I was, as I have said, a large and sturdy baby, 'fat as butter'.

My sister Lois was almost nine when I was born and had a large family of dolls of her own, which she put to bed in turn in a cradle that was a miniature replica, rockers and all, of my own.

Lois was playing with her dolls after tea one evening when I was about six weeks old, while Mam was bathing me ready for being 'put down'. She had me naked, placidly plump, pink and perfumed with powder on a towel across her lap when a knock sounded on the door of 'the shed'. Mam guessed at once who the visitor must be . . . that very same itinerant vendor of household linen from whose lips I first heard the magic phrase 'Horrocks's Calico' in time to come.

Mam did not want to see him, or to allow him across the threshold, for he was a most persistent salesman and many a woman had bought towels or sheets she couldn't afford just to get rid of him before 'the mairster' came home and found no tea waiting. On the other hand, it was already dark and cold and he had been lugging two large 'portmanteux' about the slippery fen droves all day. His visits were an embarrassment to Mam in more ways than one — especially when Dad was not in evidence.

He 'halloo'd' at the door, aware of Mam's deafness. She rose hastily and dropped me, wrapped in the towel, on to Lois's lap where she sat in the rocking chair. Though Lois had been allowed to 'hold the baby' fully clothed on her shoulder with adults standing by, it was the first time she had been entrusted with the real live baby doll. The minutes lengthened as Mam did her best to send Jeremiah packing and failed. Temptation was too strong for Lois, who unwrapped me, lifted me — and plonked me down in her doll's cradle.

Lengthwise, the cradle fitted me to a nicety. Widthwise, it was not so accommodating. It was more than a tight fit for my plump little shoulders and fat little bottom and unfortunately my sister had neglected to line it with bedding. As the ribs of the wicker-work began to cut into my rotundity, I began to protest — naturally. As my yells grew louder, Lois was afraid that even at that distance Mam might hear them, so she tried hastily to restore the situation as it had been, with me in a towel on her knee.

The fit between me and the cradle was, alas, too good. I had slipped into it easily enough, but getting me out was quite a different cup of tea. The more Lois pulled and hauled on my arms and legs, the more the wicker hurt me and the louder I yelled.

Mam heard, shut the door in Jeremiah's face and came to see what the matter was. Her tugging, lifting and pulling had no more effect than Lois's had had. My sister by this time was concerned on her own behalf as well as mine, because Mam had a heavy hand on the rare occasions that she did use it, which were usually when, as now, she was frightened, or felt guilty herself. It didn't take a lot to cause Mam to lose her cool and when that happened a scapegoat had to be found.

She slapped Lois hard on arms and thighs, setting her howling in tune with my ever more frantic bawling. Mam had begun to cry herself from helplessness and terror at my probable fate. She mopped Lois up and together they tried again to extricate me.

They tried everything — anointing me with more powder, then with best butter, to make me slippery. No result.

Then Mam sent Lois for wooden spoons and butter boards and with these they tried to prise me out of the cradle. This only produced more red weals among the rolls of fat.

In desperation, Mam tried the force of gravity. She held the cradle upside down over the sofa and shook it with all her (considerable) strength. Out I plopped suddenly, falling about three feet on to the green plush padded sofa, face downwards. And there I lay, with the pattern of the woven wicker embossed from head to heel on my back.

Mam grabbed the towel, folded it round me and applied nature's balm by stifling my sobs with her nipple. There, a few minutes later, Dad found her, dishevelled and exhausted, with an equally red-eyed and distraught Lois clinging to her. His concern at their distress was changed to guffaws of helpless laughter when the star of the performance was turned over to have her true fen-tiger cub's stripes displayed.

That's the tale as I heard it, 'many's the time', from the other three in years to come, not, I dare say, without embellishment that would prevent it from standing up to Grandmother's criterion of Truth Absolute.

I can't vouch for any of it. By the time all three of the supporting cast had recovered from their paroxysms of laughter, I had slipped into a state of blissful breast-fed slumber.

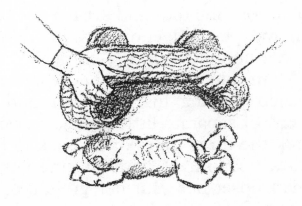

3

Rattles

My Grandad Rattles was 'a curious customer' by anybody's reckoning. Take the following as an example.

Mam, Dad, Aunt Lizzie *et al.* believed what he told them, that he was of pure Irish blood. His story was that his mother and father ('Gramp') had come over to England during the terrible potato famine of 1849 (which would, thereabouts, coincide with the date of their marriage). Mam remembered and loved Gramp, whose hair and beard she used to do up in tiny plaits while she sat on his knee and he sang folk-songs to her. She also remembered Gramp's wife, her grandmother, because when she was once staying with them and sleeping in their bed her grandmother asked her to get out and go to shut a tapping door. She did, and set her foot straight down on the pet hedgehog kept to devour the crickets that abounded in the cottage.

Now Mam adored Gramp because when she had finished plaiting his long hair and 'b'ard' into dozens of separate little plaits, he would set off to walk the three miles or so back to his own home 'down Daintree' without undoing them, rather than upset her. But her grandmother she was not very fond of and told me that she was 'a sour-dark-faced old Irishwoman'.

We all grew up accepting that this was true and that both the charm and the temper that were our grandfather's trademarks were due to his pure Irish blood. Dad appeared to believe this myth — as it turns out to be!

I actually still believed it when I began to write this book; but, as it happens, almost in the nick of time I had a letter from 'a forty-second cousin' — Gramp's great-great-great-granddaughter Christine. She had been properly researching the family and had traced Gramp's ancestors back to A.D. 1700 — all the Papworth's being born in Ramsey! Gramp's wife, Elizabeth (after whom my Aunt Lizzie was named) had been Elizabeth Grimmer, not from Ireland, but from Norfolk.

I think Christine was afraid I might be upset by being thus corrected in my beliefs — but on the contrary, I was absolutely delighted to find that instead of the three generations of fen-born folk I thought I had on my mother's father's side, I had at least seven, all born in Ramsey; and that even 'the furriner' on that side was also an East Anglian.

Well, I do think Dad ought to have suspected Grandad's tale, because he had had enough proof of what an accomplished liar Rattles was, especially when it came to spinning fantasies about himself and his doings. Maybe he did suspect, but if so he kept quiet about it. We, at any rate, believed his concocted story of our part-Irish origin. All a great con-trick perpetrated by a prince of yarn-spinners. Ah, well! Anyway, there it is as an introduction to my maternal grandfather.

'Gramp', whose baptismal name was John and great-grandmother Elizabeth lived 'down Daintree' and had in all, six children; Rattles was their third, he having two brothers older than himself.

The Battle of Inkerman was fought and won on 5 November 1854, but the news of the victory didn't reach our part of the world till the middle of January 1855, in the very week that Rattles put in his first appearance. Whatever difference the news could have made to anybody in our remote spot I can't think — but the excitement was so great, so I've been told, that the newborn baby boy only escaped having to go through life as 'Inkerman Pa'per' by the skin of the teeth he hadn't yet got. Commonsense prevailed for the moment and he was given the names of John Thomas. In the event, it could not have mattered less what names his parents chose for him. He got the nickname of 'Rattles', or to his intimates 'Rattlo-Jack'.

Nicknames were an accepted part of fen life. The men were distinguished by their nicknames from others bearing the same surname and when they married, their wives had to accept the distinction equally. So Mam, for instance, became either 'Mis' Will'En' or 'Mis' Bill-Arry', because Dad answered equally to both.

Other contemporary neighbours were 'Mis' Ponny, 'Mis' Banker, 'Mis' Ixie, 'Mis Young Uncle' — in their particular cases because their husbands, like Mam's, were all legally William Edwards. Not that 'Edwards' was ever pronounced with both its 'ds', if any. The most usual way of saying it was 'Ethers' or 'Edduds', though a family might be 'the Etherdses'.

To get back to Rattles: whatever he was called, he was a man it was difficult to ignore.

In appearance, he was 'a fine figure of a man', over six feet tall, and 'as strong as a hoss'. He was also exceedingly handsome, with a clean-cut face and a Roman nose, high cheek bones and a deep forehead. His hair was thick and springy and his whiskers and beard (which grew down over his chest) hid a firm chin and a wonderful set of teeth.

When I remember him, beard and whiskers were snowy white — and thereby hangs a tale.

When Rattles was around forty, he was out one evening on some nefarious purpose or other, accompanied by one of his like-minded cronies. (Mam, telling me the story, said she believed they were 'lark trolling', but she wasn't quite sure.) While at it, they had a serious disagreement: but they patched the quarrel up and sealed it by calling at several pubs on the way home. Too much beer made the other fellow maudlin rather than belligerent and the more he drank, the more he regretted the quarrel. He kept on coming back to it and saying that whatever happened they must never get 'off hooks' with each other again, 'Never no more, Rattles, never no more'. In this state, they at last reached the gate of 'The Carriages' where his companion put an arm lovingly round Grandad's neck.

'Goo' noight, me ol' mate' he said and withdrew his arm sharply. Unfortunately for Rattles, the hand on the end of the arm was clutching a cut-throat razor. No vital damage was done, though the cut was deep and went half-way round Rattles's neck and left a very clearly defined and jagged scar, which, consequently, he grew his beard long enough to cover.

But, so goes the tale, his blue-black hair and beard 'turned white overnight'. I interpret this to mean by the time he felt able to show his face in public again, when the wound had healed. As far as I am aware, there were no other consequences — the two men even remained friends.

Mam, though, always averred that his hair did change, literally 'white overnight' and that the incident notched his peculiar behaviour up a bit and made his already violent fits of temper worse.

It also meant that for the rest of his life, whatever variety of garments hung about his tall frame, his sartorial get-up was always completed by a scarlet 'neck 'anderchief' tied just above the collarless neckband of his flannel shirt, with the ends tied into 'rabbit-ears' under his left ear — 'in the place' Mam used to say 'as Nature had intended for the hangman's knot'. She had no patience with him, I fear, and little love. She could not forgive him for his treatment of her mother. Dad had no liking for his 'goings-on', but endless tolerance for the man who, in Dad's philosophy, 'couldn't help being born the sort of chap he was'.

I dare say that Dad wisely understood, as Mam would never have done in a million years, that opposition and/or condemnation only made Rattles's rebelliousness and unsocial behaviour worse; and that whoever it was that provoked

Grandad, the person who suffered was Grammam.

It was his eyes that gave him away to those who knew him. They were not very large, but deep-set in bony sockets; as to the colour, it changed with his changing moods. When his hair was black, Mam said, they almost startled you with their blueness: but after his hair became white they seemed a paler, greyer blue most of the time, with just a touch of hazel or green. They were blue when he was at his most vivacious, charming self, twinkling like stars on a frosty night. The twinkle became a glitter when he was in one of his crafty moods and his cold, grey-green glance swivelled from side to side with yellow lights in them, like a fox approaching a hen-house. In one of his sudden, unprovoked rages, they glowed red beneath the grey-green, just like the hot ashes under a crumbling mass of burned out peat — grey until it is stirred, when red sparks shoot from it like fire-tipped arrows. His eyes did the same, when the sullen, angry mood flipped without warning into violence. To his unhappy family, these changeable eyes were the only indication of what they had to expect next.

The curious thing about him was that when he felt like it, he could turn on the sort of charm (often Irish) we see so much of these days on our TV screens. Somewhere not too long ago, one of his ancestors must surely have smothered the blarney-stone with kisses. In this mood, he could crack even Grandmother's face into a smile. He was undeniably intelligent — though he chose mostly to employ his intelligence for the wrong reasons. He read and wrote well — a source of puzzlement to me still. Where did he learn? And as for his gift of the gab . . .

His powers of invention were little short of the miraculous. He made up tales with such pellucid ease that other folk were mesmerised into believing them, though he himself had forgotten what Truth sounded like, if indeed he'd ever known the sound of it. If he did know, then one has to say that he was as much against Truth as Grandmother was for it. His gift of story-telling was of spell-binding, Ancient Mariner quality.

There was an occasion when two brothers from Upwood, who were carpenters, came to do some work for Dad. Knowing the quality of their work and their absolute integrity, Dad left them to it, but was amazed to find nothing done at the end of the first day. They assured him that he would not be charged for the wasted time.

'We just cou'n't tear ourselves away from Rattles' they said. 'We di'n't know as he'd ever 'ad such a life as 'e's bin telling us on!'

'What's 'e bin bladging about, then?' asked Dad, a bit suspiciously.

Well, it appeared that he had been regaling them with tale after tale, full of minute and circumstantial detail, of his life as an officer of the law in 'Van Dieman Land', where, he claimed, he had been employed generally as a tracker of escaped convicts. One lurid adventure had him, all alone, against three powerful desperadoes, which uneven odds had caused him to cling upside down under a culvert for three days and nights before the baffled convicts had given up and taken themselves off.

Dad listened to all this, second-hand, from the besotted young carpenters (and much more of the same nature), until he could keep himself under control no longer. To use his own words, he had to 'bust out a-laughing', and laughed till be had to sit down on the side of the horse-trough to get his breath back.

He was genuinely sorry to have to disillusion the brothers by telling them that as far as he knew, the farthest Rattles had ever been out of the fen was to Manchester, once when he was in trouble with the law and had to do a moonlight flit.

That story will serve as well as any other to show what sort of a life Grammam had had to endure by the time I knew and loved her. Rattles was always treading very close to the verge of what was legal, not because of what the enterprise gained him, but to demonstrate his own craftiness. In this particular case, all I know is that it concerned a valuable missing greyhound.

The police connected Grandad with it two days after Aunt Lizzie was born and this event, for the moment, provided a bit of cover for him. It did not inhibit him as much as it did the police. He harnessed his old pony to the cart and in the middle of the second night of Aunt Lizzie's life, he carried down Grammam's mattress and put it in the bottom of the cart. There he placed Grammam, with the baby in her arms, Mam (aged thirteen months) by the side of her and Uncle Watson, aged two, tucked in by her feet. Covered by such quilts and blankets as they possessed and their necessary changes of clothing, they lay while Rattles clicked the old pony into motion and under the bright, full December moon they set off northwards.

Two or three of Grammam's sisters had gone to Manchester and married there. Grandad was astute enough to know that wherever he found shelter, she and the children would be given a roof over their heads.

The experiment didn't last long. He got himself a job in a quarry, but within a few days he had dropped a lump of rock on one of his feet and crushed it, so there was nothing for it but to set off back home. By the time they reached the cottage (at Mereside) that they had left, the hue and cry had died down, largely because the missing greyhound had escaped from its captors and legged it back home as well.

Now historiographers, sociologists and other academic researchers will not consider such an anecdote worth a second thought simply because it is 'only an anecdote'. How can I possibly prove that such an adventure is anything but a figment of my own active imagination? After all, my mother was only thirteen months old when it took place, so even she could not remember it. It was only hearsay to her, who heard it from Grammam.

However in this particular instance there was in the course of time, practical proof that this modern version of The Flight into Egypt did actually happen. When Aunt Lizzie reached seventy, she applied for her old-age pension and was asked for her birth certificate. There wasn't one — the midnight flit had meant that her birth was never registered! (She got her pension, I think, because her age was recorded on her baptismal certificate. She, Mam and Uncle Watson had all been christened at the same time as their cousin Jubilee Anne, in 1887. Mam was seven, Aunt Lizzie six and Uncle Watson nine.)

Rattles liked to 'oblige' people. Some of this was genuinely the effect of a streak of good nature that appeared in his make up here and there in unexpected places. On the other hand, most of it was because it often provided him with an excuse to skive off a bit of honest work, or gave him a wonderful chance to obstruct others from doing theirs. For example, a bridge across Raveley Drain was used by many old turf-diggers to get to their heavy work in the fens the other side; but it was not a public right of way and to prevent it from becoming one, the bridge had to be closed for one day a year. The owner had great difficulty in finding anybody willing to stand on the bridge all day to see to it that men who had already walked five miles from Ramsey couldn't get to work that way or home again at the end of the day. Nobody was willing to take on a job that caused their neighbours such inconvenience. Nobody, that is, except Grandad. To him it was a day compounded of power and nasty authority and he gloried in it. He was, he said only 'obliging' the owner.

Grandmother once asked him if on his travels he had ever found a source of the herb penny-royal which she used among other things for making black puddings. It was not very prevalent in our fen and she thought he might know where to find some. He spent a whole day searching for it in Sawtry Roughs and in the end found what he was looking for. On his way back he had to go a mile or so past his own home to deliver the bunch of penny-royal to Grandmother. She lifted her bombazeen skirt and her flannel petticoat and reached for the pocket kept tied round her waist among her other 'underskirts' (four). After much deliberation she produced a penny and handed it to him. He took it, raised his old cap with exaggerated politeness and gave it back to her.

'You keep it, Mis' Etherds' he said. 'I'm sure as yew need it mor'n I dew.'

Grandmother was by that time a well-off farmer in her own right. Grammam had already been stricken by the illness that in the end proved fatal. The silly incident is a sort of spotlight on both of my grandparents and I would not care to have to judge between them. Neither ever forgave the other for it.

Rattles showed a hearty contempt for work if there was any way possible of keeping a bob or two for beer in his pocket without it. He was 'agin' an honest day's work on principle — not because he wasn't a good workman. When he did consent to lower himself to accept work, he made it his business to show other men just how it should be done — mowing an acre of standing corn with a scythe in less time than it took anybody else and thereby showing them up as weak or lazy, or both. He spent a good deal of his time 'wizening' out ways to avoid work, or getting paid for something he hadn't completed. While 'wizening', he sat in his high-backed chair by the side of the hearth in the lean-to kitchen of 'The Carriages', with his old short clay-pipe in the corner of his mouth — upside down. Many men smoked their clays with the bowl turned downwards. In Grandad's case this resulted in the snowy whiteness of his beard having on it a bright orangey-yellow patch of stain. Another symptom of some plot being hatched was that he would gather up a few strands of his luxuriant white whiskers, roll them between his fingers and tuck the end of the roll into the corner of his mouth to chew on while he cogitated.

He called himself 'a higgler', that is, one who took on small tasks for others. For this 'business' he kept a placid old pony and a 'light' cart. The cart would often be empty when he left home in the morning for a pleasant day out rambling round villages on the other side of the Great North Road, but it would rarely be empty when he returned. For one thing, he never travelled without his double-barrelled gun and he was an excellent shot, besides being an experienced poacher. Aunt Lizzie taught me to sing, after I was about three, a tune with a chorus that went:

Does your mother want a rabbit?
Skin her one for ninepence.

It could have been Grandad Rattle's signature tune. His gun helped to keep something in the pot for his wife and children and the pig and the fowl down at the bottom of the garden helped as well. But the old pony, the pig and the fowl also had to be fed. The work of feeding them fell to Grammam, but the provision of their food was up to Rattles himself.

Dad was by no means the only farmer or smallholder who was occasionally surprised at the rate at which the contents of his corn or pollard bin was being used up. Not that Dad ever wondered where it had gone. As the chief sufferer, he knew what the others only suspected, but short of catching the old villain red-handed, they had no proof: and if they had had, what could they have done? 'Had the law on him'? They had enough sense to know they would come off worst. Tackle him physically about their losses? Grandad's philosophy was that if folks would leave unconsidered trifles lying about, they must expect them to be snapped up.

He thoroughly enjoyed his days jogging about behind the old pony, stopping at as many pubs along the way as he had money for and entertaining strangers with tales of his adventures in the colonies — for which spurious inventions his beer mug was often replenished. (He must have read a good deal, I think, to have had enough foundation of fact to support his pile of fiction.)

Meanwhile, it fell to Grammam to do everything else to support the family. Like most other women, she tended the garden and fed the domestic animals. Most of her neighbours had been bred to such work and expected to labour alongside their menfolk whenever constant child-bearing would let them. They 'set-off' the turf-diggings as their men dug the peat, set and 'picked' potatoes, made 'bands' for sheaves in the harvest field even if they didn't gather up the cut corn and tie it as their men mowed. Later on (in my own youth) they weeded onions and singled sugar-beet and 'dropped', even if they did not actually set, the precious and expensive celery plants.

(Mam refused point blank ever to work in the fields, before she accepted Dad's offer of marriage. It did not worry him, but it sent his mother and oldest sister nearly crazy with anger and jealousy.)

Dad himself saw nothing wrong with women doing 'light' jobs about a farm, but did not care to see them expected to cope with dangerous jobs like gault-digging, or working in the turf-fen. Many had to, to feed their large families. A woman at work would often be heavily pregnant and be accompanied by two other babies, a toddler and the last baby who couldn't yet walk.

As in Grammam's case, their work was often essential to keep their family fed and clothed. The difference was that in many cases they grew up expecting this to be their lot in life. Grammam, from the age of four, had been the petted darling of the well-off childless aunt and uncle who had taken her and brought her up. When her aunt had died young of cancer, her uncle had taken to gambling and was soon ruined. Only eighteen, she found herself without a home and made the mistake of falling for the handsome young John Thomas's charm.

To Grammam fell the task of keeping her children clothed 'respectable' for school, and 'well-dressed' for high days and holidays. She went out washing to the bigger farmer's wives and took in washing for others: she went setting potatoes in spring and picking them up in autumn, besides her everlasting chores at home of patching and mending, making meals out of very little and making a home sweet and clean and even pretty until in one of his rages Rattles wrecked it all — time after time.

Her pride in her own appearance never faltered and she was always one of the best-dressed women when there was any 'occasion' to go to. She was often deprived of the pleasure that a Good Friday tea, or a chapel anniversary Service of Song might have given her, by the fact that Rattles had pawned her best frock or her new hat. (On one such occasion, she was so disappointed that Dad cycled the twelve miles to Peterborough and back again to redeem her frock in time for her to go.)

She also did her utmost to keep Rattles as well turned out as other men, at least for 'workaday' clothes. He had a clean pair of 'bluette' or 'drabette' trousers for every Monday morning and a clean shirt for every Saturday afternoon, after she had bathed him by sluicing buckets of dyke water (heated in the copper) over him as he stood in the tin bath in front of the hearth. He was quite pernickety about personal cleanliness, which at least is one good thing that can be said for him.

The worse of Grammam's trials and tribulations was his tendency to fits of passionate anger for no reason other than a delight in violence and the power it gave him over his defenceless family. Until the temper burnt itself out, he seemed utterly incapable of controlling it.

The scenes that it caused when Mam was a child had burned themselves like scars on her memory and she would recount them to me in detail until, even after eighty years, she could find relief in tears. She had always been afraid that in one of these fits of violence he would do her mother some serious bodily harm. She never dwelt on any fear for herself, though obviously it must have been ever-present. She was always a splendid raconteur and even with tears slipping down her face, would remember to include the humour that inevitably accompanied such outbursts. It wasn't all misery for the children, though apprehension never left them for long.

Grammam sang or whistled as cheerfully as a bird whenever there was any peace from worry or anxiety and when 'Jack' was in a reasonable mood. If the children had to go to bed before their father came home from one of his daily jaunts, Mam would say to her 'Whistle, Mammy, so we know you're alright' and she would keep up a tuneful singing of folksongs and hymns, or an equally tuneful whistling of the popular songs of the day, as she moved about getting a meal cooked against their father's return. Better still it was for them when they were in the old lean-to kitchen with her while they waited for him to

91

come home. They loved this part of the day. The room was in twilight, often with a haze of blue peat smoke and the only light the glow from the hearth. They were warm and cosy for the first time all day, because if they got wet or cold on their long walk to school, they had to stay like that. They played with what few pieces of toys they had — a broken slate and a slate pencil, an old wooden or rag doll, bits of broken china and empty cocoa tins to 'play house'. The smell of the meal cooking on the pothook over the fire added the pleasurable expectation of being well-fed for the first time that day. When it got too dark to see, their mother lit the paraffin lamp and stood it on the middle of the table. At last the sound of cartwheels announced Rattles's arrival home.

If he'd had a good day, he too, was likely to come in singing — usually folksongs that he must have learned from his parents when he was a boy. Mam could remember only snatches of them, but according to her, they knew he was in a specially good mood when they heard: (Jubal? I have never been able to trace this and guess that Mam may have heard it wrongly or put her own interpretation on it, as children do.)

Whatever its origin 'O what have you got in your bag?' must have seemed to her a very appropriate accompaniment to her father's homecoming.

And in this pleasant atmosphere the family meal might begin — until Grammam sang or whistled a tune Rattles didn't care for, or dished him up herrings when he'd expected pickled pork, or even put one too few 'taters' on his plate. Then the coin would be flipped over and he would rise from his chair with blazing red eyes bawling curses and imprecations and bring his huge fist down on the table with such force that the oil-lamp would jump up and go out, leaving them all in lurid twilight lit only by the smouldering turves on the hearth. While their father swept both meal and crockery from the table with great swings of his shapely arms, the children scrambled to their mother, both for protection and to protect. When the ruin was complete, Rattles would slam the door behind him and make for the pub. Then Grammam wept over the broken bits of the last of her remaining 'chiny' and tried to gather from the wreck of the meal enough food to make sure the children didn't go to bed hungry, even if she did.

There was one tale Mam used to relate at least once every year, when the anniversary of the event came round again. The details of this tale never varied in all its poignancy or all its humour. She never got through it without tears trickling down her face and dropping from her chin, for of all her memories it was the one that hurt the most because of what it had meant to her mother. It was the one story of all her store that she laid an embargo on, that I should not put it into print; and until now I have honoured my promise to her. I shall not tell all the details even now, but I include it here for two reasons. One is that she broke the embargo on its publication herself; the other is that it contains one of the most extraordinary examples of folk-memory that I have ever met.

Though this was obviously a memory too close to her heart to want it treated lightly, Mam would on occasions tell it to people, even strangers, whom she liked and whose sensitivity to understand she sensed. One such person was the late Henry Treece, the novelist, who sat entranced at her side while she exhibited all the dramatic panache she was so capable of. She was already eighty-five when that happened, but sadly outlived him by four years. Another visitor privileged likewise was a radio producer named Reggie Leigh-Crutchley. He had come north to interview me and was trapped in the web of Mam's skill as a raconteur like a fly in a spider's web. He switched on his tape recorder and to my utter astonishment, she went on to tell the tale she always called 'the time we went on tramp' — in all its detail, sad and funny. He played it back to her and asked her permission to broadcast it. I was even more amazed when she agreed, and broadcast it was.

I feel that the broadcast released me to make my point about it if I ever came to need it.

It was after such an outburst on Grandad's part as I have just described above that Grammam's courageous spirit broke at last.

The date was 1 March 1890 and the tempest rose as Grammam was getting Jack's breakfast, while the children were still in bed. As soon as they heard the noise, they scrambled out and threw on enough clothes to cover them — the old clothes they had been playing in the night before, while their school clothes dried. They bundled down the three wooden steps to the kitchen, to find Grammam in her hat and coat, about to close the door and walk out on her miserable life, and them.

They rushed to cling to her, begging to know where she was going without giving them their breakfast on such a bitter morning, when a black frost wind with a hint of snow in it was sweeping relentless across the open fen. She told them — away, for ever.

They went with her, just as they were. Uncle Watson was in his breeches, unlaced, and his shirt. Aunt Lizzie had a whole frock on, but the 'play' frock Mam had grabbed up was one with a frill round the bottom, only about half of which was still attached to the skirt. All had shoved chilblained feet into their school shoes drying on the hearth and Mam, who suffered constantly from terrible earache, looked round for some head covering. The only thing handy was a 'play' hat, a summer straw affair with a very high crown and a broken brim. Thus attired, they rushed out after their mother who was resolutely striding with set white face towards 'the high road'. What desperation she must have been in, not to turn back and at least see them properly dressed against the weather!

She had only a few pence in her purse, but her intention was to get to Peterborough, where the old uncle who had brought her up still lived — the only person in the whole world she felt she could go to for love and sympathy; though she knew he was old and ill and without any visible means of support himself. She had been broken away from her brothers and sisters when 'Uncle Coggy' had taken her, aged four, to bring her up as his own. She had been the object of their jealousy then and when Aunt Jane died and tragedy struck, she was not welcome to go back home. Moreover, some of her sisters had married very well (her oldest sister was a doctor's wife) and her brothers all 'doing well'. They did not want to be connected to Rattlo-Jack and spurned her after her marriage. Her pride was indestructible, praise be! (Like the rest of us born 'down the fen'.)

She had, during the week just passed, been doing some work out in the fields for the landlord of the riverside pub (where 'the high road' crossed the Old Nene over a hump-backed bridge), but she had not been paid.

By the time they reached the bridge, all three children were frozen with cold. As they crossed the bridge, Grammam spoke for the first time.

'Throw your hat in the river, Kate' she commanded. 'Let him think we have all been drowned!'. Mam demurred and clung to her broken straw hat. Her ears were aching badly enough as it was.

Grammam was going to the pub to ask for the few shillings the landlord owed her. The children took shelter from the icy wind under the arch of the bridge, getting colder and colder without the exertion of walking to keep their blood flowing.

Grammam was gone a long time. The landlord demanded to know why she wanted her money, where she was off to, and why. He was a kindly man and needed no telling about Rattles in his rages. He was full of sympathy for her, but also of common sense. He tried to persuade her to go back home while there was still time, even refusing her the money to try to make her change her mind. But she was beyond reason, beyond endurance, beyond any thought except that somehow she must get away. The landlord reluctantly gave in, paid her seven shillings and away they went again 'on tramp', as Mam always put it. They had only reached about the halfway mark to Peterborough when darkness fell and it began to snow. They took refuge in a stable with an old horse whose warm breath, and the heat of his body, kept them from freezing. In the morning the world was white, but they had to go on. Grammam unpinned the woollen shawl from her own shoulders and tied it round Aunt Lizzie: she removed from under her skirt her red flannel petticoat and made that into a cloak for Uncle Watson, who had only his ragged shirt to keep out the wind. Mam, having at least got her underclothes on beneath the torn frock and a hat to keep her head warm, had to go on as before.

There was no succour for them at the end of their journey. Uncle Coggy was dying and utterly penniless himself. It is at this point I deliberately skip the rest of the terrible details — for Mam's sake. A woman connected with the Salvation Army took in the three children and fed them till Grammam was rested enough to start on the return journey. There was nowhere else on earth she could go.

They were away three nights altogether and it was late on the fourth day when their poor home

97

came in sight again. It was only at that point that Grammam's courage failed altogether, for she had little hope of being let in when she got there. Grammam told Mam afterwards that if Grandad had refused her entrance, they would have all gone straight on down to Raveley Drain, where she would have dosed them with laudanum she had acquired in Peterborough and drowned them before drowning herself.

The cottage was in darkness in the fading light, but when she lifted the latch, the door opened. She shut it again quickly and gave the children their orders. When she opened it again, they were to slip behind her into the kitchen, up the steps as silent as mice and get into bed just as they were. If it was possible at all, she would try to bring them a hot drink later on.

They did exactly what they were told. Exhausted and hungry as they were, Uncle Watson and Aunt Lizzie sank at once into sleep; but Mam lay shivering and crying, deliberately keeping herself awake in case Grammam should need her, or try to slip away again without them. She had only her ears to tell her what was happening and she was already deaf in both.

There was no light in the kitchen and no fire on the hearth, but by the side of the dead ashes sat Rattles in his high-backed chair, leaning forward with his head in his hands. He neither spoke nor moved.

Grammam took off her sodden coat and boots and lit the lamp. Still he did not look up. She fetched kindling and turf and lit a fire on the hearth. Still no response. She filled the old black kettle and hung it over the fire. As far as she could judge, everything was exactly as it had been when he had slammed himself out four days before. She picked up the broken crockery, righted the table and emptied the caddy to make herself a cup of tea. When it was brewed, she dared at last to pass close to him on her way to her own old wicker armchair. As she did so, he looked up. His hair was dishevelled, his eyes sunken in, his cheeks gaunt and hollow. They held each other's eyes, each waiting for the other to speak first. It was he who finally broke the silence.

'If all the stars in heaven had have fell, I should never have believed as you'd ha' left me, Mary' he said.

She answered 'If they do, I shall never go again.'

The silence being what it was, even Mam succumbed at last to weariness and warmth and went to sleep. When Grammam found enough cocoa and stale bread and butter in the cupboard to take them all the promised hot drink, she couldn't rouse one of them to take it. All three were dead to the world, and no wonder.

As the years passed, there were many more times when she and Aunt Lizzie implored Grammam to leave the old devil and take refuge under their safe roofs; but she had given her word, and she would not break it.

She reproved her daughters, sadly if gently, that they should suggest such a thing. 'You mind what you're a-saying, my gel' she would reply. 'Remember, whatever he is, he's your father' or, if Mam was very distressed for her, 'Don't you worry about me, my gel. Them as keeps mad bulls knows best how to deal with 'em.'

To Dad, who loved her and did his best in practical ways to protect her from the worst consequences of Grandad's outrageous tantrums and general way of life, she would speak a different language, knowing that he would understand.

'Jack is my cross, Bill', she would say. 'No cross, no crown.'

The cross was heavy and the way was long.

There were so many sides to Rattles' nature that to try to present him as any sort of entity is, as Dad would have said, 'like eating vinegar with a knitting needle'. What made Grammam's life with him such an endless anxiety was not so much his disinclination to work and the poverty it caused, but the constant fear that one day his 'unkisliding' would land him seriously on the wrong side of the law. If he could get something for nothing, it was not the value of what he got that pleased him, but the 'wizening out' how to do it and the pleasure in carrying it through. So he didn't care who he did down, or whom he involved. It just pleased him to think himself cleverer than other folk. Of all the people who dealt with him, the one most tolerant of his capriciousness was his son-in-law, my Dad. Dad was the possessor of a keen intelligence allied to a deep philosophy that engendered unbounded tolerance of other people's foibles. He also had a spotless reputation far and wide. He and Rattles made strange bedfellows and one would hardly

100

have expected them to be partners in any sort of enterprise; but as an example of my grandfather's skullduggery, the story about digging a well is as good as any other.

Somebody wanted a well dug. Rattles offered to do the job. The farmer, well aware of Rattles's reputation, warned him that a sharp eye would be kept on his performance. It was to be a well twenty-feet deep, and therefore too dangerous for one man to complete alone. Rattles agreed to find somebody to help.

Grandad did not lack physical strength and the owner was pleased with the rapid progress made. Grandad had reached the point when help must be brought in. The farmer asked whom Rattles was intending to apply to for help, since most of his cronies had little better characters than he had.

'I'll tell you what', said Rattles. 'I'll ask Will'En if 'e'll gi' me a 'and. 'E'll find time some 'ow, if I arxt 'im, I reckon.'

He reckoned right. Dad wasn't at all pleased, because he had more than enough work to do already; but if Grandad was willing to do a bit of honest work that would bring in a bit of help for Grammam, Dad was not the man to deny it to her.

The work went well and they were within six feet of the required depth. The time of day had come when Dad had to knock off and attend to his yardwork at the farm. Rattles declared he should go on working by himself. Dad had no option and was very worried about the safety factor, but next day Rattles was all right. The

101

same thing happened again — until Rattles announced to a very surprised Dad that the job was finished. The farmer was invited to come and see the depth measured for himself.

With a very anxious Will'En as witness, a very cocky Rattles let down the tape and proved the well to be its full twenty feet deep. Quite satisfied, the farmer paid up, leaving the two workmen to tidy up the top and clean up their tools. It was only then that Dad discovered that at three separate places in the tape, a foot or more had been most expertly removed.

To Rattles, this was nothing short of triumph — a triumph of wit over 'a bee'ing farmer'. To Dad, it was a thorn in his pillow for the rest of his life. He had done a man a wrong and there was no way he could 'rightle' it.

Furious though he was, he could not help being amused by his father-in-law's ingenuity — not in cutting the tape, which appalled Dad for its dishonesty, but in foreseeing that he could get away with it simply by using Dad's absolute integrity and spotless reputation as an insurance policy against being found out.

Of course, Rattles's own reputation was as black as Newgate's knocker and everybody knows that once you give a dog a bad name, you may as well hang it.

The shadow of his reputation as a plausible rapscallion, a light-fingered scoundrel and a charm-filled villain with a ferocious temper floated ahead of him like the shadow of a cloud across a stubble-field on a sunny day; a fact that proved of great advantage to many another petty crook. Why look for any other wrongdoer, while Rattles was about, larger than life and twice as boastfully natural? In any case, his very presence served to make the local police officers partially-sighted, because he made sure that they always had one eye on him.

He rejected and detested authority in any shape or form, from the Almighty down. Schoolteachers, ministers of religion and above all policemen were the outward and visible signs of authority against which his whole being rebelled. It gave him wicked delight to lead the police on wild-goose-chases while the real culprit had time to dispose of any damning evidence — knowing all the time he could turn the tables on the police and prove himself 'innocent as a babe unborn'. His crafty intelligence was too much for them most of the time and his fiendish delight in slipping through their fingers just when they thought they'd got him infuriated them. It made them determined to pin anything and everything criminal on him and caused him to sail nearer and nearer to the wind in order to outwit them.

It was not in his nature to consider the effect all this had on his wife and children. Grammam spent her entire life in apprehension of his being picked up for some serious crime for which he had no alibi. Aunt Lizzie had enough roguery in her spirit to take some vicarious pleasure in his exploits. Mam's only concern was for her mother and but for that would have wished her father to perdition. She could never understand Dad's tolerance of 'the old Rattle-Snake' try as Dad

103

might to explain to her that her father was as he was and that condemnation was what kept him going. He *liked* being painted blacker than he was. 'There's more good in him than in a lot o' folks who go to church on Sunday', Dad would say. 'You must give even the Devil his due!' Poor Mam. She had nearly as much difficulty in understanding her unusual husband as she had in trying to fathom her reprobate of a father!

He didn't always come out on top, of course; but in general he was so much like Bob Pretty that if ever W. W. Jacobs had been in our fen, one would swear he had taken Grandad as inspiration. Just like Bob Pretty, he managed to leave the law with egg on its face even on the few occasions when they did manage to catch up with him.

There was, after all, something slightly ludicrous when they jailed him for a month for stealing a cat he'd happened to take a fancy to one day when he was visiting The Fox at Catworth (on the road between Huntingdon and Thrapston). Of course, Dad had to keep Grammam and all the rest of Grandad's livestock while he was inside; and Mam suffered agonies of shame, because ever afterwards her mother-in-law and Aunt Harriet could hurl 'jail-bird' at her at the height of any internal family quarrel.

Another incident was much more serious.

He had been out one day with his old pony and cart, accompanied by one of the less desirable of his mates and had stopped for a drink at The Woolpack, just by the Holme-Glatton crossroads on what was then the Great North Road. A stranger came into the tap room, 'flown with insolence and wine', having had a good morning's dealing in Peterborough market. In paying for what he ordered, he pulled from his pocket a bag of coins and groping in it, somewhat befuddled, managed to spill seven golden sovereigns on to the floor. Rattles politely and helpfully picked them up and restored them to him. The man then replaced the purse in his jacket pocket and ordered some victuals. When the food came, he took off his jacket and hung it over the back of his chair. His morning spent tippling caused him to take frequent trips 'out the back' in a hurry and when, finally, he prepared to leave The Woolpack and to pay his score, the purse was no longer in his jacket pocket. By that time, Rattles and friend were well on the way home; but he had been at the scene of the crime at the crucial time. The police were jubilant. They'd got him, fair and square, at last.

He was committed for trial at Norman Cross on the grounds of his reputation, his knowledge that the money was there and the opportunity there had been for him to take it. Moreover, another customer in the pub gave evidence that he thought he had heard the man with Rattles say in a low voice 'If you see a chance, mate, you want to dive in.'

What Grammam suffered while awaiting that trial! She was already mortally ill, half-starved and overworked. The disgrace was more than she could endure, yet she bore her cross with patience and dignity. Aunt Lizzie rushed home to be with her, consoling and doing her best to recharge Rattles's own depleted bombast. He had very little hope that he'd escape the full rigour of the law this time. There was a difference between an old cat and seven golden sovereigns! Dad, as usual, footed the bill for everything while Grandad skulked in his corner and Mam stayed away as much as she could, ashamed to show her face in public. She had no doubt whatsoever that Grandad was guilty and said so. Grammam was hurt, Aunt Lizzie furious and Dad uneasy, telling her it would be best to keep her thoughts to herself until her father had had a fair trial. So she sulked.

Dad, of course, had been expected to attend the hearing, because somebody had to bring the old pony and cart back if Rattles couldn't. For some reason I have never understood, Aunt Lizzie had been called as a witness.

When the morning of the trial came, Dad did his yardwork at Grandmother's (who nevertheless stopped him his day's wages) and then went straight to The Carriages early. Aunt Lizzie was distractedly getting herself ready for her ordeal in the witness box, dosing Grammam with *sal volatile* to ward off one of her swoons, abstractedly assuring her tearful father that the God he most surely didn't believe in would this time answer his prayers and trying to cook Dad's breakfast in the iron frying pan hung up the chimney, all at the same time.

Dad's sense of humour was always extremely delicately balanced and in spite of his genuine anxiety about the outcome of the trial, he was nevertheless observing the scene with more and more amusement as the minutes passed. Then Aunt Lizzie plonked his breakfast down before him and when he discovered that his fried egg was neatly decorated with a coil of combings from Aunt Lizzie's jet-black hair and that between his rashers of bacon lay four well-fried postage stamps, he could contain himself no longer. The pent-up laughter burst out of him and when Aunt Lizzie inspected the plate he was holding out to her, she sat down weakly and joined in. Grammam, who hadn't got much to laugh about, caught the infection all the same and laughed till her sides ached though she had no idea at all what they were laughing at.

Grandad was so low that he hadn't enough spunk left even to curse them. He just sat through it all like a sack of wet feathers, mumbling prayers under his breath.

But at last they came to themselves and got the accused dressed in Dad's second-best suit (not quite long enough in the leg), with a clean 'neck 'andkercher' and his hair and beard washed white as snow and combed to look as much like Abraham's in the bible as makes no difference. They climbed into the cart and drove off, leaving Grammam alone. (It seems that even Mam deserted her that day, though she had promised to be there when the cart came back without Rattles.)

Towards the late afternoon, the strain began to tell on Grammam, so much so that when one of Grandad's relations that she both disliked and distrusted appeared at the door, she was glad to welcome even his presence as a distraction. He was a bird of similar feather to Rattles and normally she strove to see that they did not have too much to do with each other. But this day, she actually asked him in and he sat down in Grandad's own chair, heaving mournful sighs and glancing continually up towards the mantelshelf above his head, on which sat two orange and white china dogs. 'They'll nab 'im this time, Polly,' he said. 'Ah, poor ol' Jack! They'll nab 'im alright this time, yew mark my words.'

This was not the kind of cheer Grammam needed. The pain in her chest and diaphragm was made no better by these gloomy predictions.

After a few minutes, her Job's Comforter began again. 'Ah. Poor ol' Rattles. Yew wou'n't see 'im again for a longish while, that yew wou'n't. They've got 'im proper, an' I reckon as they're gooin' to keep 'im, this time. Got 'isself nabbed at last, I tell yer.'

And so on, and so on — every despairing comment accompanied by swift apprehensive glances upwards towards the pair of china dogs. All this 'nervoused' Grammam to such an extent that she began to wonder if he knew something she didn't, and at last she plucked up her courage to ask him what made him so certain of the outcome of this trial.

'Well, Missus, when I were at 'um this mornin' by misself afore I comed 'ere, arter I see Jack an' them goo, them ol' china dugs on my mantelpiece started a-jumpin' up an' down o'

108

their own accord, an' I knowed what that meant. Jumpin' china dugs is allus a bad o'em. It's a sign as bad as bad can be, jumpin' china dugs is. Yew watch you'rn. Soon as they reach a verdick them dugs on your shelf'll start jumpin' up an' down an' all. Yew'll see!'

After that, they both sat and watched the dogs with fearful fascination, though never a jump did they discern. And then, suddenly, there was the sound of cartwheels crunching the old brick rubble that made up the gateway leading down the side of the house. It was Grammam who jumped up and rushed to open the door. The cart contained the same three figures as it had done when it set out. Having taken that much in, she collapsed in tears of thankfulness and joy, all pain forgotten in gratitude and relief.

Rattles got down, puffed up to his own size again and twice as jaunty as usual. He took it ill that the visitor showed obvious surprise at seeing him back home.

'I thowt as they'd nabbed yer this time, bor', the visitor said. 'On account o' them jumpin' dugs on my shelf. I've never knowed them jumpin' dugs to be wrong afore.,

'Damnation seize your bloody jumpin' dugs!, roared Rattles. 'I'll give 'em something to jump for if yew ain't orf my gateway afore I git my coat orf. I'll jumpin' dug yer, frightenin' my missus like that! Bloody jumpin' dugs! You can see as the o'em wa'n't meant for me, so yew'd better look arter yerself next time they jump.'

Dad and Aunt Lizzie went to put the old pony away, letting out their relief with another session of laughter as Rattles 'scienced about' making feint punches into the air till the neighbour had sidled by him and reached the gate. They could not keep such a gem of humour to themselves and before two days had passed the concerned old neighbour might as well have forgotten he'd ever had a proper name. He was known ever after as 'The Jumpin' Dug'.

It was a bit much for Grandad to turn his exuberance at being acquitted against his old friend's 'o'em', for he was himself more superstitious than most folks around there and that's saying a lot. As far as I know, he never acknowledged any religion and neither did his brothers and sisters. He hated both the Church of England and the non-conformist chapel equally and never set foot in either except for his wedding to Grammam when he was twenty-one.

Grammam found peace and consolation for an hour in chapel on Sundays, when Rattles was in a good enough mood to let her go. But he was dead set against her having anything to do with it and on one occasion strode in after the service had begun and ordered her out. She herself took great comfort and strength from her belief in Jesus, who, she declared, often made himself visible to her. 'He touches me,' she said, 'and the pain fades away; but He'll never let me touch him.' She never told Rattles about these visitations. He would probably have suspected the visitor's intentions and stayed around waiting to 'haux Him off'. Grandad was afraid of her humming to herself as she so often did:

Cross over the line, it is only a step
A step between me and Jesus.

She was only in her sixty-third year when she finally took the step and left him to carry his own burden, including cancer, for another five years without her.

4

The Fenland Habitat

There is a good deal of misunderstanding about 'The Fens', which perhaps I ought to clarify for those who do not know the area intimately.

The Fens (note the capital letters) is the term used for the great shallow basin extending over several hundred square miles and stretching from Lincoln to Cambridge north to south and from Huntingdon to The Wash from west to east. A large area of flat land under huge skies, unromantically described by one writer as 'the piss-pot of thirteen counties'.

The fenman, born and brought up there, does not use the word 'fen' in any general or all-inclusive way. He is aware that 'The Fens' is correctly used in the plural. There are dozens of different 'fens' in this larger area, each with its own characteristics. The fenfolk distinguish always between one fen and another.

Nor does a fenman use the word 'fen' loosely to include any place where in former days the fenland floor rose above the water level, creating little islands or peninsulas of 'upland' clay or gravel. With successful drainage, the water surrounding these islands has been removed and the 'highland' areas are no longer immediately to be perceived as islands. Strangers can, if they wish, make fairly accurate guesses by noting the number of villages whose names end with 'ey', the mark of a former island e.g. Ramsey, Thorney, Swavesey: sometimes 'ea' as in Manea and Quanea is substituted. Sometimes a village may be spelled both ways, as Whittlesey and/or Whittlesea.

By 'fen', the fenlander himself means only the true fen, that is, the deposits of silt and clay and the layers of peat laid down *in water* in times past.

My concern in this book is with a tiny area approximately one mile square, on the very edge of The Fens, so that on its southern side it begins to rise gently towards 'the highland' where a belt of clay stands, almost imperceptibly, above the adjacent 'fen' and 'mere'.

This slightly higher ground was, quite appropriately, called 'the heights'.

When I attended the elementary school in our scattered hamlet, which by that time had been given the name of 'The Heights', we were told by our teacher that our 'village' got its name because 'heights' was derived from an older word 'aits', which in turn was a form of a still older word 'eyot': and that an 'eyot' in Old English, was defined as 'an island in the middle of a river'.

Well, as we all know and Pope wrote, 'a little learning is a dangerous thing'. My father was about the most tolerant man who ever lived. Anyway, his tolerance did not stretch to accepting this example of 'a little learning' on the part of our teacher. It infuriated him to hear one of us trotting out this explanation for our homeground, which was on an average three feet below sea-level, being called 'The Heights'. He regarded it as almost a personal insult that 'a bit of a gal' who happened to be a school teacher, should so take it upon herself to teach her grandmother to suck eggs. As he said, he knew every inch of the land concerned and had done so since the day of his birth: and he would aver with his last breath that since mankind had had the gift of language, the part referred to correctly as 'the heights' could never have been an eyot, an ait, or an island entirely surrounded by water. It was simply the very edge of The Fens and it was on this patch of higher ground, next to the waterlogged fens, that the little community which later became 'The Heights' first grew; partly because the clay provided better foundation for dwellings than the adjacent peat or silt of the fen proper and partly because the clay itself began to be used as raw material for brick and tile making.

So to the initiated, such spots of somewhat higher ground are neither 'in the fen', nor 'down the fen'. In our particular case, The Heights was 'The Heights', Lotting Fen was Lotting Fen and not to be confused with the heights, or with Ugg Mere, or Wright's Fen or Jackson's Fen or any other fen that had its own boundaries and its own identity.

This square mile or so of my home-land was amongst the last bits of the huge fenland basin to be drained. A map dated 1833 shows that within an area roughly two by two-and-a-half miles there remained three shallow meres still

114

undrained — Whittlesey Mere, Trundle Mere and Ugg Mere. About two-and-a-half miles to the north-east was Ramsey Mere and all of them were surrounded by wide borders of marsh and 'raised bog'. (Sir Harry Godwin[1] says that raised bog was more prevalent hereabouts than anywhere else in The Fens.)

Besides these freshwater lakes, there were others that dried out in summer, but were filled with water in winter: Benwick Mere, Brick Mere and Dray Mere, as the sketch map shows. This is the area wherein my genetic identity begins. The meres that dried out in the summer produced verdant pasture and were used for sheep and cattle grazing. They were, sensibly, referred to as 'summer lands'. There is a much publicised belief that the fenmen of old splodged through their surroundings on tall stilts. How anybody with the intelligence of a gnat, who pretends to 'know' the fens, can believe this nonsense absolutely beats me! Walking on high stilts is difficult, very nearly a circus act, even when the ground below is firm, hard and level. The most obvious explanation of what has almost become a sacrosanct myth, is that when the 'summer lands' were grazed by wandering sheep, their shepherds raised themselves up by using stilts on 'the roddons', from which vantage point of height they could keep an eye on the precious

---

[1] *Fenland: its Ancient Past and Uncertain Future* by Sir Harry Godwin F.R.S., Emeritus Professor of Botany, University of Cambridge, pub. C.U.P. 1978.

flocks. ('Roddon' is the term given to the clearly definable banks of ancient rivers that existed in the pre-glacial era. These roddons stand slightly proud of the surrounding tilth even today and are firm with compacted sand and clay.)

The same stilt-walking was — perhaps still is — used by shepherds for the same reason in 'Les Landes' in the Bordeaux region around the Garonne in France.

It was to this still undrained corner of the great fenland basin that my great-grandfather emigrated to escape a terrible outbreak of cholera in Ramsey in 1829–30, when, according to folk-memory still extant in my own youth 'the grass growed green up the High Street for want o' folks to wear it down'.

Tucked in between the boggy margins of Ugg Mere and the Raveley Drain, lying next to the higher ground on the edge of the fenland basin, was a fen as yet uncultivated. It was in the process of being drained and dykes criss-crossed it, cutting it up like a chequer-board into fields averaging about four acres in area. The going price for such a field was five shillings and a gallon of beer. Its value to any purchaser at the time was calculated more on its potential yield of reed, sedge and peat (possibly workable as a turf digging), than on its use as agricultural land.

Great-grandfather, who, (according to my oral family sources), was one of the first purchasers, chose the highest and driest field and paid for it with seven sacks of potatoes. Who the vendor was, I have not yet discovered. Maybe his plot contained a roddon, because he built himself a

116

house in the field, the only house for many a year to have a second storey. Other, later colonists had to be satisfied with the two-roomed, low walled cottages, which sank lopsidedly into the soft peat after a few years.

Some 'lots', of course, were better than others: the little fen acquired its name, Lotting Fen, this way.

At around this time, however, 'the heights' was becoming a growing, if tiny, community of dwellings. According to my father's own observations and investigations as a child, attempts had been previously made to commercialise the clay there for the production of clay pipes.[1] Then it became the start of a successful brick and tile-making industry. When my father was born, in 1870, there were three separate brickyards all in full swing, but some had already been worked out. My grandfather (John Edwards) was born in 1837 and when he married he went to live in a cottage converted from a disused brick kiln, and was not its first occupant, either. It was in this converted brick kiln that my Aunt Harriet was born in 1860, Dad in 1870 and my other aunts Eva and Flora Mahala (Loll) at two-year intervals later. The gap from 1860 to 1870 is accounted for by the birth of two other boys, both named Samuel and both doomed to death at a few weeks old. When Dad was born, he was also provisionally called Samuel, but it was then that Aunt Harriet (aged

---

[1] Ibid.

ten) first exhibited her Cassandra-like propensities. She dreamed and woke up screaming that if her new baby brother was named Samuel, he, too, would die. My grandparents, superstitious to the hilt in spite of their strict Wesleyanism, took the hint and called him William Henry instead.

The brickyards made the colonisation of Lotting Fen possible. The clay was dug by local labour, the kilns fired by local peat dug by local labour and the bricks and tiles were made by hand, thus providing a lot of work for local women as well as for men. Families who owned a 'lot' could work it themselves and still take regular work in the brickyards.

Packing the kilns with green brick or tile was a very skilled job and firing the kilns with peat even more so. The workmen who undertook these tasks were respected, full-time employees. When fired, the brick or tile was transported by water to its destination anywhere within reasonable reach, though mostly in the area of the interconnecting rivers and canals of 'The Middle Level'. One old horse plodding along the tow-path (or even a donkey) could haul a whole string of barges, or 'lighters'. Farm produce (in the course of time) was also transported by barge and raw materials brought back on the return journey.

Dad went into partnership with his friend Charlie (Uncle John's brother) when they were about seventeen and set up a business as watermen. Dad always said that no other sort of work ever gave him half as much pleasure as that

118

of being a lighterman.

The brickyards flourished. Sometime c.1875–80, one of the brickmakers invented a wooden mould to shape the bricks more accurately and more quickly than hitherto. Finding his invention unappreciated at home, he took it to 'Americky', sold it and made a large fortune besides founding a dynasty of mechanical engineers. He took his fenland wife with him and other members of the family went too. So did a lot of other skilled brickmakers, including Fred Bedford and one of Rattles's brothers, Stephen Henry.

Both these characters returned fairly soon to the rigours of the fen, which they preferred to those of the strange country around Philadelphia. They were revered for their daring and ever after retained a certain aura of 'difference' because of their excursion. Being of the same breed as Rattles, Stephen Henry had, of course, a good many astounding tales to tell and was always known thereafter as 'Americky Stiv' or 'Pennysylvania Pa'per'.

Perhaps the sudden exodus of skilled workers had something to do with the decline of the brickyards, though it was much more likely to have been the transport by rail of cheap coal to the larger brickfields at Whittlesey and Fletton that finished them. The decline must have been sudden and swift. The owner for whom Dad worked most often became deranged in his mind and the failure of that yard was put down to this cause. My guess is that cause and effect were the other way round. He owed Dad and Charlie a lot

119

of money and gave them the chance to take out their dues in brick instead of cash. That is how Fern Cottage came to be built and waiting for Dad's bride.

I also have a bit of evidence of my own as to how sudden the end of the brickmaking business must have been. One of the three brickyards belonged to the Summers family. From the time I first started to attend school, after my narrow escape from the Bottomless Pit, my constant companion was the youngest daughter of 'the Summers family', a girl of my own age named Joyce (still, happily, a friend!).

When it was my turn to go to play at her home, our playground was most often the forsaken brickyard. There, clustered around the old kiln, were the former drying sheds — long, low hovels with open sides to allow the air to dry the brick and tile to firing state.

Under the beautifully tiled roof of each hovel were shelves and racks upon which the brick and tile were placed; and when Joyce and I used to play there, those shelves were still full, with hundred upon hundred of 'green' tiles that had never got into the kiln at all. They had crumbled, fallen and smashed as wind and rain had reduced the hovels to ruin, but they were still where they had been put to await firing. Even the tools of the trade still lay about there, as I know because one 'dockey-time' Joyce and I were discovered by her mother using them to make 'mud pies' from a sack of unslaked lime and we had unearthed in the corner of the shed we had chosen that day.

I can date that incident fairly closely, because at Easter in 1924 Joyce and I together became pupils at Ramsey Grammar School, after which we had better things to do than make mud pies. I guess that that memory comes from around 1921 when we should be eight years old. Close to the kiln and the sheds were several little cottages, all tiled, like the sheds, with home-made wares, as was the 'big house' where the Summers family lived. Joyce's grandfather, who had been the last of the brickyard owners, lived at Peterborough. He was the one and only man I ever saw actually driving his own coach-and-four.

I loved those little cottages. In one of them lived Dad's best friend, 'Uncle' George. It was as clean and bright as springtime, with a hive of bees in the garden and flowers all round the low, whitewashed walls. Inside, even in summer and after many years since peat had been burned on the hearth, there was always the lovely faint aroma of peat smoke — a lovelier perfume to me than anything Chanel could ever produce. After the end of World War II, I conceived a desire to buy that particular cottage, so as to be able to keep one foot among my own folk, but I took my eye from it and when I next went down The Heights Road, the whole lot had been condemned as unfit for human habitation by Ramsey's District Council — not only the cottages, but the kiln, the hovels and even the house were gone! Brash post-war Britain was all for 'progress'. There was not, as far as I could see, the least reason for this wholesale demolition. It was just that in those days 'sentiment' was a dirty world and 'nostalgia' even worse. The fen was MUD, metaphorically as well as literally. Who, in his right mind, could even want to preserve anything that had ever been there, let alone go and spend time there voluntarily? Archaeology had not yet taken notice of such vanishing ways of life as our humble fen so it was lost, except in the memory of people like me.

It seemed, suddenly, that everybody left in the fen or 'down the Heights' was clamouring to go and live in Ramsey, or at least demanding a modern council house on 'the high road'. Maybe they were being uprooted by 'fashion' rather than desire, because some of the other old fen-tigers I know well now agree that they would rather not have moved and that their hearts, like my own, were left in the fen. It was at that time that our clan, or tribe, was largely displaced and dispersed.

And that mention of 'clan' and 'tribe' brings me round to a bit of amateur anthropology. We were — or are (perhaps there are enough of us still left to justify the use of the present tense) a closely-knit community largely inter-related, practically all descendants of those first few pioneers who colonised that square-mile of undrained fenland during the first half of the nineteenth century.

Geographically, this district was enclosed by the Old Nene river to the north, the Raveley Drain to the west and 'the high road' on the east. To the south, as I have already said, the land began to rise out of the fen. It was a sort of self-contained unit, with its limits well defined.

The scattered hamlet had to have an address.

Its original centre was 'the heights', for the reasons already given. In the time of my parents' childhood, addresses didn't matter much, because few people were literate enough to write letters, or read them. If a letter was sent to anybody in our fen, it was delivered by the draymen to one of the public houses and notice was sent by word of mouth to the recipient to come and collect it. (This was during a sort of illiterate hiatus, which did not last long.)

However, once schools had been established, after the 1870 Education Act, letters became more frequent and a postman was sent out from Ramsey on foot to deliver all round the fens. The post, as well as bread, was still being delivered daily on foot up and down the droves until the mid-1930s.

Postal officials required addresses and it was decreed that The Heights should be the name of our hamlet, including Lotting Fen (still, of course, mostly below sea level in spite of its incongruous official address).

But by that time, other factors had entered in. Ugg Mere having become cultivated, the population was no longer concentrated at the southern end of the square mile. At the northern end, where the high road (it was called that to distinguish it from the unmade, 'sluddy' droves that ran parallel to each other between it and Raveley Drain) — where this high road crossed the river (the Old Nene), a school had been set

123

up and was kept going by the charity of the Fellowes family of Ramsey (later, the Barons de Ramsey). The school served not only the community on our side of the bridge over the river, but that on the other side as well (the Herne and Daintree).[1]

Facing the school across 'the high road', the Fellowes family also built and endowed a church, which was dedicated to St Mary. It was not long before a chapel was erected 'down the heights', on the Heights Road — a former drove which was then gravelled, or more correctly, granited, as far as the chapel. There had been a chapel farther down, before the new one was built in 1871.

The Anglicans definitely had the whip-hand, though the Wesleyans had greater numbers. The Anglican parson, far removed in social class (and his own estimation) from either farmer or labourer, was the figure-head of our 'parish'. He was also, until 1902, the *de facto* head of the school, in spite of the teacher who had been

---

[1] *Note on 'The Herne'*: Godwin states that the word 'mere' was applied to any complex of shallow freshwater pools as well as to the large freshwater lakes; but he goes on to say that such complexes of pools had other names, among which was 'hurn'. My guess is that this is the origin of the name given to that part of Ramsey St Mary's which in my youth we called 'The Herne'. I imagine also that the heron (hern, hernshaw or 'harnser') got its name from that of its habitat among the shallow freshwater pools.

124

appointed. Moreover, he held over us all the ultimate sanction — only he could marry or bury us. The chapel had no graveyard and was not licenced to marry until c.1930. The chapel 'baptized' and the church 'christened', but marriage or death drove us all into the church's arms.

It was no doubt a contributory factor to my Grandfather Edwards, Grandmother, Aunt Harriet and Uncle John all being taken 'for a bloody j'y-ride' to Ramsey cemetery, instead of being allowed to lie, with the rest of us, in St Mary's churchyard.

The post office then put a spoke in our wheel. It decreed that the northern end should become, officially, 'St Mary's', while the other end still remained 'The Heights'. I don't know where the official demarcation line was, though I think it was probably the Green Dyke Bank. Soon, we were both annexed to Ramsey and so became 'Ramsey Heights' and 'Ramsey St Mary's'. The anger that was generated when, subsequently, Ramsey Heights was subsumed by postal decree into Ramsey St Mary's still rumbles on and no wonder; but the bureaucrats had not finished with their interference yet.

As my map shows, the eastern side of our square of land is bounded by 'the high road'. This road must once have been an ancient trackway on the very edge of the impassable fens, along the 'upland' by the side of Ugg Mere. When it became used more and more, (I guess in the middle-ages when the huge abbey at Ramsey was largely occupied by Norman monks who spoke Norman French), it acquired the name of 'Ugg Mere côte road', that is, literally, the road or track *by the side of Ugg Mere*. Officialdom and bureaucracy, however, had little knowledge of or concern with history. Somebody, to whom Norman French might just as well have been Sanskrit, translated what he heard into what he thought he had heard and wrote it down as Ugg Mere *Court* Road. (Our teacher used to tell us that this was its correct name.)

Now where 'in the Lord's blessing' as Aunt Harriet would have said, did they think the word 'court' had come from? In connection with Ugg Mere? A less likely location for a court — of either variety — than Ugg Mere would really be difficult to conceive. But authority had spoken and Ugg Mere Court Road it became.

No wonder we old fen-tigers were, and are, angry and upset at this latest attempt by officialdom to teach their grandmothers, as in their modern jargon they would undoubtedly phrase it 'to instruct a parent's mother to extract the embryonic juices of an egg by suction'.

Folks who a few years ago lived in The Heights, Ramsey, Huntingdonshire may never have moved house, but are now obliged to give their address as:

No. 'OO', Ugg Mere Court Road,
Ramsey St Mary's,
Cambridgeshire.

Excuse me while I growl!

It all began with the building of St Mary's

126

church. Not one in ten people who went to either place of worship could have told you why. If asked, they would probably have answered, 'Well, don't yer see, I were born chapel', or 'Cos my fambly's all'us bin to church. I dunno.'

There was little communication between chapel and church in my young days, though the parson's wife ran 'The Girls' Friendly Society' which was open to girls from chapel as well as church. Both Lois and I (in turn) were members. I always felt that I was there on suffrance and only attended in a mood of belligerent reluctance because Mam said I had to go.

However, of my two Grammar School cronies, Joyce was chapel and Jess was church. (Her family was then and still are, the pillars of St Mary's.) I went to church one Sunday evening, with Jess, when we were about eight (before Grammar School days). I, of course, had been 'born chapel' and baptised there. Gerald and Lois, though both 'born chapel' had been properly christened in church, so perhaps they had a foot in each camp.

I must, I think, have been a rather unusual child, though fifty years working in primary education have taught me that most children are far more observant and thoughtful than adults give them credit for. Certainly, at the age of eight, that visit to evensong with Jess gave me some amusement and a lot to think about. I can recall every detail of it!

The building itself awed me. I was in the presence of a very different sort of god from the

127

one I knew so intimately in chapel. This 'church' god was aloof and cold, lodged somewhere in the huge empty space over my head. He was Awe-ful and Watch-ful and I was Fear-ful and above all, Respect-ful. His Silence was dread-ful and His ways quite incomprehensible. The congregation around me were full of righteousness and dignity and as I sat wriggling, waiting for the service to begin, I half expected to be turned out as an unworthy intruder.

Then followed utter confusion, which gradually filled me with what I then felt was terrible, wicked amusement. The proud ladies in their best Sunday hats and the stiff men in their stiffer Sunday collars all began such a performance of bobbings up and down, that it turned into a sort of party-game, as far as I could judge, accompanied by mumblings I couldn't follow. Jess did her best to come to my rescue, finding the place in the prayer book I had been provided with and pointing to the passage we had reached, while still performing her own bobbings and mumblings. From rump to feet, from feet to knees, from knees back to rump, from rump back to knees they bobbed. I tried to copy the people in front of us, but was always a fraction too late in my anticipation of what the next move would be. Likewise with the responses, in spite of Jess's help. By the time I had found the place and started to read, everybody else was finished.

Then there were the hymns. I was used to a chapel jammed full to the gallery with people, all opening their throats and mouths to let rip in such volume as to make sure 'the Lord' heard either prayer or praise. The squeaking of our broken-down American organ was there to give us the note and was drowned by our uplifted voices. If the organist didn't happen to turn up, we sang just as heartily unaccompanied. Not so was the congregation's singing in church, as I found. The voices, for all I know, may have been just as hearty (if a little more prim) — but the sound of the pipe organ drowned them and they disappeared into that space above me like the mewing of newborn kittens or the squeaks of terrified mice. I stopped singing, because the organ (with my teacher at the keyboard manual) sent such thrills of pleasure through me that I didn't want my puny screechings to spoil it. I was interrupted in one of these moments of intense pleasure by having a little bag presented before me, to receive my contribution to the collection instead of the open plate I was accustomed to. Then I suffered agonies of embarrassment, because it appeared that I was supposed to take the bag and pass it on to Jess. What if I dropped it?

I knew the clergyman by sight, of course, from his occasional appearances at functions and his even more occasional visits to our house — we were, in spite of being 'chapel', his parishioners. I had even seen him once or twice before, in his cassock, dog-collar and surplice. I rather liked the look of him, actually, though he seemed that evening to have a dreadful cold that made him sort of sing through his nose. I was sorry for him and wondered if he would have to have his tonsils and adenoids removed. He seemed all right though, when we sat back to listen to the sermon, which I found extremely dull. I was used to histrionics.

(When I was about fifteen, the parson who so engaged my thoughts that evening walked out of his vicarage, went into the garden shed, put a double-barrelled shot-gun into his mouth and somehow pulled the trigger. His ghost thereafter roamed the road between the churchyard and the river and was encountered by several people I know. It once tried to pull Gerald off his motor-bike. I simply state that as I was told it — about the ghost, I mean. Who am I to confirm or deny it as truth?)

The next time I went to church was on a sad family occasion — the 'funeral service' for my cousin Vernon. Not the burial service itself, but THE FUNERAL SERVICE which always took place on the first Sunday following an interment. I suppose there was also a funeral service for Vernon at the chapel, but if so, I don't remember it. This one was in St Mary's Church. My entire family was present, all clothed in deepest black.

All the feelings of dread and awe I had experienced on my first visit were intensified by the Great Silence being punctuated by sobs. This was NOT my first experience of death. On the contrary, but it was my first participation in the trappings of woe — a very different matter indeed.

All Vernon's relatives were dyed-in-the-wool Wesleyans, yet his burial oration had been made in church.

There was no doubt, however, that in those days the *dignity* of the church added a touch of the ritual that everyone craves in times of stress, such as at a funeral, or in times of celebration such as at weddings, baptisms, thanksgivings and the like. This longing for ritual was not a Victorian hangover. It was (and is) atavistic. Death, for instance, was older than the god housed in either church or chapel. Superstition revealed itself in trivial matters.

For example, we had in our house a pair of large pictures, Victorian sepias, framed in elegant wood frames. One depicted a droopy-looking female in insubstantial clothing, crowned with flowers and drenched with tears, embracing a marble gravestone made in the form of a cross. Below the picture, in beautiful Roman lettering, were the words, 'ORA PRO NOBIS'. I became aware both of the picture and the legend when we moved up to New Fen and asked what the words were. How I loved that magical phrase, ORA PRO NOBIS! It mattered nothing that I didn't know what it meant. I remember stamping up and down the path beside the house with a pliant and obliging kitten, dressed in my doll's clothes, in my arms. As I stamped along, I addressed the kitten in my new-learned phrase — Ora pro nobis: ora pro nobis: ORA PRO NOBIS! Mam heard and rushed out to stop me. She knew what the words meant and in any case the picture had a gravestone in it. It made her uneasy and I was forbidden to go on saying it. The poor persecuted kitten took the opportunity to leap out of my arms and fell heavily on to the path, being hampered by the yards of exquisitely embroidered lawn christening gown that it was attired in. My latest doll being life-sized, I had been given for its use what would now be family heirloom. The kitten was a most beautiful long-haired grey tabby and I'm sure it looked prettier in that finery than any of us ever did. My kittens always appeared extraordinarily obliging in being dressed up and pushed about in dolls' prams. At any rate, I found any kitten more likely to lead me to God than a picture of a silly girl clinging to a gravestone.

The other picture was of a very similar looking female who had apparently escaped in the middle of the night to go and clasp a similar gravestone, because she was clad in a very flimsy 'bed-gown' and surrounded by headstones. That night, I felt, was not very suitable for such an excursion, because the distraught girl was clutching a lantern to enable her to find the right tombstone in the very thick, murky brown fog that enveloped the graveyard. The legend on this one was 'Lead, kindly light' — which had no spine-tingling effect on me whatsoever.

Now all of us, without exception, detested these pictures — especially Mam herself, who for some reason seemed afraid of them and therefore caused us children to regard them with unease as well. We begged her to take them down, but she would not.

It is only of late years that I have realised what a large amount of superstition was connected with pictures and mirrors, both of which, of course, 'produce images'. Mam must have subconsciously feared the bad luck (or punishment) that might follow the deliberate removal of a 'religious' image. If she recognised this fear, she probably connected it with the remembrance of ever-present death, which was obviously just what the Victorian artist had intended; but it is my contention that the roots of this superstitious unease went much, much deeper.

Grandmother, for example, would have been very indignant at any suggestion that she ever broke any of the Ten Commandments, always so ready on her tongue. Yet in spirit she broke the first of them 'Thou shalt have no other gods before Me', every day of her life, because she clung instinctively to superstitions that must have had their origin farther into the past than Christianity, or the bible in its English translation. Did she truly believe that it was either Jehovah or Christ that sent her omens by bird and beast? By making 'coffins' grow on candle-wicks, or sending glowing coals or sparks of burning peat bounding from the fire onto the hearth? By hollow knockings (always in threes) on doors and windows or from the insides of cupboards?

Where in the Christian bible is there a decree that a corpse must be left in its own dwelling for at least three days after death — however distasteful and terrifying this made conditions

133

for the living? Whose servant was 'the Black Dug', who must appear three times to somebody before the death it portended actually took place? Why were dreams of insects (especially head-lice) so dreaded? Why was a single candle left burning by the head of a corpse and a bowl of salt placed under the bed on which it lay? Why (if possible at all) was a 'corpse watcher' employed to sit by the head of the coffin during the three nights before burial? And above all, who was 'The Hooky Man' who lay in wait wherever there was standing water, to claim children as human sacrifices?

There were too many bits of folklore and superstition left in our neighbourhood for it to be coincidence. All rural areas tend to be conservative and cling to the past, but in the face of all our superstitious beliefs and ritual, Christianity, even as practised by Grandmother, seemed only skin-deep. It was a Sunday religion, made more so by the opportunity it offered for social intercourse; a chance to listen to the grand words of the bible again; to listen to and join in the singing and to take part in ritual praying and praising.

Nevertheless, Christianity lay only on the surface, as a layer of peat may be found lying on a bed of more ancient fen clay. It really mattered little whether it was an Anglican or a Wesleyan mask my forebears and their neighbours wore below their Sunday headgear. Most of the week they were still pagans, relying on pagan gods. My guess is that as

134

blood is thicker than water, in our case Celtic blood was still holding its own against the water of Christian baptism.

I advise all academics who abhor amateur dabblers in any discipline to skip the next bit!

5

A Celtic Heritage

Yesterday is history — but 'History is what you remember' (according to Messrs Sellars and Yeatman). They were speaking of school history, that muddled mixture of facts without sequence that the great majority of us leave school with and which forever after has to serve as the backdrop against which all other momentous events of past or present are seen.

When I attended The Heights elementary school, history was allotted half-an-hour per week as a subject on the time table. It does not surprise me at all to consider all that we did not learn. It amazes me to recall all that we did.

In that period (1900–1930), history began with The Romans. (The fashion of beginning with 'the cave men' and never getting beyond 'the Vikings', came later.)

The Romans, of course, came and saw and conquered. No wonder. All they had to do, as far as I could make out, was to subdue a few decrepit old men called 'The Ancient Britons'.

This, I learned, came under the heading of a *Good Thing*, mainly because the Romans knew how to build long straight roads such as Ermine Street, on which famous road some of us had actually set foot at Huntingdon or God-manchester. Connected with these Romans there was also a queen named Boadicea who came to a nasty end because of some intriguing mystery concerned with what the Romans did to her daughters. If we had been given details of what it was they did we should have been no wiser, so innocent were we all; but naturally we were not told. All the same, I had a soft spot for Boadicea, because she came from Norfolk and I had also been in Norfolk once on a day trip to Hunstanton. That served to give her some sort of reality, spatial if not temporal.

After her was a chap called Alfred, whose chief contribution to our island's story did not blend very well with the concept of the path of duty being the way to glory, since it appeared to consist only of a dereliction of duty that caused somebody else's cakes to burn. I sympathised with the poor woman, mainly because of all comestibles I detest the burnt currants on an overcooked fruit cake the worst. I wrote Alfred off as an unreliable idiot.

William the Conqueror, it seemed, had enough sense to grab a couple of handfuls of British soil when he had the misfortune to trip over while getting out of a boat as he landed to do his bit of conquering, showing him to be a resourceful man who deserved more than Harold Hardrada's six feet of English ground.

After a few other such isolated incidents, mostly intriguing scraps mainly on account of their utter inconsequence to us, we were shown a map of the world and thereafter got down to the serious business of learning when, how and by

137

whose efforts so much of it came to be coloured red.

I give you my word that what I have written above about the ancient Britons was the sum total of my knowledge of them for the next three decades. My ignorance did not bother me. I imagined them, if I thought of them at all, decrepit old folk, all male, a bit like old Henry Etherds bent double after a lifetime of turning turf, except that they were naked, which lack of clothing caused them to paint their skins blue and let their hair and beards grow long enough to keep them warm. I can hardly conceive of the degree of indignation I should have felt then if anyone had suggested to me that these wild and disreputable old men were my direct ancestors. By the time I had begun to read historical novels and romances for myself, I should have desired to be descended from 'a civilised Roman' or 'a black-avised Norman' — even 'a fair and comely Saxon' — anything, indeed, other than a woad-painted Ancient Brit. It was a good three decades later that it was brought home to me that I was, in fact, pretty nearly a full-blooded Celt.

In strict fairness to my wonderful grammar school at Ramsey, I must exonerate them from any blame about the gaps in my historical understanding. I learned a lot of history there, eventually taking it as one of my main subjects in the Higher School Certificate in 1932. But what the Oxford Examination Board required of me was knowledge of Palmerston's Foreign Policy: the Unification of Italy: the influence on future

138

history of a man of ideals such as Cavour compared to that of a man of action like Bismarck: and the moves in the political game of draughts played out between Gladstone and Disraeli: I also had a smattering of knowledge of local history, mainly because of Dad's passion for it; but there was never an Ancient Briton in sight, even on the very perimeter of my interest — that is, until an extraordinary incident that happened to me one October evening in Cambridge.

The Second World War had moved me and my parents out of our native fen forever. After a very sad and difficult patch in my personal life, I was earning my living as a teacher in a one-teacher village school in Cambridgeshire and to help me to do so because I had a small daughter, my parents were forced by my plight to uproot themselves and come with me.

I loved my new village and I adored the school. I had turned it from a derelict anachronism to a show-piece of creative education, to which visitors from all over the world came. In doing so I had saved myself, too. In fenland parlance, I had got back my 'dossity', which means that I was bursting with good health, energy, vigour, ambition and confidence. The only thing I was missing was intellectual stimulation — except for the great shining star of Nan Youngman's art classes.

The Village College Scheme, the wonderful brain-child of our former education officer, Henry Morris, had been put gradually into being, but so far there was no 'community school' in our area. I read with envy the list of adult classes offered to those in more fortunate areas and when I saw that a course in English Literature was to be offered at Bassingbourn village college, I blew my top and wrote an impassioned letter to the then education officer about my deprivation. Bassingbourn was less than twenty miles away, but I had no transport, nor was there any public transport — even if I could have been allowed to gate-crash out of my own designated educational area. Bassingbourn was as much out of my reach as Tierra del Fuego.

My letter impressed our chief and what is more, he did something about it. If I could find transport of any kind, the education budget would foot the bill! The person who came to my rescue was the then adult tutor at Bassingbourn Village College and the man who was himself conducting the English Literature course — David Holbrook. He did the round journey twice to pick me up and deliver me home again. I was able to go. (David's decision and Nan Youngman's interest changed the whole course of my life, but that is another story. I just want to take the opportunity of paying grateful tribute to Nan and David in passing.)

It was not to be expected that David could continue this time-consuming journey for long; but I had had a taste of what I wanted and I wanted more of the same stimulant. So I took a huge gamble, cashed in my only available asset and bought myself what would now be described as 'an old banger'. I was mobile and independently so. I continued to attend the class for the second year and a third. The summer vacation was over and we were coming up to the beginning of the fourth year. It was the practice to begin each new yearly session with an inaugural lecture given to all the adult students, whatever classes they had decided to attend. The mixture was varied, from classical music to car maintenance, from local history to cake-icing, from our own study of *King Lear* and Eliot's *Four Quartets* to carpentry. The inaugural lecture might be relevant to some, or to none. It was a get-together of those willing to be educated in their own time. I doubt if few were looking forward with more pleasure than I to that first Friday in October.

During the afternoon of that day, David telephoned. He was in difficulty, because he had arranged to pick up the lecturer for the evening, but his car refused to start. Could I, and would I, go via Cambridge and pick up the lecturer on my way? I could, and I would. He would be standing on the corner of Selwyn Gardens at 7.15 p.m. and David would notify him of the change of plan. I guess David told him that his new chauffeur would be a village schoolteacher. To a man of his age, the image was stereotyped — a tall, angular maiden lady of uncertain age, with rimless glasses and greying hair pulled back into a bun, wearing a uniform of a grey suit with white blouse.

I was in my early forties 'and 'tho' I say as shouldn't', a pretty reasonable specimen of middle-aged womanhood. The large, dark,

141

bouncy, well-dressed woman who got out of the car on the opposite side of the street to our retired professor did not fit the stereotype of the village governess.

I identified him easily enough and as I crossed the street on foot to introduce myself, I was aware that he had noticed me and was watching me with a penetrating intentness that became almost uncomfortable. I reached the opposite pavement still some twenty yards from him and turned to walk towards him. He, too, turned to watch me, but gave no sign that I was the driver he was expecting. When I was about five yards distant from him, he raised a large gloved hand, just like an old-fashioned policeman on point-duty and said, loudly and very distinctly, 'STOP'.

I stopped. What else would one do, in such circumstances? I looked again at him. There could be no doubt that he was my passenger, especially as he carried a clip-board with notes attached under one arm and held a carrier-bag full of exhibits in his other hand. I, too, had a stereotyped image of the absent-minded professor, but I had never before encountered one of such eccentricity. My mind raced round for some explanation of his strange behaviour, but the only thing I could come up with was that he had mistaken me for a prostitute out early on my beat. I stood quite still, wondering what line to take.

Then he began to move, slowly and deliberately towards me, his keen eyes scanning me from dark head to small feet and back again, his expression changing visibly from mere interest to genuine pleasure. He reached me and stood directly before me, peering into my face. A look of disappointment crossed his face as, at last, he raised his cap and spoke.

'Oh!' he said. *'Why haven't you got blue eyes?'*

Curiouser and curiouser. I had begun to wonder which of us, if not both, was mad. I felt obliged to make some sort of response.

'I'm sorry' I said apologetically, adding, as a sort of inane douceur. 'But my brother has!'

This was, in fact, not true. Gerald's eyes were grey, though they did have a blue-ish tinge and a blue rim round the iris. Could such a white lie matter? As far as I could judge, the Mad Hatter's tea-party had nothing on this incredible encounter. All the same, it seemed that my inconsequential rejoinder had satisfied my interrogator. He proceeded to walk all round me, mumbling to himself words that I occasionally caught. I understood that he was, in fact, going over my points, exactly like a horse-coper at a fair.

'Short tibia' . . . 'thick femur' . . . 'only the eyes wrong'.

He came out of his trance with an apologetic start, raised his cap again and began profuse apologies.

'You took my breath away!' he declared, by way of excuse. 'So very nearly the perfect specimen!'

We had begun to walk back towards my car and I was, quite naturally, intrigued.

'Perfect specimen?' I asked. 'What of?'

'The Fenland Celt' he replied.

Our speaker for the evening was, in fact, a well-known anthropologist. Before we had reached the outskirts of Cambridge, he had given me a breakdown of my genetic origins. He told me that he was pretty sure I had my roots 'somewhere in the Ramsey district of Huntingdonshire'. Being assured that he was correct, he begged leave to question me, rather than to inform me, for the remainder of our journey. I was more than willing to play the part assigned to me.

What size was the family from which I came? Only three. Some disappointment, because 'it was one of the characteristics of Celtish women that they were extremely fertile and produced large families'. (The contraceptive pill was not at this time generally available.)

Did I know anything about this aspect of the generation to which my parents belonged?

I could have laughed aloud. Of course I knew — have I not stated that pursuing genealogies and kinship ties was the staple female conversation in the fens — well, male conversation too, except that men didn't have quite so much time for it, or quite such a nose for the 'less respectable' aspects of other people's 'famblies'.

As it happened, it was also a bit of a coincidence. Just a short time before Dad died, this very subject had arisen over our tea-table. Dad had been sitting 'mosing' during the afternoon and at the table suddenly said to Mam 'I'm just been a-counting up how many first cousins I'm got, or at least, had. I knowed there must be a whull hussle on 'em, but I di'n't think

144

there'd be so many. I make it seventy-four. Tha's got you beat, Mam!' He was teasing her. She hated to be bested on any subject. 'I mean', he went on, 'just look at Uncle Smooker's lot. There was Julie, Allie, Polly, Johnny, Eddie, Arthur, David, Walter, Leslie, George, Clara, Anne and Ernie — Ernie were the thirteenth and Aunt died of him.'

But Mam wasn't listening. She'd accepted the challenge and was counting her own first cousins. Rattles had been one of six children, but the Papworth side had not produced vast numbers of offspring. On the other hand, Grammam's side, the Strettons, had made up any deficiency.

'Aunt Marthe had fifteen' Mam mused aloud, to my intense interest. 'She drowned herself in the end, poor old Aunt Marthe did, in the middle o' the first war. I know that's right, because six of her own sons in uniform got compassionate leave to come and carry her to the grave. She had womb trouble, you see, and she was in such misery she couldn't bear her life. She kept threatening to do it, so one or other of her daughters used to sleep with her and tie their wrists together with a strip o' rag. But Aunt Marthe bided her time and picked the knot undone one night while her daughter were asleep. They found her next morning in the pond, poor old gel. So there's fifteen, to start with.'

Mam went on and on enumerating, till she announced in triumph 'I make my count seventy-five — well, seventy-six if you count that last one of Aunt Liza's, as she had in the change. She'd had twenty-one already, you see and I reckon by that time she thought she'd laid her laughter; but then when she were over fifty, she fell for another, though it was either born dead or only lived a few hours. So she had twenty-one, then twenty-two then twenty-one again. And if anybody asked her or Uncle Billy how many children she'd had, they used to make a joke about it and say as she'd had 'twice twenty-one'. So she had, if twice twenty-one means the same as twenty-one twice! Anyway, that last one makes my count two more than yours.'

I related this tale to my inquisitor in 'my old fen twang' and almost diverted him from his original purpose by switching him on to the subject of dialect. He was particularly interested in my use of the word 'laughter' (pronounced 'lorter'), though this is not a word peculiar to the fens. It can be found in any dictionary, meaning the number of eggs laid before a hen-bird begins to incubate them. It is an example of how isolation had succeeded in preserving words once in common use, but which had elsewhere been forgotten or neglected.

The questioning went on and on. Did I know how many of these first cousins on both sides had remained in or near to their birthplace? Yes, I knew a good deal. Dad's uncles and aunts fell into two groups. Most of them were still to be found around Ramsey — at Upwood and Raveley (where they still flourish) and Holme. However, another group had emigrated to Bardney in Lincolnshire (the emigré being forever after referred to as 'Bardney Bill') and from there his progeny had wandered to the steel mills around Sheffield, where, true to their nature, they had sought out other emigrés who had gone there direct from the fens. The result was that, in spite of their removal, they followed the genetic trend and married each other, thus establishing a sort of sub-clan in and around Tinsley.

Mam's counsins had, more or less in the same way, established a pocket of kinship in and around Bacup, Manchester. I don't know so much about that side, because Grammam had been broken away from her family when young. However, some of the Strettons (of whom more later) were frequent visitors to our house and from the first time I ever heard him mentioned, I could not forget that I had a great-uncle who rejoiced in the name of Abelol Spencer. Another knife in the bible, surely, to have found a name like Abelol for the baby?

We had reached Bassingbourn. It was I, not my professor, who had learned most. I had Celtish ancestors.

Many classical writers speak of them as being 'proud and fearless in battle, but despondent in defeat'.

Ptolemy tells a lovely story about a group of Celtish warriors going as a deputation to negotiate with Alexander the Great (fourth century B.C.). The Celtic envoys, 'men of haughty bearing and tall stature', having finished their business, were relaxing with Alexander, who in the course of conversation, asked them what it was they, the Celtish race, most feared.

'We fear no man' said their spokesman. 'There is but one thing that we fear and that is that the sky should fall upon us.'

The oath by which the Celtish envoys bound themselves to Alexander contains the same phrase:

If we do not keep our word, may the sky fall upon us and crush us, may the earth open and swallow us, may the sea overflow and overwhelm us.

In *The Book of Leinster* (twelfth century A.D.) is the story of Tain No Cuailgne (c. eighth century A.D.). In this story, some heroes of Ulster were in a tight spot in the middle of a tribal battle. Their king told them he would have to leave them to it, to go to meet a new enemy on a second front. They replied to him

Heaven is above us, the earth beneath us and the sea around us. Unless the sky fall with its shower of stars upon the place where we are camped, we shall not give ground.

What was it that my Grandad Rattles said in the hour of his greatest despondency? '*If all the stars in heaven had have fell*, I should never have believed you would have left me, Mary.' The ultimate sanction, still. No wonder we fen-folk think such a lot of our great wide-open skies, our glorious sunsets and the immense expanse of stars on a frosty night!

Other facts about the Celts (Gauls or Ancient Brits or whatever) are not so palatable. Their religion, for one thing, appears to have demanded human sacrifice as propitiation to their triad of elemental gods — earth, sky and water. We know that at one of their seasonal festivities they constructed a huge effigy of wicker-work, into which hollow cage they stuffed as many sacrificial victims, men, women and children, as it would hold. They then set it on fire.

A lot of research has gone into Celtic religion in the past century, but the results are still nebulous, to say the least, especially with regard to any named gods or goddesses. The underlying religious beliefs are most easily deduced. They seemed to believe in the indestructability of 'the soul', or (to distance it from any Christian connection) of 'the spirit' with which all things in the natural world are endued. If men scorned death, it was because they felt assured that their spirit would be assimilated back into nature and soon given a new habitation of life. One classical writer noted how similar in this respect their belief was to that of Pythagoras and his belief in the transmigration of souls.

The spirit of a man, they thought, reposed in the head, because from the head came speech, that vehicle of all human emotion.

This notion added a curiously cruel streak to their barbarity, making them head-hunters. They rode home from tribal battles with the heads of their defeated foes slung from their saddles — as

Thomas Love Peacock said in *The War Song of Dinas Vawr*.

Ten thousand head of cattle,
And the head of him who owned 'em.

They hung up the trophy heads of battle and those of their sacrificial victims, in sacred grooves dedicated to gods or goddesses. They impaled them on spikes at tribal meetings; if one story is to be believed, they occasionally plated the skull of an important enemy with gold to use as a ritual drinking vessel. (Is this akin to the patriarchs of the Bible 'making their enemies their footstool'?) Possession of the head meant possession of the spirit, at least for the time being. Rattles feared the camera because it might steal his spirit, right up to the time of his death in 1923.

It was 'the spirit' that these proud, passionate people revered and it was the fruits of the spirit that they gloried in — 'subtlety of speech': poetry, song and story: music: in rhythms, dance and ritual. They were proponents of all that we now lump together under the term 'The Arts'.

My own definition of 'creativity', (with which I have been associated throughout my professional life), is 'the ability to create symbols of one's own experience'. It seems to me that the ancient Celtic races did this all the time. Symbolism overflows into magic and blends with it until they become one and often the same thing. The Celtish religion appears to have been based on magic, a magic in which all living things had a

150

part and which created a link between men and their gods. Hence, no doubt, all sorts of superstitions involving animals, birds and insects as carriers of omens, or warnings from the gods.

I have often wondered what possible connection there could be between Aunt Harriet's ominous dream of head-lice and death. It occurs to me now that the explanation is not far to seek. The heads taken as trophies or used as sacrifices must often have been infested with lice, growing, as it were, by magic on the head and from the head and probably continuing to multiply on the severed head after death. From mouth to mouth through forty or so generations, the association of head-lice with death has continued down to my own day.

Another characteristic of the iron-age Celt was his tendency to think in triads — possibly linked with the elemental triad of earth, sky and water that appears in his oath to Alexander. I had not realised how significant the triad was to us until I read a review of my own book *The Silver New Nothing*, which is an account of the childhood of my brother and sister in Edwardian times. The reviewer remarked that 'everything seemed to happen in threes'. It was so natural to me that it took a reviewer to point it out to me!

Archaeology has proved that dogs were of special significance to the iron-age Celts. Skeletons of dogs have been found, sometimes in pairs, placed deliberately in the foundations of Celtic dwellings. Shuck, the Black Dog, is a common phantom all over East Anglia, but our fenland Black Dog is not Old Shuck, though he may be a relation. In our fen, dogs in general carry warnings of death, the Black Dog being only the chief of them. A dog howling for no reason still sets spines tingling 'down our fen' and even 'china dugs', it seems, can indicate bad-luck approaching.

I am also inclined to deduce, without any of that documentation so necessary to the academic historian, that some of our customs and annual rituals, to which we looked forward with such great pleasure, had very sinister origins.

Another custom, extraordinary insofar as I know of its existence only in the Ramsey — Whittlesey area, had attached itself to Plough Monday. This was strictly an adult ritual and consisted of parading the Straw Bear. Men spent the middle of the day dressing up one of their fellows in bunches of straw and at night paraded him from house to house on a chair. (The custom, which had already died out by my childhood, has recently been revived in Whittlesey.)

My parents were well acquainted with the custom and Aunt Lizzie remembered vividly the occasion when Rattles was selected as the Straw Bear. Dad gave me a detailed description of the way the chosen man was dressed in the straw. As tall a man as could be found was selected and the straw was applied in such a way as to extend his height and practically double his girth.

It was only when, quite recently, I saw on television a reconstruction of the wicker man in which Celtic sacrificial victims were roasted alive that the horrid truth occurred to me. It was to that wicker effigy, containing live human-beings, that our Straw Bear was related, surely? Had folk-memory simply been unable to dismiss that terrible figure from its consciousness?

Plough Monday is in January; one of the Celtish festivals fell in February — a lunar month could contain them both, so it would have been all too easy to combine them.

I wonder, too, about the origin of our 'Hooky Man'. While some Celtic deities appear to have been tribal, others were general. One such important god was Cernunnos, 'the horned god'. He is depicted on an iron-age bowl, seated low upon the ground, with arms outstretched. On his head is a pair of antlers, branched with many 'hooky', curved tines. In one hand he holds what appears to be a golden torc, but with the other he grasps a huge snake by the throat.

We used the word 'hooky' as an adjective for anything bent or curved — for instance, we always took with us a 'hooky-stick' when we went blackberrying, to pull down the best and most luscious fruit, always too high for us to reach without its aid.

Was it upon Cernunnos's 'hooky' tines that so many fen children were caught and held down in the water till they drowned? 'The Hooky Man' was a very real and ever-present danger to all children in our fen and we were constantly warned to stay out of his reach. Another reason for avoiding the flower-studded dykesides as a playground was 'that there ol' King Snake' which lived there.

Snakes, of course, were by no means rare, but

153

we very soon learned to differentiate between the harmless grass snake and the venomous adder. When Aunt Harriet, or any other of her generation referred to 'that there ol' King Snake', I took it for granted that it was the dangerous adder to which she referred. It was, in any case, a piece of folk-lore more or less forgotten by then and I think few of my own contemporaries were aware of it — though they all knew about the Hooky Man. However . . .

When Dad was an old man, concerned to pass on to me as much as he possibly could about the fen before it was too late, he suddenly launched into a tale I had never heard before. He had, he said, one day in his youth, been coming home from the fen where he had been digging turf and, as usual, had jumped a dyke that was in his most direct path. It was a bit wide to leap without a spade or some other tool to act as a vaulting-pole, but he had done it many times before and did not hesitate.

This time he missed and came down among the reeds and sedge of the opposite side, grabbing whatever came first to his hand to save himself from a wetting. To his horror, he found that he had his hand upon, and was actually grasping a huge black snake such as he had never seen before and never saw the like of afterwards. It was, he declared, at least six feet long and just about as thick as his (quite large) hand could encompass. From head to tail it was glistening, shiny, ebony black. As he moved his hand and recoiled it slithered away among the reeds and he confessed that he did not stop long enough

154

thereafter to investigate it further.

'I never told nobody about it,' he said, 'because I reckoned that nobody would believe me. But if I didn't meet that old King Snake that day, nobody ever has done.'

I should be called to book quickly and severely by the few left alive who still remember Dad if I suggested that he was incapable of inventing or telling a tall tale, or embroidering an incident to make a good tale out of it if he could get a bit of fun that way; but I cannot believe a man of such life-long integrity could invent that tale about the snake to tell me, when both of us were taking the whole recording of past fenland life so seriously.

Obviously, I cannot vouch for the truth of it. Dad himself was still very puzzled by the remembrance of it, sixty years after the event. Perhaps some ophiologist may one day clear the mystery up by discovering the imprint of some now extinct species that Dad's King Snake could have belonged to. In the absence of such scientific evidence, one cannot help remembering the huge snake old Cernunnos is grasping in his outstretched left hand!

Research during the 'Keltish Revival' in the late nineteenth century supports the assertion that our particular locality was colonised by the Iron-Age Celts. Land-hungry like all other invaders as they were, they were forced by water to give most of The Fens a miss; but there is evidence that they did colonise as close to the boggy margins of the fens as possible. Sir Harry

Godwin's team[1] found evidence of husbandry in Holme Fen and Trundle Mere 'in Neolithic, Middle Bronze and Roman Iron-ages'.

I imagine that it was isolation that thereafter kept the Celtic genes dominant in our neck of the woods.

The re-establishment of Christianity in England in the seventh century A.D. left traces of Anglo-Saxon influence in our dialect, but it was not until the Normans began to build their magnificent abbeys and cathedrals on the sites of the old Anglo-Saxon religious houses that our fenland area began to be of much significance to the country at large — as witness the old rhyme about the local monastic houses:

Ramsey the rich of gold and fee;
Thorney the flower of many a fair tree.
Crowland the courteous of their meat and
    drink:
Ely the gluttons, as all men do think.
Peterborough the proud, as all men do say,
And Sawtrey, by the way,
That old Abbaye
Gave more alms in one day
Than all they.

(Sawtrey was 'by the way' of 'the Knights' Road' to London, later the Great North Road and now the A1.)

Even so, in Norman times, there was not much commerce between the Normans and the

---

[1] *Op cit.*

indigenous fenmen, so that those who lived on the little islands and around the margins of the fens were left very much to their own devices, until such time as the great drainage schemes were put into operation and the water began to recede.

The true fens had always provided occupation for those living on the islands and around the margins — fishing and wild-fowling, harvesting of reed and sedge for thatching and the cutting, as well as deliberate husbandry of osier-beds for the wicker-work already so widely used in the Celtic iron-age.

It was the fear of losing these occupations that made the fenmen so set against drainage in the first place; but when faced with the drainage as *fait accompli*, it made sense for those who could to add new occupations to what remained of their old ones. When the region around Ramsey and Whittlesey meres became dry enough in summer for the peat to be cut for fuel, turf-digging in such fens as ours became a way of life for a lot of people who still lived on the higher ground on the island of Ramsey or the edge of the uplands at Upwood (for example). They could not yet dwell close to their work, but those near enough went backwards and forwards to it every day. 'Near enough' meant, on average, no more than five miles each way, and this had to be done on foot, by 'frog-and-toeing' it. A long walk, one might think, at the end of a long day often spent up to your ankles in water, surrounded by swarms of mosquitoes whose bite could, and did, often bring on an attack of fen ague.

The journey, however, was not exactly walked:

the peat-diggers evolved their own way of taking it at a steady jog-trot, behind their empty turf-barrows.

Let no-one imagine that this apparently idiotic custom implies that those indigenous old fenmen were brainless oafs. Indeed, one of the purposes of this book is to refute, with everything in my power, the idea recently promulgated by our local media that the 'fen-tiger' is a music-hall figure of fun.

The turf-diggers of the half-drained days were, in fact, living up to the quick-witted inheritance of their Celtish forebears for seizing on new ideas.

Turf digging was an exact science, each 'cess' having to be cut exactly to size while wet and then put through an elaborate series of processes in order to achieve the exact state of thorough dryness that made them into saleable fuel. People who have not had immediate and first-hand knowledge of peat as fuel may not be aware that turves not properly dried in the first instance, or those that had subsequently been wetted and dried again, will not burn, but only smoulder dully with too much acrid smoke for comfort. The top 'peelings' of a new turf digging were simply pared off and thrown aside. When dry, they were collected (free) to serve those who could not afford the usual price of a penny for six 'cesses'. Most households had a heap of this 'clunch' to use for keeping the fire on the hearth smouldering while they were out at work, or even overnight.

When wet, the newly dug cesses had to be handled with care, and when successfully dried, had to be transported from the digging to a rick by the side of a drain or other waterway from which it could be loaded on to a lighter. For this purpose, a special barrow was designed. It was, in fact, a long, low slatted platform, with a slatted back of approximately the same proportions. It stood on two short legs and had a small, narrow wheel, with handles to allow the propellor of it to tip it to such an angle as to throw a good deal of the weight of its load on to the high back. When fully loaded, the barrow held 120 turves.

Fenland waterways, of course, usually lie between high banks that have been raised to prevent flooding. The lighters, therefore, lay well below the level of the banks and the turf was loaded on to them by way of a plank about ten inches wide, resting between the bank and the barge. To negotiate a heavily-laden turf-barrow up and down such a narrow plank was a balancing act requiring surefootedness and speed, because as every cyclist knows, balance depends upon speed. The loader, therefore, approached the planks at a jog-trot, holding the handles of the barrows high in order to keep the narrow little front wheel on the sloping plank. Even on level ground, this rhythmic jog-trot made the balance easier to maintain and became the accepted gait of a man behind a turf-barrow.

When 'knocking off' time came, the same men faced a five-mile journey home; but walking was not their natural gait, though they were not used to the jog-trot without their barrows. They did the sensible thing and trotted home behind empty barrows, returning to work next day in the same fashion.

When the brickyards began to flourish on the clay of 'the heights', a few intrepid folk left Ramsey and Upwood to live nearer the turf diggings, to become brick-and-tile makers and even to begin to cultivate the drier fields in Lotting Fen. There were only a few families, all of them in the first place from the same root-stock. As the tiny community began to grow, it did so in even greater isolation than the island villages in the fen had been used to, with the inevitable result of much intermarriage between the few families. Even when young men did seek brides out of their own immediate community, the girls came from no further distance than Ramsey, Holme, or Upwood — in essence, of the same group of families to which they themselves already belonged.

Of course this constant inter-marriage means that sooner or later, everybody in the community is 'kin' to everybody else. We are, truly, a tribe, which is why strangers, even today, characterise us as 'clannish'.

The genealogies, becoming more and more complicated as generation succeeded generation, were remembered in all their intricacies by the womenfolk and cropped up in every conversation. Indeed, they still do, wherever and whenever two or three of the tribe are met together.

Strangers to the area, especially those from towns, find it both amazing and amusing that we should still care about who is related to whom, and how.

It was necessary, in the literary hiatus caused by the first colonisation of an area with no schools, for all details of births, deaths and

160

marriages to be recorded in memory, as they had been in the distant past (especially in the case of the non-literate early Celtish tribes). Many of the older people I knew in my childhood were completely illiterate and could not have recognised their own names if they had faced them in letters of gold a foot high. Yet they could tell you the date of birth of everybody within our scattered hamlet and sort out the genealogies back for four or more generations. The district was, and still is, full of 'Etherdses', all descended from the Welsh blacksmith and therefore all 'kin', though it may now be necessary to go back more than the six generations anybody can actually ever remember in the flesh, to find a common ancestor.

Anyway, whatever their origin, after a couple of generations they were all 'fen-tigers'.

Little do those who throw that appellation at us as a term of contempt know its origin, or the people to whom it can truly be applied. Even educated people who should know better still declare, given a chance to air their views on radio and television, that fen-folk are so called because of their wild, savage and even cruel behaviour. Some will tell you that it refers to their behaviour in the face of the first attempts at drainage, others that it arose from the Littleport riots of 1816 and still others that its origin was the habit of the first lucky fen-farmers of wearing tiger-skins as cloaks. It is, of course, none of these things.

The only things we have in common with the tiger are the attributes of strength, intelligence and pride — pride above all, and like our

161

ancestors 'afraid of no man'.

The term 'fen-tiger' is, in fact, just another anglicisation of a foreign word. Within our dialect there are many instances of the transmutation of consonants — 'd' and 'th' being a good example. The beaten-down track by the side of a dyke was not, as one would expect, a 'path', but a 'pad' (exactly as in the Dutch). We did not go further to see our father and mother: we went 'furder' and see our 'farder and mudder'. We did not go up and down ladders — we went up and down 'lathers' (as Fred Tatt said, 'The longest lather I ever went up were down a well') and, of course, the Edwards clan were 'Etherses' or 'Etherdses'.

Now, as every schoolboy knows, the Fens were drained by Dutch engineers, who constructed canals with steep banks — 'deichs', in fact, and the indigenous folk who did the actual labour were 'deichers'. Change the 'd' to a 't', harden the 'ch' to 'g' and what do you get? 'Tiger' instead of 'deicher'. Alas, nothing more romantic than that!

The illiteracy in 'our' fen may have been matched by the same lack of schooling in other isolated fens drained late. The well-established towns and villages on the islands were, in contrast, above average in the matter of literacy, probably because of the monkish influence in so many of them. Ramsey was well provided with schools and Upwood had its 'dame school' to which grandmother went and my great-grandmother Edwards before her. My great-grandfather married and bought his first field in

162

Lotting Fen in 1829. My grandfather John was born in Lotting Fen in 1837 and at the age of twenty-one married Grandmother (Rachel Voss) who had been born in Upwood c.1837. She was a good scholar, he completely illerate because there was no school, not even a Sunday School, that he could attend. So Grandmother took it upon herself to teach him to read by making use of 'the book' — that is, the Bible. Dad remembered that to the end of his life, Grandad read like a child, pointing with his finger to the words and spelling them out. 'T-O — toe, D-O — doe' etc., just as he had first been instructed. Very few of his contemporaries born in our fen, could read at all. Even in Dad's own generation those who could not read far outstripped in numbers those who could. This was largely because there was an exclusion clause in the 1870 Education Act excusing children who lived more than two miles from the school from attending. A lot of families took advantage of it, especially where families were large and even small children potential wage-earners. What did they want 'eddication' for? Perhaps there was still an in-built racial resistance to writing things down?

This inability to read and write in no way inhibited their natural 'subtlety of speech', on which in his own time, Cato commented. It vexes me almost beyond bearing when I hear, or read, of the natives of East Anglia being tongue-tied yokels whose conversation consists mainly of grunts punctuated by 'AHs'. It may be more true of those East Anglians whose genes are predominately Anglo-Saxon — though I doubt it. From what I know about the Anglo-Saxons, they were as fluent in speech, as fond of the subtleties of language and as devoted to story and poetry as any Celt, if in a different way. I do not, however, presume to speak for the whole of East Anglia.

What I do know is that any true-blooded fen-tiger, male or female, given the chance will 'talk the leg off an iron pot'. Not, you notice, 'the hind-leg off a donkey'. Iron pots were precious to the Ancient Britons.

My particular tribe are all tremendous talkers. They love the sound of their own voices — but they are good listeners as well, and never get tired of hearing old tales or fishing up new ones, especially about each other. A strange or curious character, especially one with a particular turn of wit, is never likely to be forgotten. Perhaps, sadly, I ought to begin to use the past tense. The days of our isolation are over, our tribe has been dispersed and newcomers to our fen are 'kin' to nobody.

There are still enough of us left to meet occasionally and bring the past to life again, but what we have to talk about is incomprehensible even to the young of our own families, interested though they may be. It occurs to me that our diminishing group is made up of those who still speak, and even think in, the dialect that has been educated out of the last two generations; for with dialect goes idiom, with idiom goes natural metaphor, with metaphor goes symbolism, and in symbolism is reflected a philosophy of life and an attitude towards death not easy to find among the young of today.

164

I do not intend to allow myself to be led astray on the subject of dialect yet, but I do need an example of my tribe's continued 'subtlety of speech'. It is shown in the variety of words we have at our disposal to convey what is being said, and the mood and context of the conversation too. The distinctions among all the words meaning, in general, 'to speak' are so subtle that it is difficult to convey them in 'standard English'.

Speaking or muttering 'under your breath' especially if there is an element of complaint contained in what you are saying, is 'puttering'. A child making a few protesting comments about a firm female parent is met with a large raised hand and the command to 'Stop puttering — or else!'. Now if the same child (or adult), actually voiced his complaint aloud and kept it up, he would be 'chuntering'. 'Chuntering' contains an element of disgruntlement, so that the word cannot be substituted for what nowadays would be termed 'nattering' or 'rabbiting on'. The word in our vocabulary that comes nearest to that is 'chelping', which does mean to keep up a stream of desultory conversation; but 'chelping' can also mean 'answering back'.

'Don't you chelp at me, bor, else I'll kelp your airse!'

When the talk is general, it can be termed 'chelping'; but if it turns inward and begins to consist more particularly of reminiscences, it becomes 'bladging'; but 'bladging' has also a different meaning in a different context. Again, we have the substitution of consonants, the 'd' for 'th': make this change and you get

165

'blathering' or 'blethering' — 'chelping' in a perjorative sense. A person with too free a tongue, one too anxious to pass on a bit of salacious gossip, or one not at all careful with the details of the truth on a serious matter, can be accused of 'bladging'. One who cannot be trusted with secrets is also scorned as 'a bladger'.

When mischief is afoot, and bad-feeling is aroused, the already high-pitched female voices are raised a tone or two higher and a decibel or two louder. This acrimonious sort of speech becomes 'yawping' and is seldom used of men except when drunk or otherwise out of normal control of themselves. It is mostly women who 'yawp' especially if they are show-offs who desire to be noticed. Such noticeable females can be said to be 'yawping about' even if there is no element of disagreement between them.

If, however, a real verbal battle is taking place, the bitter edge added to the raised voice turns 'yawping' into 'yanging'.

Now, how is that for an example of 'the subtlety of speech' 'heired' from our forebears? Six different words, some with variations, all indicating a different mode of speech? It is all part of the general love of words that is inherent in the breed. This love of words found a natural outlet in chapel more, I think, than in the Anglican church, because the free churches gave more scope for audience participation at a higher level of passionate involvement. There, in chapel, it was less the meaning than the sound of the great rolling periods of the King James version that left them forever ringing in our ears and ready on our tongues. There were many occasions when the preacher in the pulpit at our chapel could no more read the passage he was reciting than many of his congregation could. Such preachers had learned much of the Bible 'by heart'. When literacy became more general, those who could read made the most of it. There was not much money to be spared for reading matter, but sharing made a penny-paper go a long way and offered value for money. Women walked the five miles to Ramsey to fetch the weekly copy of 'Peg's Paper' and its male equivalent. The magazines then went from cottage to cottage till they fell to pieces. Most of Dad's close friends, though not quite so print-crazy as he was, were dedicated readers, if only of the Bible. Reading aloud on Saturday evenings was a looked-for pleasure in our house, especially as one of the weekly papers was carrying the Claybury and Cudford tales of W. W. Jacobs, as well as the adventures of one 'Ally Sloper'. A cartoon figure? I don't know, because I was too young to remember much more than the names and the constant allusions to the characters thereafter. 'Bob Pretty's pantry' as a synonym for plenty is something I grew up with.

Grandmother abominated fiction and read only her Bible or other 'good works'; but her children put their noses into books and kept them there. I wish I knew how and where Dad encountered Dickens and Twain in the first place. It gave him a kind of proprietory pleasure to remember that he was born on the very day Charles Dickens died. Words, spoken or written, held us all in thrall.

Hymns had their own, special fascination — words in rhythm and metre, set to music. There was no inhibition in the singing of a chapel full to the gallery with fen-folk! They threw back their heads, opened their throats and sang their hearts out.

Sing to the Lord! Exalt him high
Who spreads His clouds along the sky;
There he prepares the fruitful rain,
Nor lets the drops descend in vain.

He makes the grass the hills adorn
And clothes the smiling fields with corn.
The beasts with food His hands supply
And the young ravens when they cry.

What is the creature's skill or force?
The sprightly man, or warlike horse?
The perfect wit, the active limb?
All are too mean delights for Him.

This particular hymn was a universal favourite, perhaps because it was such a wonderful compromise between non-conformist Christianity and an inherited religion of magic in nature. The music, too, was universally enjoyed. There was never enough hymn-singing to satisfy the chapel congregation. After the evening service on Sunday, the children played outside in summer, or 'the big 'uns took the littl'uns um' while their parents and grandparents stayed on to a prayer meeting.

This gave everybody, individually, a chance to raise his or her voice in public, in prayer or

168

supplication, thanksgiving or praise. There was no tongue-tied lack of language, or of passionate emotion. It was the men, mainly, who spoke aloud, while the women kept up a low, murmured chorus of assent and amens. Such people had no need of others to speak for them. They were quite capable of communicating direct with the Almighty, whoever He was.

And *still* they had not had enough! Sunday was, after all, a day of rest and rejoicing. They left the chapel in small, self-selected groups, to gather in some cottage and end the day by singing more hymns. Most families boasted some sort of musical instrument and a musician to accompany the singers. 'Uncle George' had a harmonium, which both he and 'Aunt Rose' could play: 'Gaskin' Allpress had an accordion and Joe Skinner a banjo: Aunt Loll had an American organ and we had a piano. The concertina was a maid-of-all-work, played by Old Henry at chapel and by many another for pubs and other secular get-togethers. Dad 'did not know a note of music', though he had been 'foosterer-in-chief' for the village in his youth, using fiddle or concertina as it pleased him (his old concertina is by my side as I write this). There were also dulcimers, mouth-organs and Jews' harps. Music 'came natural' to most fen-folk. Gerald could get a tune out of anything. Lois concentrated on the piano, though she also played a mandolin. My cousins were mainly organists, though one was a good violinist. I, alone, of all our family, was without musical skill on any instrument and there is good reason for this; but what I lacked in executive skill on a musical instrument, I made up for with my feet. Like the rest of us in our tribe, I had an excellent ear and a sense of rhythm so exquisite that it almost hurt. Dancing was built into us and I count it among the many privileges I have been granted that I spent my youth in 'the dancing years' of the twenties and thirties. But long, long before I had reached the stage of putting on a long dress and being escorted to a proper dance by a dinner-jacketed young man, I had partnered Dad in a cross-hand polka, or 'Haste-to-the-Wedding' at a village social, or had been swung off my twelve-year-old feet by a couple of neighbouring small-holders in a rumbustious 'basket' movement of a set of Lancers. Music in all its many aspects was as much a part of our fen life as the purply-soot-coloured earth, the black-frost winds, or the rustling reeds and cat-tails down the dyke-sides.

6

Fen, Food, Facts and Phobias

I am accused of romanticising and glamourising the past. I refute the accusation. I am not viewing it through the rose-coloured spectacles of nostalgia. It is a fallacy to believe that Time, like distance, must necessarily '*lend enchantment to the view*'.

There was, indeed, very little to glamourise, or romanticise about, especially if viewed through eyes accustomed to the standards of the late twentieth century, and with regard to such matters as housing, hygiene, health and poverty. But therein lies the dilemma of all historians. They can make valid comparisons but they cannot make valid judgements. The latter can be made only by those who knew the conditions at first hand and had to cope with them. Real history resides not in pitying comparison with what we are accustomed to, but in somehow discovering what the people of the time made of their conditions themselves.

The general standard of living was low, the housing deplorable, amenities non-existent. Disease was rampant and medical help out of reach, both financially and geographically.

Food, always basic and never over-plentiful in the labourer or smallholder households, became very scarce in time of flood or frost, especially for

171

the labourer who had no smallholding to back up his wage, because when men could not work, they were not paid. It was hard — too hard to throw much glamour on — when mothers had to tell their hungry children there was nothing to eat because 'ol' Jack Frost had frez the cupboard doors to'.

In such 'unhygienic' conditions, and such a state of 'poverty' (both qualified below), it was little wonder that epidemics raged across the fen like the plagues of Egypt one after another. Until very recently, a gravestone standing in St Mary's churchyard told the sad tale of a family of my brother-in-law's relations. Its inscription proved the five members of one Emmington family must have lain dead in the house in one and the same week. 'Consumption' took its toll every year: drownings were frequent, and those who survived an immersion often only did so long enough to die of pneumonia. Sooner or later, almost everybody succumbed to 'rheumatiz', if not cancer.

As far as I can judge, there is no way of standardising 'poverty' or 'cleanliness', for any age other than the present. To be 'below the poverty line' in the last decade in the second millenium A.D. (in the UK) is to lack the amenities of a television, a video-recorder and a telephone, according to a letter in *The Times* recently by the distributor of a charity to whom an appeal had been made by a well-known association on behalf of a family. But what is 'poverty' in Ethiopia, El Salvador or any of the South American Republics?

172

One did not apply the word 'poverty' lightly to any family in our fen. It carried too much of a stigma with it — it was part of our stiff-necked pride to 'manage' somehow. For anyone else to acknowledge a family's need (except in the case of severe illness) would have added an extra blow, a final cut, to their suffering. Hurt pride takes longer to heal than hurt flesh and leaves a deeper scar.

The same applies to the question of cleanliness. What is 'cleanliness' but the ratio between what is possible under prevailing conditions and what is actually achieved?

No dwellings in our fen had space set aside for ablutions. There was no water supply except for what 'soft water' was caught in wooden butts or galvanised tanks or dipped from the dykes. The soft water was kept for washing hair and very special clothes. Drinking water was often from the dyke and the weekly wash was done in 'sody-lea', that is, dyke water to which a large handful of carbonate of soda had been added the night before to soften it. It would be of a brownish tinge having drained through the peat, and very difficult it was to keep your heavy twill sheets clean, however long you boiled them in the copper in the lean-to. There was no such thing as a 'toilet' or a 'w.c.'! *Water*-closet? In my Dad's childhood, there was no provision at all but the great outdoors where one 'went broadcast'. By my time every cottage had 'a closet' — a sort of wooden sentry-box set at the end of the garden, as far from the dwelling as possible because of the inevitable stench from

173

the deep earth vault below the wooden seat.

How does one judge the standard of cleanliness and personal hygiene under such conditions? Poor, by today's standards: but you can take my word for it that it was excellent under those that then prevailed. People who had been working in appalling conditions all the week were, on Sunday, metamorphosed to a surprising degree of 'spruceness'. Take, for example, the men who made up the team that accompanied 'ol' Freddie Jackson's' threshing tackle. They spent long days with a coal-fired steam threshing tackle, walking the distance between the farm employing the outfit and their homes every night and morning (anything up to five miles). They were soaked with sweat, coated with dust and as black as miners at the coal-face by the end of each day, as well as being decorated with straws, chaff and, worst of all for discomfort, barley-awns. Their hands were black and calloused with work and ended in broken, black-rimmed nails. Thus they might appear on their way home on Friday evening or more likely, Saturday afternoon.

At 10.00 a.m. next morning, they would be in chapel for Sunday School and morning service, without a vestige of the grime or sweat of the working week. They would be dressed in suits (kept for Sundays) and clean shirts, even if these were collarless. The hair would have been washed and brushed and hands scrubbed and trimmed so as to be fit to hold 'the Word of the Lord'.

Women, of course, had extra problems of

personal hygiene to cope with, especially those who worked in the fields. There were no disposable pads or tampons for their use. The best they could hope for was an adequate supply of home-made 'diapers' cut from their own wornout petticoats, old sheets, or the tails of their menfolks' shirts. Babies' nappies had to be gleaned from the same meagre supply, which was why a lot of babies went 'bare-arsed' until it was time to 'breech' the boys; the girls' skirts 'kivered' their nakedness a bit longer. The women's diapers had, of course, to be handwashed in dyke-water, ready for the next month — and many, many were the silent prayers that they *would* be needed.

The women, however, were in general more particular about personal cleanliness than the men. They did their work, indoors or out, in 'hessen-eppens' (hessian aprons), which were discarded in the afternoon when they 'had a good wash'. For this they used the house-place, in front of the hearth, setting a bowl of water on the table and stripping to the waist. This was an absolute necessity for those working out in the fields: they suffered agonies from sweat-galls under arms and breasts, for which soap and water was (and still is) the best cure, though it was often aided by homemade ointment composed of lard and fuller's earth powder. They then attended likewise to the lower half of their persons — as they used to say 'Down as far as possible and up as far as possible, with a good goo round possible if there was time'. Time was important, because they strove to get these private ablutions carried out while their men were still at work and before the older children came in from school. Folk-lore may have prevented a very high standard of hygiene for women, because it was absolutely taboo to wash hair or feet, let alone take a bath, while menstruating.

The daily washdown completed, they donned their working clothes again, but topped them with their 'afternoon eppen' — white, bibbed and starched, like that worn by nurses until a few years ago. They were now ready to cook 'the mairster's' tea and see to feeding the backyard pig and chickens, drying the children's wet clothes when they came in from school and doing the rest of the hundred-and-one jobs that fell to the woman of the house to see to. As the old saying went:

A man's work is from sun to sun
But a woman's work is never done.

It was part of a wife's duty to wash her 'mairster's' person, as well as his garments. (I must explain the use of the term 'mairster' in this context. There was no hint of subservience in it, though the men, as chief breadwinners, were accorded a bit of respect and a few extra privileges. When a woman called her husband 'my mairster', she simply meant 'my man' exactly as the man would have used 'my missus' for 'my wife' or 'my woman'. 'My missus' has survived as a general colloqualism and 'my mairster' has been dropped — that's all.)

176

Since I must report the whole truth, even on this matter of personal cleanliness, I have to state that the one part of the body that did not receive much attention was the feet. People now in high-places often tell me that their forebears hailed from the fen. They almost always cap their assertion by saying 'You know — they only washed their feet once a year!'. I believe them; but considering the pains fen-folk took to keep the rest of their persons clean, there surely must be a good reason for this anomaly. One reason was probably that it was much more trouble to wash the feet than any other part. Washing, even in the late innovation of the tin bath, was performed standing up. This 'up-and-down' washing, carried out with an old 'flannel' cut from a shirt tail and a rock-hard bar of yellow soap, stopped short at the knees. Washing the feet was almost a ritual, requiring a chair, a bowl big enough to put the feet in, and above all, time.

There was also another, even more practical reason. If there was one hardship more than many others endured by men, women and children alike in the fen, it was sore feet. Men's boots were made of leather, with heavy soles hob-nailed to make them last longer. They were knee-high, the sides laced tightly over a leather tongue to keep out the 'slud' of winter or the water when roding dykes or digging soggy-wet peat. (Hence the need for a lace-hook by every hearth-side.) At the end of each winter day and a lot of summer days, too, these boots would be sodden and set on the hearth overnight to dry before morning. Such treatment hardened even more the already unyielding cheap leather, so that after a time they became instruments of torture to the wearer. The men suffered unending pain from blisters, callouses and corns, particularly 'soft corns' between the toes. These were caused by the feet being wet most of the time, in spite of the boots. The conclusion naturally drawn was that feet must be hardened to cope with the rub of the footwear and that immersion in hot water, which had a softening effect, was to be avoided.

Wives acted as chiropodists for their 'mairster', cutting hard corns with old cut-throat razors; but soft corns defied such treatment. One old fenman, in desperation at the never-ending pain, fetched hammer and chisel and amputated his own toe. Toothache was cured in the same drastic fashion by a willing neighbour with a pair of pincers.

Stockings worn by men were also knee-high, made to reach the top of the boots. They were knitted by wives and mothers in their 'spare' time. Darns were not encouraged by the wearers, because even the most neat and careful darn raised a slight ridge that added to the chafing. A hole was preferable, until there was so little of the foot left that they went back to the knitters to be refooted, often with a yarn of different colour from that of the original legs. The legs of stockings beyond further refooting were pulled 'down' for refooting purposes, or turned into 'slivers'. Between their stockings and their boots, most men also wore a pair of 'slivers'. These oversocks were usually the cut off legs of other old stockings (or sometimes the feet, since a few holes did not matter) and were never washed. The more thick and matted they became, the greater protection they provided. They were only thrown away when utterly worn out or so matted and odorous as to be unbearable.

Those who could possibly afford to, kept a pair of ankle-boots for 'best', which were supplemented by leather leggings for Sunday morning chapel or the very rare trip to market. Sunday evening services merited a suit, however old and however many times handed down. Funerals brought out the family's bowler hat.

Women worked long days in the fields, either in cold and wet or in scorching heat, so that their earnings could provide their own 'best dress', their children's shoes and the obligatory new outfit for Sunday School Anniversary Sunday.

By the time I was in my teens and riding through the fens to school at Ramsey (1924–32), farmers were employing female labour in gangs of ten to twelve women who crawled up and down the black soil side by side weeding onions, setting potatoes, singling sugar-beet and the like. This phase of ganged female labour could not have lasted long, and was eventually made obsolete by the first attempts at mechanised farming. It did, however, while it lasted, produce one of the most extraordinary 'fashions' I have ever encountered.

Women who worked on the land in my grandparents' and parents' era did their best to shield their complexions from sun and wind by wearing a bonnet fitting close round the face,

179

drawn tight under the chin by a draw-string. This produced a frill that covered the forehead and shaded the eyes, while another longer frill protected the throat and the back of the neck.

In the gang period, somebody had the idea of adding a peak to the front of the bonnet to shade the whole of the face. This peak was made of cardboard and covered with the same material as the home-made bonnet. Then the peak grew and grew in length till it reached twelve or more inches. In shape it resembled an old-fashioned flour or sugar scoop, inverted. The women made their own 'hoods' and seemed to take pride in out-doing each other in the size of them.

A gang of women working in a field presented a row of ten or twelve behinds if viewed from the back; but all one saw from any other aspect was a row of these enormous hoods so long that as the workers bent their heads to see their work, the ends of the peaks only just missed the soil. I don't know whether this extraordinary fashion spread to other fens, or if it was a phenomenon peculiar to ours. Peculiar it certainly was!

Many women made their men's shirts by hand, partly to save money, but partly because the shops could not or did not provide the sort of shirts men in the fields were accustomed to. These were voluminous creations with gussets under the arms (to allow freedom of movement), gathers across the front set into a band at waist height — again, to accommodate the extra width of material that allowed unimpeded movement. The tails of the shirt were wide and very long, so that when the front tail had been tucked down well between the legs, the back tail came through from behind and overlapped the front. All was then enclosed inside a pair of 'trouser linings', over which trousers of 'drabbette', 'bluette' or moleskin were donned. Linings and trousers were washed so as to be clean every Monday morning. Shirts were usually changed on Saturday afternoons, when 'the mairster' had his weekly 'bath', which usually meant an 'up-and-a-downer', unless he chose to stand in the tin bath while his 'missus' poured handbowls of heated dyke water all over him. When at work, the trousers were usually 'hootched-up' below the knee. They were made wide above the knee, to allow free movement, but once the wearer began to sweat, it was necessary to trap air around the knees so that the damp material did not stick. The garters worn below the knee were traditionally made of eel-skin — partly because of its elasticity and durability and partly because it was firmly believed that eel-skin garters would ward off rheumatism. These garters have a variety of names, the most usual being 'lallygags' or 'galligaskins' in other parts of East Anglia. For some reason that I have never discovered, they were usually referred to in our fen as 'eye-dusters'. At least, that is what Dad and all his friends called theirs.

Most farm-workers simply went to bed in their shirts, though some, like those who worked the treshing tackle, kept a worn-out one as a night-shirt. With one accord, Dad's generation detested the introduction of pyjamas and most refused absolutely to wear such uncomfortable,

181

inconvenient and unhealthy garments. I guess their judgement was sound — one eminent academic assured me only a few years ago that he still had long red-flannel nightshirts specially made for him!

The 'closet', 'little house' or 'petty' at the end of the garden was kept as clean and fresh as possible, though nothing could reduce the stench, not even the liquid 'garribolic' or 'powered carbolic' that those who could afford it kept handy. The tiny tarred wooden boxes with tin or corrugated zinc roofs got as hot in summer as they were cold in winter. The only light let in was by the holes cut in the top of the door, or by the dog-tooth seration there, both of which also allowed a bit of ventilation if the door was ever completely closed upon its occupant. Usually, it was left a few inches ajar — after all, there were few close enough to see inside. Such a 'closet' was a very scary place to a small child to visit alone, for the wooden seat was made high enough to accommodate grown-up legs, just as the hole in the wooden seat was too big for a little bottom — and below the hole was that huge, deep, horrendous vault! A few of the newer and larger houses were equipped with a double-holed seat: and one plutocrat of toiletry actually had a 'three-bear' arrangement, with holes cut to fit father, mother and baby bear to use all at once.

Women saved the offcuts of their sixpence-a-roll wallpaper to use on 'the closet' walls. The resultant montage must have been quite artistic (by modern standards) if anybody had desired to stop there long enough to admire it.

The horror of such a 'necessary' to our pampered sensibilities can be illustrated by the story of what happened to my first ever little friend. Her parents were my parents' dearest friends and we called each other's parents 'aunt' and 'uncle' respectively and regarded ourselves as cousins. Aunt Sis was a most beautiful woman, outstanding because she was Norfolk born and Anglo-Saxon in stature and appearance, with an English-rose complexion, blue eyes like cornflowers and such masses of thick flaxen hair that it did, literally 'crown' her. When Marjorie was born, tragedy had already struck the family and seemed determined to go on doing so. Uncle Herb was one of Jackson's threshing-tackle team and they lived in a group of cottages close by Jackson's yard on The Heights proper.

They had one little son, named Ailwyn (a name popular in Ramsey for historical reasons) who was almost three when Aunt Sis gave birth to another boy. In spite of the birth being quite normal, the mother's swollen legs prevented her from getting up before the midwife left: so Ailwyn, the toddler, was left to his own devices to play round house and garden. One day, he accompanied a fourteen-year-old back to Jackson's yard 'to look at the bullocks' and wait for his father, coming from work, to take him home. The older boy missed him, and concluded that he had toddled off home to his mother. So he had, wearing a little bright red outdoor coat. When the inevitable search for him began, it was his father who caught sight of the flash of red beneath the dark water of the pond in the small field through which the path to the cottage ran. The Hooky Man had claimed yet another child sacrifice. I remember Aunt Sis saying 'I didn't need telling what had happened, as soon as his dad carried him in at the door. I could smell the mud!'

She struggled downstairs to see him lying in his little coffin on the 'house-place' table, before they screwed it down. Such a tragedy should surely have been their share, but it was not.

Aunt Sis began to suffer dreadful attacks of asthma (it proved to be cardiac asthma and killed her at forty-two). At the time of Marjorie's birth, it was diagnosed simply as 'asthma' and necessitated the doctor's bills every fen household dreaded so much. However, Jackson's threshing teams were paid better rates than farm labourers, and once the family had recovered from the shock of Ailwyn's death, they prospered for a while. Even the attacks of asthma seemed to grow less frequent. Then spiteful fate singled them out again.

Marjorie was three and had proudly learned to manage the elaborate arrangement of buttons on her calico knickers (not so easy a task as it may sound). Our knickers were open at the sides, with fullness gathered into a waistband back and front. At each end of both waistbands was a buttonhole. The front waistband fastened on to a button sewn on to our 'liberty bodice' (often home-made from father's worn-out flannel shirt and quilted by hand). Then the back-flap of the knickers overlapped the front and fastened over the same button. The waistband had to be unbuttoned before the back flap could be let down — a difficult task for little fingers to achieve by touch only, especially with little legs crossed in desperation. Doing the buttons up again was even more demanding, which often resulted in the child trotting back to mother with the back-flap of her knickers trailing round her ankles. Marjorie had taken herself down to the closet, proud of her ability to manage her buttons. Then Fate stepped in. The grocer arrived on his bike, and was asked into the house while Aunt's brown paper parcel of groceries was unpacked, checked, paid for, and the next fortnight's order given. Only when he had left did Aunt miss her little girl.

What had happened was that Marjorie had barely got inside the closet before a gust of wind sweeping across the fen had slammed the door shut with such force that the latch so rarely used had dropped, and trapped her. It was already growing dusk outside, so the little holes in the top of the door let in hardly any light at all. She was not tall enough to reach the latch, even if she could have lifted it. Once outside the house, her mother could hear the frantic screams coming from the petty, and went to the rescue.

But it was hours before the terrified child could be calmed. During the week that followed, both parents noticed that the little girl was developing a squint, and as the defect worsened, her eyes became increasingly red and sore. There was no help for it; she had to be taken to the doctor, at Ramsey, of course. From where they lived, on The Heights, it would have been silly to think about going by train, because besides the cost of the train fare, by the time they had walked to the station, they could have been half-way to Ramsey already across Biggin Fields.

There were two doctors in Ramsey, ours and another who had the reputation of being 'good with eyes'. So to him 'Aunt' took her little girl. Marjorie told me only yesterday that she remembered the first few visits with pleasure because Biggin Fields were a mass of wild flowers and she gathered cowslips, 'cuckoos' (wild orchids), 'milkmaids' and the like on the return journey. But the eyes got worse and worse, ulcerated, very painful and sensitive to light. 'Aunt' was, in fact, leading an almost blind child to and from Ramsey every other day — nearly five miles each way.

Dr Fisher was extremely concerned for her sight and made the desperate suggestion that the little girl should be sent to hospital in London.

It takes a good deal of imaginative effort, in our days of welfare and ease, to understand the choice put before those two honest, hardworking, loving and caring parents. They had already lost one child: London, then, was as far away in real terms as Australia is today: German bombs were falling on London, in any case, because the year was 1917: Aunt Sis was suffering more and more with her 'asthma' and needed treatment herself. The amount of walking to and from Ramsey forced upon her could hardly have helped an already damaged heart. Most of all, there was the cost. The doctor's bills they were running up were already stretching them to the limit. And yet, in the balance, lay the chance that their baby girl would be blind for the rest of her life.

They had no option. London was out of the question, so Marjorie would have to take her chance. Dr Fisher, though, seems to have been a man of integrity as well as skill. He had to accept their decision, but decreed that Marjorie must stay somewhere in Ramsey, so that he, personally, could dress the ulcerated eyes with hot fomentations three times every day.

For once luck was on their side. 'Uncle' had a cousin whose wife cleaned and looked after the Wesleyan Chapel, and lived in the Chapel House, more or less opposite the doctor's. She took the little invalid in, now quite blind from being swathed in bandages, and so for six weeks it continued until at last some improvement was achieved. When Marjorie was at last taken home again, she was still blind from her bandages; but the day came when they could be taken off for a few minutes each day. The light was unbearable to her, but ingenuity found a way out. The table was covered with a tablecloth that came down almost to the floor, and at tea-time this became an improvised 'dark room', where Marjorie could sit and eat her tea under the table, in semi-darkness, bandage-free.

The eyes got better at last, though Marjorie has been condemned to poor sight through thick-lensed spectacles ever since. Being a true daughter of the fens, she does not grumble.

'After all,' she said yesterday, 'I might have been blind, but I'm not.'

One can only wonder whether it was the trauma of being locked in the lavatory, or some germ picked up there as the frantic child rubbed her eyes that caused the trouble. There were hazards everywhere — even the carbolic fluid must have constituted a danger in its own right.

Another problem was to find enough paper of any kind to do its duty in 'the closet'. Toilet tissue, like scented soap, was a luxury we had never heard of. Daily newspapers did not find their way into our fen until the twenties, (we took *The Daily Mail*) — but most people did not, or could not, afford the cost. Sunday papers were proscribed by the fourth commandment and were not allowed on moral grounds. They went with all such other wicked occupations as playing with toys, knitting and sewing, reading fiction, or rendering any music other than hymns in any sort of way, even whistling. We were very naughty about this last prohibition. Mam was deaf, and as soon as Dad actually left the house, Lois would nip into the front room where the piano was, and try out the latest popular song such as *Margie or Dancing Time*.

One paper only was allowed in our house on a Sunday, *The Joyful News*, distributed at Chapel.

The joyful news of sins forgiven
Of peace on earth, and hopes of heaven

it said, under its red headlined title. I don't remember anybody, even Dad, ever opening it to read what was inside it; but that paper ended up, like the worn-out Peg's Paper etc., torn into little squares and hung on a nail inside the petty. For this use every scrap of precious paper was hoarded, whatever kind it was. Grocers wrapped their goods in stout blue paper, expertly making up bags for such dry goods as sugar, rice or currants, and little cones for small amounts of such things as spice or a pennyworth of aniseed balls. (When the 'New Art' hit primary schools in the 1930s, it was this very same paper we used as part of the revolution. We called it, truthfully, 'sugar-paper', and at first it came only in the same blue colour as the grocers used.)

When our grocer unloaded from his cluttered cycle the brown-paper parcel containing a household's fortnightly supply, the woman of the house decanted everything into jars or tins saved on purpose, so as to salvage every scrap of paper for further use.

To be 'taken short' and rush down the garden to the petty, only to find that the last scrap of paper had already been used, was a real dilemma. As usual, (in our fen) such a situation tended to be immortalised by a bit of impromptu if crude doggerel, home-made on the spot.

'Mairster Paul' (so called by his rather better-off and socially-superior mother) was going to market at Peterborough, and had to make the usual long walk to the station. Nevertheless, he found he had 'to pay a visit' before he set off. Alas, the last scrap of paper had been used. In his own words:

189

Here I am in a terrible caper,
Got to the house without any paper.
The train won't wait. I must not linger,
So, here goes. I'll use my finger!

(How the rest of the fen applauded this bit of scatological humour!)

There's a story about Grammam, too, while she was still well and full of life and vigour. She found herself one day in the same 'terrible caper' as Master Paul.

She was, however, still wearing her 'hessen eppen', and hopefully searched its voluminous pocket for anything that might serve her in her need. She had just been unwrapping her groceries, and, sure enough, had absent mindedly shoved a scrap of blue sugar-paper into her pocket.

Thankfully, she smoothed it out, and applied it. Next moment, her assembled family (which by chance happened to include Dad) were treated to a spectacle they never forgot, or allowed Grammam to forget. There she was, whooping and shrieking up the garden, taking high leaps into the air with both hands clutching her backside.

The smoothed out paper had been a cone containing two ounces of cayenne pepper!

Dear old Grammam, how she loved a joke! That in this case the joke was against her only added to the fun of it. She and Dad had the same outlook on life, which was that you made the very most of anything that occurred to balance the inevitable hardship. No wonder they loved each other. He was in most ways far more like his mother-in-law than like his own mother, and Grammam never stopped thanking her God that He had sent her such a son-in-law as 'Will-en'.

I'm quite sure that Grammam's antics as she careered up the garden that day were both enlarged and embroidered as the years passed, when Dad would relate the story, with suitable actions, while Grammam wiped the tears of laughter from her eyes with the corner of her white afternoon apron. It was one of those silly, intimate family jokes that we never got tired of hearing, and which made our childhood home-life so contented and happy, even between the storms that occasionally threatened us when Gerald and Lois were in their teens. Mam, it was then found, could not brook much opposition, even from her own children.

So much for cleanliness and hygiene.

One also has to ponder the nature of poverty, for of that there was no shortage, either.

It 'came natural' to me to take in, and think about, any phrases that I heard and learned at first hearing. Many of the more memorable of them were words heard in chapel and later, at school, including long passages from the Bible, and from hymns. I began to question 'the Word of the Lord' a bit, especially as continually quoted at me by Grandmother and Aunt Harriet. As I have hinted once before, I began to use my reason at a fairly young age. We learned 'The Sermon on the Mount' by heart at school, and had its tenets explained to us. I spent a good deal of time trying to fathom its meaning. What did 'Gentle Jesus' mean by it? I acknowledged him as 'meek and mild', but it seemed to me to be overdoing it a bit for him to declare

Blessed are the poor in spirit.

For all its Sunday-go-to-Chapel face, if there was any characteristic heartily despised in our fenland society, it was lack of 'spirit', by which was meant the courage to face up to things as they were and the pride to overcome hardships. I knew nobody in our chapel set, or any of our friends and neighbours, liable to inherit either heaven or earth if to be 'meek' and 'poor in spirit' was the passport.

I wonder now if Christ ever said anything of the sort. If he was not actually advising political agitators to pipe down and await their time, then my guess is that whoever reported it transposed the order of his words.

'Blessed, in spirit, are the poor, for theirs is the kingdom of heaven' makes comforting common-sense. When people lacked the material things of life, as most of us did in our fen, they balanced deprivation by turning to those things that cost them nothing — the things of the spirit — good talk, old tales, music in which they could participate and the poetry both of the Bible and the grand old hymns.

They might work 'every hour God sends'. They might 'rise with the lark and bed with the fowl'. They might get up from the table still hungry, or, for the time being at least, aware of

192

the adage that 'what don't fat fills'. They might go to bed cold, and be forced to supplement their thin coverlets with old coats, or even the pegged rug picked up from the floor, on nights when 'a black-frorst wind' blew across the fens direct from the Ural Mountains with nothing to stop it. They were certainly 'poor' by our modern standards, but they didn't harp on it as applied to themselves. Were not most of their neighbours in the same plight? And they were not by any means 'poor in spirit'. I don't want to leave the impression that they accepted 'meekly' whatever hardships 'the Good Lord' had seen fit to bestow on them — only that they stood up to them with courage and 'ol' fen pride'. There were certainly among them those who were very much concerned with material things — however often they might sing in chapel.

Take my silver and my gold
Not a mite will I withhold.

Grandmother was one of them. By the time I was born, she was, by the standards of the time and place, quite a well-to-do old woman; but her reputation for meanness was proverbial. I could fill pages with instances, but perhaps the one that sticks in my gullet most is the time, when Dad still worked for her, that he came down from topping up a stack in scorching weather so exhausted that his tachycardia actually frightened him, and he more or less collapsed on to the hearthrug. Mam, and I, though only about three, were present. Dad was striking his chest and showing signs of distress. Mam, panicking as she so often did, knelt down beside him and said to Grandmother 'Have you got a drop of brandy he can have?'. Grandmother lifted her petticoats, found her pocket, extracted a key and unlocked the chiffonier. Then she went to the pantry and fetched an egg-cup and carefully measured out a tot of brandy.

'There', she said, holding it down to Mam. 'I should think that's about a shillingsworth.'

Maybe it was his disgust that cured Dad's attack rather than the brandy — though having inherited his tachycardia, I know that it goes as suddenly as it comes, in any event.

Another story concerns a visit from one of her nieces, who had walked from Raveley to see her. She was not a welcome visitor, being a disgrace to the family for producing a child we should now recognise as suffering from Down's Syndrome. Even Grandmother felt she could not let her walk back to Raveley without offering her some food. So she set the table with cups of tea and bread and butter only. (Bread and butter, not slices of bread-and-butter.) Agnes did as requested, and helped herself. The next moment she spat out her first mouthful, and said 'Well, Aunt Rachel! Your bread's mouldy, and your butter stinks!' This meanness was the one characteristic of his mother that Dad could not condone, or make excuses for. She had been through some very hard times, and he made allowance for that; but she seemed to put her good fortune down to her righteousness, as one to whom the jealous god was 'showing mercy'.

194

Another such was as great a pillar of the chapel as 'Old Rachel'. He was known as the man who got married in the morning and then escorted his wife to the station to put her on the train to go to Bridlington for a honeymoon — by herself, while he went back to work. A much greater stain on his character was that he did not spare time to get down from his cart to help a poor fellow subject to epileptic fits when he saw him fall off his bike on to the verge. Had he been turned over, he would probably have lived. As it was, Johnny drove on, and Jimmy died.

It was Jimmy's mother from whom I first learned that people could have different standards of living, where food was concerned.

Dad's partner in the lighter business had been his good friend Charlie: so when they had to take their debt out in bricks, Charlie had also had a plot of land to build on, next to ours.

The two houses were at first identical, but Charlie had his extended to make another dwelling for his parents. When he died young and his parents, too, departed, his house became occupied by one of his brothers, and the extension by Charlie's sister-in-law's parents. Jimmy was their epileptic son.

Though they were 'next door' to us, each house had a wide yard, and there was a dividing hedge between.

Ol' Mis Marshall never grumbled about her helpless son, or about the 'onion dumpling' that made their main meal six days out of every seven. She would have been highly insulted if anybody had suggested that she was among 'the

195

poor', let alone 'poverty-stricken'. She liked her daily 'ungen dumplin' . . . and so did I.

Compared to Ol' Mis Marshall's, our standard of living was high indeed. We always had a ham in cut, and sides of home-cured bacon adorned the pantry walls. We always had 'butcher's meat' for Sunday, or 'an old fowl' from the farmyard or from the poultry we kept at the back of the house. We had plenty of eggs, and vegetables galore. We had no dairy of our own down Lotting Fen, as we did at the farm later, but Dad sometimes carried a can of milk home on his handlebars or in his flagon-basket or Gerald was sent to fetch one from Banker Bill's; and our backyard pig provided lard for a roly-poly pudding most days.

I was the one not satisfied with my lot! Mam could keep her jam-roll, or currant pudding. I had discovered fare I liked better. One day when I was three-and-a-half, I found a hole in Ol' Mis' Marshall's hedge, crawled through it and went up to the door to visit her. She was just dishing up the dockey, at approximately 10.30 a.m. She was dressed, as always on weekdays, in a long black skirt 'dolloping' over her broken boots and covered with a hessian apron. She had a knitted shawl pinned round her shoulders with a bent hairpin, and a man's cap sat firmly on her head of thin and straggly white hair. When I went in, she was just lifting a basin out of an oval iron pot hung over the turf-fire by a pot-hook. She put it on a plate and delved into the top (suet) crust with a knife. By this time, I was in the room and leaning on the table. She said few words to me, but she fetched another plate and fished a small helping from the basin on to it. I ate it standing up — as many children in large families still had to.

Thereafter, I managed to be standing by the table on a good many days when Ol' Mis' Marshall dished her dockey up. I hope I didn't rob her of what she needed, because it was herself she robbed for my portion, until Mam found out and somehow excused me from the old woman's generous hospitality.

I was distressed. I couldn't understand why we didn't have anything as delicious as Ol' Mis' Marshall's 'ungen dumplin' at home. Ham? Definitely over-rated, even though it was Mam's best home-cured. I think so still — especially the tasteless, fatless, wafer-thin cardboard sold as 'ham' nowadays. How can it possibly be compared with a basin lined with a suet crust and filled with sliced onions flavoured with a tiny cube of pickled pork and a good spoonful of mixed dried herbs — or in spring, with fresh sage-leaves chopped into it?

Hospitality is a sacred duty in our fen. Perhaps my visits to Ol' Mis' Marshall gave me the first inkling of that, and of my own obligation to keep my fen inheritance intact.

There were, of course, times when even the bare necessities of life were in short supply, especially where there were large families, and most especially when the man of the family was taken from them by illness or accident. Then life for the widow became very hard indeed, and I remember two or three occasions when subscription lists or raffles were set up for the sole purpose of benefiting a family reduced to the level of actual starvation, and, sensibly, not too proud to accept the sympathy, such as they could afford, of their neighbours; but such occasions were few and far between. A less ostentatious and more acceptable source of a bit of help in time of trouble were the 'Helping Hand' Clubs run by most of the pubs. It was a constant source of contention between my parents that Dad did not go down to 'The Ram' on Saturday evenings 'like other men'. Mam tried to drive him out.

'Why,' he would argue, reasonably 'should I leave my own chair and my own fireside to sit on a hard old settle and drink cold beer as I don't like?' (What he really meant, of course, was why should he leave his book.) But he made a point of going once a month, to pay his 'Helping Hand' shilling a week. This was after we went to the farm in New Fen: I doubt if the weekly contribution was anything as much as a shilling from anybody until the twenties.

As a family, we never experienced any sort of need, and very few of our wants went unsupplied. There were two reasons for this. Dad had got a good start, being thirty-one and owning his own house before he married. He thereafter worked 'like distraction' to get Mam (and us) everything we desired. He was his mother's horsekeeper (at eighteen shillings a week, plus a few perks). He had a smallholding at the back of our house, and he ran the Lotting Fen Drainage Mill, which job brought in another ten shillings a week. The workload on him told in the end, when he developed the heart trouble

198

that gave him such discomfort ever afterwards. It may have been aggravated by a severe attack of diphtheria, and by the dreadful summer of 1912, when he spent forty-four nights in succession at the mill, losing the battle in the end when the bank 'blowed' and flooded the fields in which the corn had already been reaped and 'stouked', right up to the bands. Our other asset was Mam's taste in the good things of life. Where most other women saved and scraped, even in good times, to 'get a bit put by' if they possibly could, Mam knew what she wanted and got it while the going was good. She was always 'the flaunting, extravagant queen' — especially in the eyes of Grandmother and Aunt Harriet. Grandmother once took her severely to task about her 'goings on', and the way she 'fooled Bill's money away'. Mam had overcome her diffidence where her in-laws were concerned by this time, being quite secure in Dad's protection. She reared like the proverbial 'fried-bread' at these strictures, and with the terse repartee for which she is now fabled among us, replied 'If God gives Bill the strength to earn it, I daresay He'll give me enough strength to spend it!' He did, too! 'Largesse' in all its possible meanings was Mam's trade mark. So as a young child, no sort of deprivation came my way; but I did learn the true meaning of poverty by observing its effect on others.

My parents, gregarious and popular, had many friends, but naturally there were some closer and dearer than others. 'Uncle George' and 'Aunt Rose' for instance, who lived by the Catchwater

Bridge and to whose house we often went on Sunday nights to sing hymns, after chapel.

Banker Bill and his merry brood of sons and daughters (one of them so full of fun and mischief that she became my first 'crush') provided a different kind of Sunday treat when we went there for supper. Banker was not a chapel-goer, though he lived almost opposite, but we called there often on the way home. The couple closest of all, however, were little Marjorie's parents.

In spite of Ailwyn's death, Marjorie's long struggle to regain her sight, and her mother's weak heart, they recovered after each setback and faced the world again with pride and courage. Like everybody else, they desired to 'better themselves', and strove towards it. When chance arose, Uncle Herb took the bull by the horns and moved from their cottage on The Heights to our house that was for sale — including the land for a smallholding. The word 'mortgage' was not on everybody's tongue then as it is now, but all the same money had to be borrowed. When Dad bought Grandmother's farm, he had a 'capital redemption' policy, which is how I came by the phrase to put into my collection of 'sayings'. Uncle Herb was able to borrow from his in-laws, but the burden of interest plus paying back capital was still heavy. It grew heavier and heavier as Aunt Sis required more and more medical attention and doctors' bills became more frequent as well as greater in amount. The first year after their adventurous move reduced them almost to penury. Not that any outsider would ever have known, because they were always well dressed, neat and almost over-clean, so spick and span was Aunt Sis herself and Marjorie, at school or Sunday school.

We reached the first Christmas after my rescue from the Bottomless Pit, and I sent many a note up the chimney to Father Christmas for a doll that had jointed limbs and closed its eyes. Marjorie seemed uninterested, although I urged her again and again to make her desires known because I knew that when at last Christmas came, our two families were going to spend it together at our house.

Father Christmas had heeded my requests with a vengeance. By the side of my bed, in addition to one of Dad's long stockings 'bowged out' with goodies and little toys, I had found the very first *Chatterbox* Annual I ever had, and the doll. Not only was the doll itself all I had ever dreamed of, but it was clothed in every garment that a real baby could ever need, right up to an exquisite, embroidered lawn christening gown. A shawl (knitted by Lois), a satin bonnet, and, best of all, a fine embroidered net veil that went over all the rest. I do not know to this day whether it was at that time (1920) a general fashion everywhere to veil new-born babies, or whether it applied only to our fenland district where it was indeed a very wise precaution against the swarms of mosquitoes. 'Little strangers' lacking the immunity children gradually built up, were as likely to be bitten and made ill as grown-up, visiting strangers were.

Anyway, the cup of my happiness flowed over.

As soon as our large cooked breakfast of fat and juicy pork sausages well covered with gravy in which strips of sage leaves floated had been cleared away, I took my doll and went outside to watch for our visitors coming up the drove to dinner with us. I walked up and down the path at the side of the house with my doll in my arms, every other minute climbing the steep grass verge from the gate to the granited road — because from the road, some six feet above the level of house and garden, I had a clear view right across the fen.

That Christmas Day had dawned as perfect as ever was depicted on a card. There had been a frost overnight and everything glistened with rime. The sky was a clear, distant, almost transparent blue and every grass-bent leaned over like a lady weighed down with the weight of sparkling jewels. I could see the row of 'black popples' that fringed Raveley Drain on the western side, and it was from that direction that our visitors would eventually come. Then at last, there they were, the little group making its leisurely way up the mile-long drove. I forgot my instructions to warn Mam and Dad when they were close at hand. Instead, I stood on the roadside clutching my doll in mounting impatience and excitement. As soon as they were near enough, I went to meet them, calling 'Did Father Christmas come? What did he bring? Look what he left me'. My little friend neither answered nor left her parents' side to come towards me. I looked enquiringly into Aunt's face and at last she found her voice. 'Oh' she said, almost

202

casually, 'He didn't come to our house last night! Is that doll what he left you? My, ain't she a beauty!'

What does one do when the sky seems to fall on your head and the stars rain down and smash into fragments at your feet?

I could not believe what I had heard, or bear the hurt (alone) of the pain on all our visitors' faces. I turned and ran, back down the path, to find Mam. Our visitors plodded slowly after me.

Mam was in the pantry, busily preparing lunch, but my cries of distress were loud enough to reach her, and she came out wearing her huge white cooking apron. I laid my doll down on the table, and buried my head in the apron's folds. I was crying and incoherently explaining the cause of my distress. Dad had welcomed the guests at the house-place door, and they all stood just inside, exchanging greetings. Marjorie stood, stolid and stoically expressionless, examining but not daring to touch my doll. When at last I took my face out of Mam's apron and looked up at her, I could see that her eyes were full of tears, and that aunt's, too, were moist as they looked at each other. Then Mam pushed me away clicking her tongue as if in annoyance.

'Dear-oh-dear!' she said, wiping my face with a clean corner of her apron 'fancy me forgetting! I've been so busy getting the dinner on I clean forgot it. Dad (reproachfully) you might ha' reminded me instead of sticking your head in that book, and saved all this hormpologe!' (She always found some way of including Dad in any blame, but I guess it was all part of the

203

camouflage on this particular occasion.) She looked down at me but her glance was also meant for our guests.

'This morning, when I cleared the plate up that you'd left Father Christmas his mince pie on, I found a bit o' paper under the wine glass. It said he'd got late going round the fen last night and had missed a chimney out. But he guessed if he left something here, the little girl it were meant for would get it alright, 'cos she were coming up here to her dinner. I put what he'd left under the stairs to keep it safe, and then I clean forgot it!'

There was silence as she disappeared into the dark little cupboard under the stairs, which had replaced the bread oven at Fern Cottage as our 'glory hole'. She backed out again holding a doll that was twin to my own, except that it lacked the glory of a long christening robe, a shawl and a veil.

The sky was in place again, and the stars restored to the heavens. We had a wonderful Christmas Day. I think neither of us children truly accepted Mam's bit of spontaneous fiction, but we were too wise to say so. If I had done, I do not think the memory of that incident would have been burnt so indelibly into me. Marjorie already knew the truth about Father Christmas, anyway.

I am afraid there will be many who will regard my story with the squeamish contempt that so many cynical twentieth-century critics bring to bear on anything that delves deep into human emotions. They will consider that I have turned a molehill of nostalgia into a mountain of sickly sentimentality, Dickensian in its heart-wringing, eased by a happy ending.

It depends where you want to draw the line between sentiment and sentimentality. I see it in its true context, as an illustration of what poverty was, and is. I see other things too. I see the pride, and the courage, and the lack of envy that carried these two parents, heart-broken with misery, towards the plenty of our house, their own gift-less child sure to be greeted by an over-indulged one — me.

I see also what compassionate foresight, what loving-kindness and tact my own parents had displayed, ingeniously finding a way round a situation they feared but knew they could not presume to prevent. Hurt pride would have been harder to bear than poverty. Deliberate 'charity', even on behalf of a child and from such near and dear friends, would have been an insult. If my little friend had found even so much as a sixpenny toy from Woolworths by her bedside, the second doll would have remained unseen in the glory-hole; but once Mam's excuse had been made, and the doll was in the child's arms, pride went down before all-conquering love. The gift was accepted.

And dear, beautiful Aunt, whose anguished heart had not failed her that morning, had so few Christmases left to her! She died at the age of forty-two in my Mam's arms, when her physiological heart suddenly did fail. That, too, was a scrap of history, that such children as we were then came face to face with death and sorrow at an early age. Perhaps it made us cling all the more tenaciously to memories of time of pleasure.

But what is history? Perhaps T. S. Eliot got it right when he wrote in *Little Gidding*

History is a pattern of timeless moments.

Like that Christmas morning, 1921, in New Fen.

My other memory concerns abject poverty and has no such Dickensian touch, nor such a happy ending. I was, I guess, about twelve years old when, through no fault or intention of my own, I was forced to witness a scene I cannot forget.

Dad went through life with a maxim of his own invention, which was 'Never lend anybody anything that you can't afford to give them.'

If he did ever refuse a loan on the grounds of his oft-quoted maxim, I never heard about it. Maybe he was lucky enough to go through life well enough off (in fenland terms) never to have to put his own bit of philosophy to the test. Mam's heart, in spite of her often belligerent manner, was as soft as cart-grease. Together, they were 'a soft touch' for unscrupulous scoundrels like Rattles and one or two other ne'er-do-wells, but a rock in a stormy sea for those of our neighbours or acquaintances who had reached the stage at which only a cash loan could save them from bankruptcy or destitution. When the request came, Dad 'maunch-gutted' for a day or two, being no more willing to say goodbye to his hard-earned savings than most other folk are; he

206

always told the supplicant that 'he should have to ask Mam'. The outcome was never in doubt. Whoever it was got the loan after Dad had calculated carefully whether he could, safely, afford to lose it if he never got it back. There were very few cases in which it was not returned dead on time. Small loans made on Dad's maxim might as well have been given outright, but for the fact that it would have damaged the borrower's pride. There were, however, pleas for loans of a much greater size, which Dad could not afford to lose or to give; yet he was more or less incapable of saying no, and if Mam were asked, Dad found he had two supplicants instead of one to deny. There was, for example, a tradesman from Ramsey whose regular customers we were. He had somehow fallen on very hard times, and was having considerable difficulty in keeping his shop going. Moreover, he had a wife, a daughter and a son, all of them putting on such airs that, as the fen-folk said 'they didn't know which way their backsides 'ung'. Perhaps their high standard of living added to their father's financial difficulties. I don't know. Came the day, however, when the tradesman applied to Dad for an immediate loan of £50 to see him over a crisis. He got the loan, and the crisis passed, but there was no mention of repayment.

Being an honest man, he came to see Dad, confessed that it was unlikely that he would ever be able to hand over £50 in money, and suggested that we should take out the debt in goods. Dad agreed, and a careful record was kept until we had had our £50s' worth. The tradesman produced his I.O.U. and Dad a receipt — upon which the other man pocketed the receipt, and promptly applied for another £50. For the rest of the tradesman's life the scheme continued, and as luck would have it, the debt had been cleared all but for a few shillings when death cleaned the slate. As far as we ever knew, the man's family remained completely in the dark with regard to the loan or even of their father's need of it; and Lois and I (sworn by our unbreakable word to Dad to absolute silence) had many a secret giggle to ourselves when at a dance in Ramsey the tradesman's dinner jacketed, crack-jawed son would ignore us disdainfully as being 'out of the fen' and beneath his august notice. You see, it fell to one or other of us to keep the weekly tally of goods consumed against the debt! I think it does us credit that we never 'let on'.

But there was no touch of humour at all in the story I set out to tell.

If there was a scrap of envy anywhere in Dad's nature, it was for the education he never got after the age of twelve. There was, of course, a Grammar School at Ramsey, and of Dad's generation, only three or four from both sides of the bridge ever got there. One, a decade or so younger than Dad (and also called Bill), lived the other side of the bridge, on The Herne. He was not a great friend of Dad's, for they met but seldom. When they did, however, they liked each other's company. Dad loved to listen to the other Bill talk, because he knew how to use the English

208

language properly: and the other Bill appreciated Bill 'Arry's brand of philosophy.

Bill was a small farmer, at forty still unmarried, and doing well. Then, out of the blue, as it were, came 'a gal from other parts' who knocked him sideways, and he married her. Baby followed baby until there were five, and though the saying is that 'stock's as good as money' it didn't prove to be so in this case. Bill's wife turned out to be as lazy as she was ignorant of country ways, as extravagant as she was feckless. Downhill the family slid until Bill's debts forced him to sell his little farm, and go to work for somebody else (always the signal that the point of no return had been reached). I don't suppose Dad was in the least surprised to find Bill waiting for him in the yard one day, with an embarrassed request for a loan of £50. Although he was aware of Bill's sad circumstances, he made the loan very willingly, because he knew and liked the man. The loan was for six months, renewable for another six if necessary. (I can't remember ever hearing the word 'interest' mentioned on any loan except the very last one Dad could afford to make (outside the family)). Mam made no objection to Bill's loan being extended. She knew only too well what it was to be poor and even hungry when it wasn't your own fault. So time went on.

This is where I come in. If I did know about that loan at all, it was only by eavesdropping. In any case it didn't concern me because I was not required to keep a tally, this time.

I was twelve, and to get to school at Ramsey I

had to cycle about four miles each way. This meant keeping my cycle in good condition, and I was under orders to put it inside in safety each night when I got home. I rode into the farmyard gate, between two lots of black, tarred buildings, towards the small gate that led to the house. A row of buildings fronted the road, and consisted of a large cart-hovel and another small square hovel that Gerald had appropriated for his own use. He was by this time twenty-two, and as mischievous and inventive as they come. With his cronies — more often than not sort of dogsbody satellites to him — he used his 'place' to carry out all the scientific experiments for which he had a yen as well as a gift. So a visit to his workshop was always interesting.

A bench under the window facing the road was understood to be out of bounds to me, because it was there that he made gunpowder — ostensibly to make fireworks, though in fact he bored out old black-oak roots on the farm till he could get a good-sized charge of gunpowder in somewhere, and then blew it up with a terrific bang after all sensible folk had gone to bed. (Boring out, or making a hole in a black-oak root, is not as easy as it sounds.)

The left-hand wall, as one entered by the rickety old wooden door, was taken up by an old bike standing upside down, adorned with bits of meccano and other gadgets as Gerald, with one willing henchman, experimented constantly with perpetual motion. Opposite, on the further wall, was an old treadle sewing-machine. This he used to patch his own trousers, which he did far more

210

expertly and more immediately, than Mam or Lois would have done. The actual machine part was detachable, so that he could use the treadle and belt to power his other inventions. At the time I am writing about, it operated a strange contraption which sharpened pencils at one end, and grated horseradish at the other.

That left the wall of which the door took up about one third of its length. On a nail, high up, hung a rusty and now neglected dulcimer: but by Dad's decree, that wall was left clear for Lois and me to stand our cycles against. It was a matter of habit for me to put my bike away and unload my satchel, etc. before going into the house. Often I stopped to examine Gerald's latest bit of machinery, and on this particular day, that is how I got trapped. The old sagging door had fallen to behind me, but as one of the hinges was loose and the gap on that side of the door wide, I had a clear view of the yard between the hovel I was in and the buildings of the farmyard proper, as well as of the gate and path that led to the house.

While I had been unpacking my school gear and looking at the horseradish grinder, Bill had ridden into the yard behind me. Dad had just emerged from 'the pony place' with a feeding basket under his arm, and they met right outside the closed door of the place I was in. I could see them through the crack, but they, of course, had no idea that I was there, and once Bill spoke, I knew I had to be an unwilling listener.

He came to the point at once. He had not come to pay his debt, because he couldn't. As he told Dad, he hadn't been able to save a penny towards it. I don't suppose Dad can have been at all surprised, but he was a bit disappointed and disturbed, as I could see by his face. And he was silent, no doubt seeking a suitable reply.

So there they stood. Bill was as tall as Dad, and of the same, lean-faced, handsome fenland breed — and as proud. He stood erect, drawn up to his full height, his back straight and his shoulders pulled back, with one hand on the saddle of his bike, which was leaning against him. When he broke the silence it was with a firm, strong voice.

'I'm only got one thing as is worth anything at all, Will'En,' he said, 'and that's this bike. I bought it out of the £50 you lent me, to get to work on. I'm took good care of it, and it's still as good as new. If you'll take it as a bit off what I owe you, it will at least show as I'm willing to pay if I could.'

Dad looked worried. 'How are you going to get home?' he asked.

'Walk.'

'I can't take your bike!' Dad exploded. 'It's more'n three mile from your home to your work. You'll never manage without it. Besides, I don't want another bike. I'm already got a good'un o' my own.'

'Take it, Will'En!' said Bill, pleading, and suddenly pushing the bike towards Dad.

'That I shan't!' said Dad, dropping his empty basket and pushing the bike back.

Bill pushed it forwards again, and Dad rejected it by shoving it back. It would have been

212

funny if the circumstances had been different.

After two or three more tries to make Dad accept it, Bill's calm deserted him. He poured out the story of his hopeless efforts to pull his family out of their poverty, but luck had been against him. He had been ill, and unable to go to work (so, of course, there had been no wages). He already had five 'littl'uns' and had just learned that a sixth was on the way. He pushed the bike once more towards Dad, and his voice broke as he began to weep. It was the first time I had ever seen a grown man cry, except for the histrionic tears of emotion from the chapel pulpit. Never had I seen tears of such despair and anguish as those Bill shed that day. I stood as if petrified, swamped by a feeling of guilt at being a witness, however unintentional. Whatever happened, I must not reveal my presence. I wondered what Dad would do, and could hardly believe my eyes when he took the bike from Bill's hands, and wheeled it away. He took it about six yards, to the wire-netting fence that kept the hens out of Mam's garden, and leaned it there.

Without the bike to support him, Bill went limp, as if all the stiffening had been taken out of his tall frame. He drooped, his head hanging forward and his arms now dangling loosely at his sides.

Dad balanced the bike carefully against the wire-netting, taking a long time about it. Then he turned back, and I saw his face. He strode straight back to where Bill stood, put both arms round Bill's shoulders, and straightened him up. Bill raised his arms and put them round Dad's neck, clinging like a child. And they both wept.

After more than sixty years, the memory still makes my diaphragm contract with the anguish of the moment.

Then Dad gently disengaged himself and said 'Stop where you are, Bill. I shall have to go and have a word with Mam.'

Bill stood, as utterly motionless outside the door as I was inside it. I was aware of a sense of terrible awe, such as Moses must have felt when God said, '*Take off thy shoes from off thy feet, for the place whereon thou standest is holy ground.*' Time seemed to have lost its meaning.

When Dad returned at last, he went straight to the bike and wheeled it back towards Bill. He accepted it without a word, as he did the cheque put into his hand. (I learned afterwards it was 'only five pound — enough to get the child'en some grub'.) Then Bill got on the bike and rode away, and I, personally, never saw him again. Nor do I know if Dad ever got any part of his loan back. Bill took his family out of the fen and I don't know what happened to them.

Later, I heard Dad telling Mam how little he had made the cheque out for — but I took care not to show I knew what they were talking about. For some reason, I felt that I must never mention it to anybody, and I never told Dad, even when he was old, that I had witnessed it at all. There was a sort of guilt that clung to me, of having seen what nobody should ever see. I had watched a fenman's pride broken.

Fen folk may lose heart, and often do; they may even lose courage occasionally; but when

214

they lose pride — there are no words.

I have been rambling on quite long enough about the characteristics of the fen folk; but to this bit, I think, belongs something else of terrible signficance to me, personally — a matter that affects me still, and has done all my life, far more than I can ever understand or even care to admit.

Mam's overwhelming love for her mother made Grammam one of the most important people of my infancy. She was, as I have told, reprieved from the sentence of death passed on her at the time of my birth, and soon went home to look after Rattles in 'The Carriages' down The Heights Road.

We moved from Lotting Fen to take over Grandmother's farm in October 1917, and our occupation of it was baptised well and truly by a Zeppelin dropping an incendiary bomb in our field the very night we moved in. But 1918 brought the Armistice, two weeks before my fifth birthday.

We heard the wonderful news about mid-morning. Mam snatched down her own hat and coat, wrapped me up warmly against the November weather, and, dragging me along by the hand, set out as fast as she could go towards 'The Carriages'. She burst through the door shouting 'Mam! Mam! Where are you? The War's over! The War's over!'

Grammam came down the steps into the lean-to kitchen and they threw their arms round each other, crying for joy. Then Grammam sat down suddenly on the old sofa, clasping her hand to her side, and saying breathlessly, over and over again 'Thank God! Thank God! The War's over.'

'I'm going to get your hat and coat, and take you back home with me,' announced my Mam. 'We've got to spend a day like this together!'

Grammam protested that she wasn't well enough, but Mam wouldn't listen to any excuses. She dressed her mother as she had done me, warmly, if haphazardly, and settled her into her wicker 'bath-chair'. (It has just occurred to me that it was the very same one that Vernon had afterwards.)

With Mam pushing, and me trotting alongside the chair, we set off home; but before we had gone more than a quarter of a mile Grammam groaned and began to gasp for breath. We happened to be right outside the public house called The Ram.

Mam was not at her best in any crisis, having a tendency to panic, especially if Dad was not anywhere near enough to take over. This time he wasn't. The Ram was open, but for a woman to enter a tap room was simply not done, even in an emergency such as this. She grabbed me and pushed me to the side of the chair, making me hold the arm of it to make sure it did not move. Then she ran round to the back door of the pub and banged till they heard her and went from the front to investigate.

I clung to the wicker arm of the chair with all my might as Grammam gasped and choked and coughed, until Mam at last came running back with some brandy in a glass. She poured it down

Grammam's throat somehow, and the stimulant seemed to have an amazing effect. In a few minutes we were ready to set off again, but I found that my legs didn't want to carry me. Mam plonked me on the front of the chair, on top of Grammam's feet, and pushed us both. I do not think there was anything at all the matter with me at that time. I was simply exhausted by the excitement and the fright of being left alone with Grammam while Mam went to get the brandy.

Grammam never returned home again. She lingered on in our house till the February of 1919, not well enough to look after herself, but still able to get up and lie on the sofa, where she mended for Mam, and sang or whistled to me as I sat close by her. Dad had given up his place at Mam's side in bed to her, and she often went up to bed early if she did not feel well enough to cope with the hurly-burly of a farm kitchen.

It was on a Saturday night that she 'had a turn' and was helped upstairs to the double bed in the large front bedroom. As she got to the bottom of the stairs, she turned to Dad and said, 'Bill, fetch Jack.'

Dad did not argue, but went at once to run down Rattles in one of the three pubs. Next morning, it was clear that Grammam was dying. (Not to me, of course; but because I am doing my best to record truthfully the details of this bit of social history, I shall report what I now know as well as what I actually remember first hand.)

It was a Sunday in February, very cold and miserable. A huge fire was lit in the fireplace at

217

the end of the big bedroom to keep the patient warm. Grammam knew she was dying, and asked for Aunt Lizzie, who was living at Peterborough twelve miles away. In 1919 there was no telephone, and no motor transport available in our fen. Dad could not leave Mam to cope by herself, so he rode off on his bike to seek help from his friend Banker Bill, who set off at once with horse and cart to fetch Lizzie.

Rattles sat by Grammam's bed holding his face in his hands, and whispering to himself. Mam sat on the bed on the opposite side to Rattles, holding Grammam's hands, wiping the death sweat from her face, smoothing the still black hair, ready with sips of water or brandy. Dad, in his stocking feet, came and went treading as lightly as a cat, fetching coal and keeping the fire blazing up the chimney and calming Gerald and Lois who were left downstairs.

And I? I have always regarded it as a most peculiar thing that everybody seemed to have forgotten my existence that day. Perhaps they thought, even Dad, that I was still too young to comprehend what was happening — though I would have thought I had given enough proof to Dad by this time that I was reasonably quick on the uptake. Maybe they were all so accustomed to small children having to witness death at close quarters in the fens' cramped cottages that they did not consider it at all strange for a five-year-old to be there. Perhaps, even, I created a fuss if they suggested that I should go to Lois, who was fourteen, to be looked after. I don't know: but what I do know is that I was there, playing on the rug in front of the unaccustomed fire, and watching and hearing everything. It would be about 2.00 p.m. when Banker Bill arrived back from Peterborough bringing Aunt Lizzie and Uncle Bill. They were all very cold, for it had rained solidly all the journey, a stinging slanting rain with a touch of sleet in it, the penetrating sort of rain that even the biggest gig umbrella could not keep from soaking them.

They were only just in time. As I have in my mind forever a photograph of the scene when I woke up in my cradle, so I have another of the scene just after their arrival. Uncle Bill pulled off his wet coat and hat on the landing, while Mam peeled off Aunt Lizzie's and dropped them on a chair. Uncle Bill went round the end of the bed to the side of Grandad Rattles, and there dropped on to his knees. Mam resumed her place on the bed, and started wiping Grammam's face again. Dad stood at the bottom of the bed, leaning over the footboard, waiting and watching in case he should be needed.

Aunt Lizzie flung herself on to her knees by the side of the bed as close to Grammam as she could get, tears streaming down her lovely face.

I had got up at the commotion caused by their coming, and now stood only just behind the backs of Grandad and Uncle Bill, seeing the bed and the rest of the room between their two bowed heads. My ears still ring at the remembrance of Aunt Lizzie's anguished cry of, 'Kiss me, Mam. Kiss me!'

Grammam opened her eyes, and pursed her

219

lips into a kiss, first towards Aunt Lizzie, and then towards Mam. Then she shut her eyes again, and in the awe-ful silence, Grandad threw himself across the bed and cried out 'She's gone! My Meery's gone!'

I think some sort of traumatic amnesia must have seized me at that point, because I have not a single memory of the next three or four days, which must have been an agony of grief for everybody else, though especially for Mam. There must also have been a good deal of hustle and bustle of funeral arrangements, and strange sleeping arrangements with extra people in the house and the big front bedroom out of action. Yet not a single incident registered itself with me, until . . .

It would be about the fourth day after Grammam's death, and Mam, Lois and I were together alone in the 'living room' downstairs. For some reason, it appeared that there was an urgent need for one of Dad's large white handkerchiefs, which were kept in a drawer of the dressing-table in the front bedroom where Grammam's corpse still lay. Mam's nerve had gone, and she had affected Lois. Neither would venture upstairs to fetch the handkerchief. Then Mam said (and here my memory returns to me in every minute detail), 'Let Sybil go. She isn't old enough to understand.' I felt flattered at being asked to do what Lois would not, and as I had, apparently, gone through three days of complete amnesia, I did not connect my errand in any way with Grammam or the events of the last Sunday. Mam told me exactly where to find the handkerchief she needed, and off I went, up the curved narrow stairs and straight ahead at the top into the big bedroom. I was surprised to find it dark, and lit only by a candle on a chest of drawers by the bed. The blinds were down, the winter afternoon closing in. As I opened the door, the bed was on my left, the dressing table straight ahead. I went towards it, noticing as I did so a curiously shaped piece of wood leaning on the wall beside it (the lid of the coffin). It had not been there before, and I examined it with care before opening the drawer and extracting the handkerchief. Then, and only then, did I glance in the mirror. Behind me, on the bed, I could see the reflection of a long wooden box, and for the first time I remembered the events of Sunday, and connected the box with Grammam's death. I wondered what was in the box. I wasn't tall enough to see, not even when I left the dressing table and went to the side of the bed. I put my hands on the edge of the box to help me stand on tiptoe, but I still couldn't see inside. So I pulled up a chair, climbed on to it, and looked down. And there, lying in the box, was my beloved Grammam, apparently asleep. I leaned over, and kissed her.

She was cold, and she stank.

As long as I live, I shall never shake off the horror of that moment. I got down, and silently replaced the chair. I was quite sure that somehow it was all my fault for not doing exactly as I had been told, and that therefore I must never let anyone know what I had done and seen. I took the folded handkerchief and delivered it to Mam, receiving much praise for being such a good little girl. I kept my dreadful knowledge to myself — indeed, it was many decades before I ever told anybody what had happened in that terrifyingly half-lit room.

Unfortunately for me, the story does not end there. In fact it has never ended.

In the summer of 1918, our grass field was used for the peace celebrations. I won first prize in the fancy dress competiton, riding round the ring on my first tricycle dressed as Britannia. The going on the rough grass was hard, and Uncle Bill (Aunt Lizzie's husband) stepped out of the crowd of onlookers and pushed me round — though I think I was then still perfectly healthy.

It was the next summer, when I was six-and-a-half, that my life-long terror began. I had been promoted from my cot in my parents' room to sleeping in a double-bed alongside Lois. So it was by her side that I woke one night screaming with horror at the dream I had just been having. I had dreamt that I was dead, and was lying out in the open, pegged down upon the ground, my arms and my legs secured so that I could not move: and my whole naked body, including my face, was covered with live butterflies.

I screamed, and could not stop my screaming, though Lois did her best to wake me properly, and to comfort me. Dad heard me, and came, but for once his presence did no good. When Mam finally appeared, I had reached a point of exhaustion, though still stiff with horror. The butterflies were still there, though I was now wide awake. I demanded, frantically, to be bathed there and then, though I did not tell anybody why. Mam fetched water (cold) and sponged my face and body. It would not suffice — I had to be bathed, and I started to scream again.

A bath in the middle of the night was not the simple operation it would be today. It meant Dad fetching wood and kindling a fire under the copper in the back kitchen, and the tin bath being brought in before another fire kindled in 'the house place'. At last they lifted me into the blessed hot water — Dad worried, Mam inclined to be cross, and Lois frightened. They washed me all over — but the butterflies would not be washed away. I went on screaming for them to rub harder. They were all now frightened by my extraordinary behaviour, and I registered through my terror the fact that Lois, shivering in her nightgown, had come closer to look at me. Hysterically I appealed to her to fetch the scrubbing brush and scrub me. She seemed to understand better than Mam or Dad, and did what I asked. Mam had had just about had enough, and was preparing to see what a good slapping would do, when Lois kneeled down and began to scrub me. Even she hesitated to obey my command to scrub my face, until I showed signs of renewing my hysterical screaming. I kept her at it until she had scrubbed every single clinging butterfly away. In all the time it took, I never said a word about the butterflies. They had no idea what had caused such extraordinary behaviour, and very little was made of it. It was put down to 'something I had been eating' or 'the sort of thing that does happen to children occasionally'. (We call them 'night terrors' — or at least, we used to: my terminology is probably out of date by now.) Mam said nothing of it, probably because she knew that if Grandmother and Aunt Harriet heard of it, they would diagnose it at once as the result of being thoroughly spoiled, and give their unasked opinion that nothing was the matter that a good backside-tanning wouldn't cure. So the rest of the family made light of it all, and soon forgot all about it. I have never been allowed that comfort. It left me with a life-long phobia with regard to butterflies, and a recurring nightmare. On the surface, the two do not seem to have much direct connection with each other.

The nightmare, from which I still suffer, is that I have a decomposing or decomposed body to dispose of, in secret and alone. The details vary. I have found Grammam, decomposing, lying on the white enamel shelf in the dairy where normally our butter was kept till sold. I have dug graves in St Mary's churchyard, all by myself in the middle of the night, in order to bury Dad before he fell to pieces: I have dug up my Uncle John, from St Mary's churchyard (although he was not buried there), in order to find a secret grave for the decomposing corpse of a stranger whom Gerald had shot and killed: in fact, I think I must have exhumed every relative buried at St Mary's many times over, and always to get rid of some other decomposing corpse, often of my nearest and dearest, though sometimes of complete strangers. The horror of my task is always made worse by the need for speed and secrecy, because the guilt attached to the death is heavy on my shoulders. My frantic efforts at dead of night in St Mary's churchyard always take place in 'the old part' between the church and the road, or at the east end of the church, between the building and the hedge of the vicarage garden — though none of the relatives or friends that I remember could have been buried there. In some strange fashion, this unfamiliar ground adds the last touch of unbearable horror, and I wake up almost drowned in cold sweat.

(I am glad to report that since Mam's terrible death, at which my nightmare almost came true, I have been less troubled by it. If and when it does recur now, I can usually rouse myself, exhausted and sweating, enough to know that I am in my own bed, and keep myself awake again so as not to go back to sleep and repeat the nightmare as I often used to do. I still dread being in my house alone at night, though for no other reason than that I fear my nightmare and that I may wake up to find no other living soul to hold me or comfort me till I can be rid of its clinging aftermath.)

The phobia is a separate and entirely different terror. The word 'phobia' is used lightly and frequently nowadays, and has come to mean any strong dislike; but anyone who suffers from a genuine phobia knows the difference. A true phobia is a completely irrational horror (not fear at all) which robs the sufferer of all will-power and common sense, and has physical effects frightening in their own right. In my own case, they include an arrested heart-beat, a prickling of skin on arms and neck, and a stomach spasm that has often caused spontaneous vomiting. In any case, the dreadful nausea is such that instantaneous throwing-up is preferable.

There are degrees in this reaction, however. The dark body of a butterfly in flight, caught sight of out of the corner of my eye, produces at once the prickling skin, and the feeling of horror, which robs me of the power of thought — but these reactions are controllable. Cabbage whites, brimstones and orange-tips do not affect me. I can even admire them. Peacocks and red admirals put on the pressure, and I have difficulty in keeping control of my actions; but an ordinary common tortoiseshell reduces me to a screaming idiot. If any of the darker varieties or the brilliant red admiral sits opening and closing its wings in the sun, my legs become useless and the nausea rises as my heart loses its rhythm and appears to 'run down', like a chain slipping a cog. Any butterfly indoors is unendurable. If it comes in, I must get out — very difficult to achieve when one's legs won't work. But there is no compromise.

Unfortunately, the wretched things hibernate, and also die in unexpected places, which obliges me to confess that a dead tortoiseshell causes an even more violent reaction than a live one. I cannot bring myself to put on a garment that has been hanging in cupboard or wardrobe until some one else has 'vetted' it first, because I once found a dead tortoiseshell in the sleeve of a mackintosh. My family are very patient with me, because they are well aware that I am not normally one of the 'fainting female' type. For their sakes, I have tried hard to analyse my reaction, especially when there is no actual butterfly dead or alive in sight, but only something that suggests 'butterfly' to me, and the same symptoms are instantaneous. It seems to me that the common link is any overall pattern of a brown/white/orange combination. I am, in truth having some difficulty in writing this; my arms are goose-pimpled, and nausea beginning to rise. The thought of a butterfly is enough to set up the instinctive physical reactions.

My sister had a Victorian paisley shawl, which she used to protect her precious grand piano from the hot sun in summer. The pattern was too much for me; I could not sit in her sitting room until the shawl had been removed.

Perhaps the most extraordinary example of all happened one day when I was happily cooking in my own kitchen. I had boiled some milk in a non-stick saucepan, and left it a bit too long on a gas ring. I poured the milk out, and looked into the saucepan. The bottom of it was covered with a raised pattern of more or less circles in the dreaded brown and white combination. Luckily, the sink was near enough to take the spontaneous vomit, and for me to cling to until the use of my legs returned.

As one would expect, this phobia has caused much interest among my psychologist colleagues.

Each had a separate theory, most of which at least made me laugh. (I ought to explain that several witnessed the phobia and its effects, while knowing nothing of my childhood dream.)

Most of the more sensible ones alleged that a butterfly must have sat on my face while I was in my pram, giving me a very close-up view of its wings. Quite plausible as an explanation, I think, considering what a paradise of butterflies the fens used to be at that time. The most outrageous explanation was offered by an American female psychologist, who said (truthfully) that I was a very large, fat, heavy person who longed secretly to be light, slim, airy, graceful and as gorgeously beautiful as a butterfly (instead of, she implied, the absolute opposite.) That was why I hated them so much. They were all the things my dreams were made of, things that I knew I could never be. Oh well!

However, a colleague of mine who was also a friend was told about my childhood dream, and asked, sensibly, if I remembered whether the phobia existed before the dream, or resulted from it. I couldn't tell him. He suspected that the phobia was a direct result of the dream. (Again, a very plausible explanation, though it does not account for my daughter and one other member of the family at least, with whom I have very rarely had contact, suffering in the same way if not quite so badly.)

I puzzle about that dream, in any case. How many people, I wonder, know that the 'living jewels' they love so much feast upon carrion? One thing is quite certain; that I did not know it when, at the of six, I dreamt that my own dead body was being eaten by them. Then, one evening when I was travelling to a lecture with my psychologist collegue, I told him of the dream, and of my childhood experience of looking into Grammam's coffin.

'I think there must have been a tortoiseshell butterfly in that bedroom that day,' he said.

I pooh-poohed the idea. 'Come off it,' I said. 'It was February, and cold enough for snow and sleet.'

But there had been a fire of course. A hibernating butterfly could have been lured out of hiding by the warmth, and by the smell of death. Could there have been a butterfly on my Grammam's face or in the coffin with her so that I disturbed it when I leaned over?

A probability rather than a mere possibility, I think.

Or can it possibly be that we (and I in particulaar) carry some deep, subconscious race memory? In my dream, if you remember the details, I was spread-eagled, pegged-down, dead, and covered with feasting butterflies clinging tightly to me. Did not the Celts of old peg down their human sacrifices in swamps, where butterflies abound?

It used to be a common belief in the folklore of many rural areas of Britain that the soul did not depart from the body at the moment of death, but hovered there for anything up to three days. Until the soul had emerged, there was an understandable reluctance to bury the corpse, which in consequence of this as well as practical difficulties, was often kept too long. It may be this belief that originated the custom of employing a corpse-watcher, to report when, or if, the soul had departed; for in my childhood, it was held by many that the soul crept out of the deceased's mouth in the form of a bee, and flew away. A piece of folk-lore that did not comply very well with Christianity, but was among the remnants of paganism they still clung to.

My interest in the Celts has caused me to read a great deal. It seems that primitive peoples everywhere believed that the soul escaped as some kind of insect, most usually a bee. But not the Celts — they went along with the rest except in the choice of insect that bore their souls back to nature. Their poetic instincts suggested the most beautiful of all as the bearer of their souls — the butterfly, of course. So was there a butterfly there, in Grammam's coffin? Sometimes I half-believe there must have been!

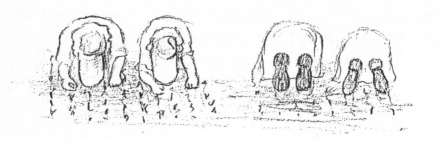

7

Mam

There's no need for me to write anything specially about Dad. He was there. He was Will'En, or Bill 'Arry, and everybody knew him. Most folks who knew him liked him, even if they thought him 'a bit of a cure'. In any case, he crops up at every verse's end in my tale.

Mam is a very different matter. If Dad was a typical fenman with a few virtues added, Mam was a fen-tigress with every characteristic exaggerated. If you knew Dad, you knew him, because he was uncomplicated, and always the same. Nobody ever knew Mam, because she was a living paradox, with both sides of every personal characteristic in her, and as many facets as one of those huge balls made of tiny mirrors that were used as decorations in my dancing days. However many facets you thought you had seen, there were always more.

I dare say being Rattles' daughter didn't help — she would have hated to think so, but she had a lot of him in her make up, particularly the tendency to be 'contrary' for no reason. His genes must have always been at odds with those of Grammam, who was born and bred a fen woman, though from Yaxley fen, and as sweet, gentle and intelligent a woman as ever married a difficult man. The family from which she came

231

all seemed, like Dad, to have 'a little bit extra' in the way of gumption, or, as she would have called it 'dossity'. They did well, and one of Mam's cousins (Uncle Harry to us) did extremely well as a builder of brickyard chimneys. He was a strange eccentric man in his later years. This was always put down to the fact that he had once been inspecting a completed chimney, had slipped inside the top, and had clung on there by his hands till rescued. Enough surely to make a man a bit queer.

He was also a part-time fireman, and loved the task. He once came to our Sunday School anniversary wearing his fireman's uniform, beautiful brass helmet and all, and a splendid sight he was. It was, though at a much later 'Anni', to which he always came if he could, that he gave me a bit of advice.

I was sixteen, I think, and beyond the stage of sitting up in the front of the chapel and 'saying my piece', but not beyond the stage of regarding the Anni as an occasion for getting a new outfit. My new dress was of blue, flowered ninon (made by Lois) with hat to match. It was sleeveless, according to prevailing fashion, and on my arm, above the elbow, I wore my precious gold bangle. Somehow, as the party set off to walk down to chapel, Uncle Harry and I fell a bit behind. It was a lovely warm afternoon, and we were not hurrying. Suddenly, without the least warning, Uncle Harry fetched me such a slap with the back of his hand on my bare arm, just where the bangle fitted tightly round it, that the pain made my eyes water.

'What's your name?' he barked at me.

'Sybil Edwards' I answered, deciding quickly that I'd better humour him.

SLAP 'What was your mother's name?'

'Kate Papworth.'

SLAP 'What was her mother's name?

'Mary Stretton.'

SLAP! SLAP! SLAP!

'There you are! You're a Stretton, and don't you forget it. STRETTONS CAN DO ANYTHING'

SLAP! (Harder than ever).

'Remember that, what I just told you. You're a Stretton and Strettons can do anything they put their minds to.'

With that he suddenly left me, running with great strides to catch the rest of the party up.

I loitered, brushing away tears of pain and trying quite ineffectually to reduce the scarlet colouring of my arm before entering the chapel. The bruise made by the bangle lasted for weeks. The advice has lasted all my life.

So, back to Mam. She was a Stretton, as well as a Papworth. I think the two sides of her were always at war with each other, just as the sudden changes in her style of life were. Her humble fearful and poverty-stricken childhood, and her increasing deafness, made her shy and diffident when she was not absolutely sure of her ground; but the Stretton confidence could not be downed for long, and the belligerent Rattles side of her was only just beneath the surface, so that on occasion she would come out fighting, especially with her tongue. In better circumstances, the slender shy girl blossomed under

233

Dad's protection into a decidedly flamboyant matron of large proportions, handsome, tall, and with a wonderfully upright and proud carriage. She was still beautiful at eighty-plus, with snow-white hair and soft, creamy skin contrasting strangely with still-dark eyebrows over dark, fiery eyes. When she turned on her charm, she could still exert extraordinary magnetism, so that strangers from all walks of life succumbed to her and sat at her feet, quite literally sometimes, enchanted by her. Unfortunately for us, and me in particular, it was the obverse of the coin that was turned towards us more often in her old age.

Her long life seemed to be punctuated with events of high drama, such as one would only expect to find in popular fiction; but at the same time, she seemed to have a genius for getting herself into utterly farcical situations. Thank goodness she possessed the same ability to laugh at her own expense as Grammam and Dad had — a quality that helped us all a great deal in the trauma of her last two decades.

Take, for example, the 'drama' of her marriage to Dad. He, aged seventeen, had watched her, aged seven, being christened in St Mary's church, and had decided she was the girl he wanted. Of this, of course, she was completely unaware, as she grew up, though like every other girl in the fen she kept a hopeful eye on the most eligible bachelor for miles around. When she was eighteen, poverty drove her into 'service', which she had so far escaped because she was said to suffer from 'green-sickness' (probably due to being half-starved). She afterwards said that she put on most of her symptoms, because with Aunt Lizzie already gone, she dared not leave Grammam alone and unprotected with her father. When she was eighteen, Rattles himself thought it was time she earned her own living, and Grammam persuaded her to return with Aunt Lizzie to Nottingham, where Aunt Lizzie was already in 'good' service as a parlourmaid. Her sister having procured a job for her in a wealthy Quaker household, Mam, ignorant, innocent, unsophisticated, shy, embarrassed by deafness and utterly inexperienced, went to her first place.

The excellent couple, pillars of Victorian society as well as shining examples of Quaker integrity, had everything a heart could wish for except the one they longed for most, just like many a couple in the old fairy tales. They even had a bevy of fine, handsome sons, but no daughter. Their beautiful, shy, country-bred parlourmaid crept into the vacant place in their hearts, and they 'spoiled' her to the very limit possible in a houseful of other town-bred female servants. She responded, using her (Stretton?) intelligence to learn fast, and return affection where it was given. The peace of a Quaker household, after the turmoil of living under Rattle's roof, made it seem to her 'like fairyland', she said.

Under their coaching, she learned a lot of social graces, and acquired a taste for beautiful things, especially china and silver, that she never lost, and indulged to the full as Dad's circumstances allowed her to. Both her deportment and her

235

taste, particularly for antiques, were black marks against her in her in-laws' book.

Her employers, watching her beauty flower as a result of good food and kindness, feared that she would not remain long unattached. Not only did they not want to lose her, they were afraid that she would marry less well than she might. Their care for her was to have long-lasting consequences, which reached out and coloured all our lives, long, long after they were dead.

In continuing this tale of high drama, I must remind you that I have only Mam's own word for what happened, and that she was Rattles' daughter. There is, I think, some truth in all of it, but not all truth in some parts of it. According to Mam, in their concern not to lose her they actually put forward the suggestion that they should send her away to be schooled, with the idea that if she turned out as they confidently expected, they would then adopt her legally as their daughter. Such a plan, of course, needed her own consent, and, as she was only eighteen, that of her parents as well. She was sent home to discuss it with her parents.

How could they possibly have imagined such a pair of parents as those, or the fenland conditions of her home? Grammam, knowing that such an arrangement must inevitably have as a condition Mam's complete break from her natural family and circumstances, unselfishly and lovingly begged her to accept an offer so miraculous; but it appears that Mam herself had not even guessed that there might be such a condition. Cut herself off from her beloved mother forever? Not for twenty such offers, with the hand of a prince thrown in! Mam's mind was made up, and all Grammam's urgings could not change it. Rattles was not told about it. They knew what his reaction would be, a violent rage against 'them rich folks as think they can buy my gal', and an even more violent tantrum on Mam's own head for not accepting it before they changed their minds.

So she returned to Nottingham, to tell her would-be benefactors that she had decided against their offer.

If all this was the result of Mam's Celtic imagination, I must say that she had a good memory. In all the times I heard the tale, the essentials never varied, nor her own distress and tears as she recounted the reason for her refusal, her anguish at the thought of voluntarily parting from her adored mother.

The Quaker couple suspected a fenland sweetheart — Mam told me she never gave them even a hint of her home circumstances. They begged her not to leave them, and she declared that she had no intention of doing so. She wanted to keep her place as their parlourmaid. She was happy there.

Relieved, they made more of her than ever, turning her more or less into a companion-help to her mistress rather than a parlourmaid. One effect this had was to make her very unpopular with the rest of the female staff, a situation that caused Mam to stand up for herself and taught her to overcome her innate shyness. The other result their indulgence had was much more

237

serious. On her days off, Mam was in the habit of meeting Aunt Lizzie, who lived on the other side of Nottingham, so that they could spend the day together in town. Both sets of employers had estates on the outer suburbs, so both the girls had a short train journey to make, which in winter involved them returning in the dark.

Mam's employers, concerned for her safety as she walked home from the branch-line station alone, ordered out their coachman with the trap to meet her at the station. He was a married man who lived in a cottage on the estate, with a wife who already had four children and was expecting another. To the man, Mam was only one of his own inferior class, a servant like himself, and he resented having to turn out to fetch her; but once he had done so, he succumbed completely to her beauty and the rural charm that had not worn off. His pursuit of her thereafter made her life a nightmare. She dared not walk out in the grounds, even when ordered to do so, lest he should leap out from behind a tree and drag her into the bushes; she could not keep her appointments with Aunt Lizzie, because it condemned her to being alone with him on the return journey. He made excuses for going into the house, where he hid round corners and in dark passages to waylay her in the course of her duties. Jealous tongues began to wag in the kitchen, at her expense. She was in a terrible dilemma, because she knew what the consequences would be for the coachman's wife and children if she appealed for help from her strictly moral employers, and told on him. He would have been dismissed immediately, and his family made homeless, since their cottage went with the job.

She did the only thing left for her to do — gave in her notice, and left, without any further explanation. It grieved her always to imagine what they must have thought of her, so to repay their kindness. She had also broken her promise to stay with them, and she was well aware that never again would she live in such circumstances of ease and elegance, such peace and pleasure. One other thought hurt her considerably — that the construction they would most probably put on her abrupt departure was that she had found herself pregnant. As her attitude towards sex all her life was as ambivalent as everything else about her, anything more likely to wound her was impossible to think of. She would far rather they had believed she had stolen all the silver! She used to comfort herself, forty years later, when recounting all this to me, by reflecting that they must have realised this was not the case when they were asked to supply a reference for her to another Quaker couple in Godmanchester, which they did. Aunt Lizzie also wanted to be nearer her mother, and left her place too — to go to her doctor's establishment.

Both of them on holiday at home at the same time, they walked together to church at St Mary's, and met Dad, as already recounted.

So — the day-dream of her adolescent years had come true. Will'En was hers for the taking, but did she still consider his offer as 'a dream come true'?

She had very mixed feelings about it. She was still only twenty: he was already thirty. He was still the most eligible bachelor, besides being the handsomest and kindest, in the whole district — but how did he, how could he, compare with the sons of her employers, the educated gentlemen who might have been her 'brothers'? Not very well. He was still a very rough diamond, an uneducated, unpolished fen-tiger. And what could he offer her? A house of his own built and paid for, but it was a mile down an unmade drove, with no water laid on, no gas-light, no vestige of the elegant life-style she had glimpsed and had come near to being part of — the sort of life, moreover, however immoral it might be, that her sister had fallen into.

Once again she was being forced to make a big decision. Against acceptance of Dad's proposal was all her revulsion at going back to life in the fens, and the knowledge of Grandmother's and Dad's sisters' contempt for her and her upbringing. For it was the delight, comfort and security it would give Grammam. Once again, it was her love for Grammam that turned the scale.

I don't want to suggest that she married Dad only for this reason. She was as much 'in love' with him as she would ever have been with any other man, and they were happy, even if Dad often got the worst side of the bargain.

The trouble was that she seemed incapable of setting off what she had got against the phantom of what might have been. However much she 'chuntered' about Dad and his curious ways, she was well aware how extraordinarily lucky she had

240

been in the marriage lottery: but she could never wipe out from her mind that it had meant returning to the fens against her inclination. When both Grammam and Dad were dead, she seemed to seize upon that as a grievance against which she measured others. She had given up all that might-have-been for Grammam, and her own love for Grammam, whom, Mam would declare, she had loved more than she had loved anybody else (by inference, more than she loved Dad or us, her children). As the years went by, she built her rejection of a different life into a great 'sacrifice' that she had made for her mother; and from this came the corollary, that she expected to be rewarded in kind for her sacrifice by us, her children, making the same sort of sacrifice for her, putting her always first, and subjecting our own marital happiness to her welfare. She built the entire incident into a huge drama, as out of proportion as she in the flesh was to the slim shy girl she had then been.

She *would* be different. This was the Stretton coming out in her — though another youthful drama over which she had no control began it. At the age of seventeen, before leaving home, she was suddenly attacked by a horrid skin disease — about the worst thing that could happen to a girl whose only asset was her beauty. It spread all over her, and the doctor, when called, was non-plussed. He bundled her into Huntingdon hospital. The fen was agog, and everyone put his or her own interpretation upon it. Dad aged twenty-seven and still living at home, was infuriated by Grandmother's and Aunt Harriet's declaration that of course it was 'the bad disease'. His anger was partly on 'his' girl's behalf, but also because of the injustice done to Rattles. Whatever his many faults, womanizing was not among them.

The hospital diagnosed the complaint as psoriasis, declaring it to be genetically inherited with migraine as an alternative form (like asthma and eczema). Grammam, when questioned could give the doctors several instances of one or the other in the Stretton family, and Gerald certainly had terrible migraines all his life. The doctors averred that it usually passed from male to female and vice versa, even when it missed a generation.

Luckily, Mam's psoriasis cleared up as quickly as it had come, leaving her skin as soft and smooth as ever — but she was warned that it would probably recur. In fact, it never did in the same way, though every autumn and spring in her middle-age brought out a small patch of the 'silver scale' on elbows and knees and the base of her spine. Naturally, every time the red spots appeared, she feared the worst: and when she had become the wife of a prosperous farmer, she sought treatment at the first intimation of its recurrence, costing Dad a fortune. Not that he grudged it — he never grudged her anything!

One year, when I was about ten, her search for a cure landed her into the hands of a quack doctor who practised somewhere close to the village of Holme. By this time, Mam (forty-three to forty-five) had her own trap and high-stepping little pony, which she drove expertly, elegantly dressed in a tailored 'costume', with hat and veil 'made a-purpose', and leather driving gloves. There was no difficulty in consulting the expensive quack, who declared that he could prevent any serious attack such as the initial one by treating her with small doses of *arsenic*. I'm pretty sure that it was the dramatic nature of his treatment, plus the fact that it was expensive and provided her with an excuse to harness up and take a pleasurable drive, that kept her going back to him year after year for more arsenic. In the end, he warned her that the treatment might have the side effect of loosening her joints, but she just added this dire warning to the drama of talking about it, and otherwise disregarded it. I have absolutely no medical evidence that she was, in fact, ever given arsenic, that such a cure was ever considered for psoriasis, or that a prolonged course of it has any effect whatever on the joints! All I do know was that except for knees and elbows, her beautiful skin was never again blemished, but that at the age of fifty-plus her knees did begin to give out, finally landing her in the wheel-chair in which she spent her last fifteen years of life.

No wonder her knees gave out, arsenic or not. By forty-five she turned the scale at approximately 15 stones: by seventy, at 17 stones, plus, by eighty at nearly 20 stones. She had a terrific appetite, and it was symptomatic of her paradoxical nature that she refused to believe that eating had any effect on size. She loved her smart clothes, and bewailed the elegance that had once been hers, and the proud carriage she

243

had maintained until her knees would no longer hold her up straight. None of us dared to press her into controlling her appetite for butter and cream, and all the rest of the fat of the land. She must have been a living parcel of cholesterol. If we ever did mention it, she would snap 'My knees are nothing to do with what I eat! You know as well as I do, it was all that arsenic I had to take to keep my psoriasis from coming back!' And she would empty the jug of cream just to prove it.

Now who, I ask you, but my extraordinary mother would be able to claim that she lived to be eighty-eight and a half on a diet of cream and arsenic?

To be utterly fair to her, and in view of what happened to her in her ninth decade of life, I must report that I, personally, followed her pattern of expansion through middle and into old age almost identically, in spite of being an inexhautible mine of energy that others found difficult to keep up with. Dieting only deprived me of my energy. It was only when I suddenly blew up like a balloon that my clever, experienced GP suspected what he himself could hardly believe, that in spite of my energy and everything else about me that went against all the usual symptoms, my thyroid gland had become inefficient. Treatment was begun at once, since when diet has worked, and four stones or more of unwanted weight have been shed. As Aunt Lizzie in her last years had a goitre, and as many of Mam's relations suffered the same problem of excessive weight, it would

244

not be at all surprising if Mam's thyroid gland was also a bit deficient. If our diet in the fen in her youth and mine lacked anything essential it must have been iodine.

Poor old Mam! She has now become a sort of fable to us, and no meeting of the family is ever complete without tales about her being told, though now she is remembered as 'Nanny', not 'Mam'. Occasionally, it is the difficult, bitter old woman that is remembered, with anger and tears; but much more usually the tears are of laughter, because the other side of her was such fun, such delight, so ludicrous; and her unexpected ability to laugh at herself only failed at the very end. She was just as willing to relate the farcical episodes as the dramatic, while still in her own control.

It surprises me considerably to remember, for instance, how the shy, diffident woman she so often appeared to be, ever drove that high-spirited young pony we had, called 'Jack'. Jack bolted with her several times. Once in the shafts he would rear and buck, and on a few occasions took it into his head to proceed in the opposite direction to that she intended. Then a battle of wills took place that was exciting, if frightening, to behold, and which resulted in the whole equipage turning round and round in the middle of the road like a cat chasing its own tail. She always won. We were too scared to ride with her, and Dad worried himself into an attack of tachycardia as soon as the trap was out of sight. Mam herself never turned a hair!

In the same way, she would take herself off for

a two-week holiday at the seaside all alone, or set out happily for a day in London — something which in all my life I have never done voluntarily. Such outings would inevitably end in farce.

Once when Lois was staying with friends in London, Mam decided to spend a day there being shown the sights. They agreed to meet on the steps of St Pauls. Mam got there first, and climbed to the top of the steps. Before Lois and her escort arrived, a huge crowd had collected for some official function. The police moved the crowd back to the sides of the steps, leaving a wide space for the VIP to mount. Mam, from her vantage point, saw Lois in the crowd on the pavement at the foot of the steps. Absolutely uninhibited, she stepped out into the cleared space — all fifteen-stones-odd of her, waved frantically, and called out (as she always did, in a high-pitched, squeaky little voice) 'Pip-ip! Pip-ip!' to attract Lois's attention. Then she turned to descend the cleared steps — but twisting her ankle on the top step before any astounded policeman could prevent her royal descent, she fell flat, horizontally and parallel to the steps. Then she continued to roll from one step to the next down the top flight until caught and hoisted to her feet by two hefty policemen. Lois's subsequent hilarity in recounting this extraordinary feat was marred a little at the remembrance of her own embarrassment at having to step forward and claim her mother.

Another such trip to London was highlighted by her stepping off the platform of a moving bus in Piccadilly, and travelling on her face in the gutter for thirty yards or so because she refused to let go of the distressed conductor's hand. Still another perhaps contained the most farcical incident of all. Late for the homeward train (as she invariably was) she somehow or other climbed into a compartment clearly marked 'Out of Order'. There she enjoyed enviable seclusion till the train reached Holme station, where she had to change for Ramsey, and tried to get out. The door on the platform side was boarded up. She banged and yelled on it till she attracted attention — with the result that she had to be extricated by a posse of hastily-summoned railwaymen bracing themselves to manhandle her huge posterior down on to the track of the 'up' line. I know how it looked — I was with her!

She was always missing trains. Twice she got stranded in a strange town, having missed the last train home. On both occasions she was absolutely without money or identification, the first time having left her handbag on a market stall, the second having spent out except for a 'threepenny bit'. There were no telephones in our fen, so it was impossible to let us know she would not be coming home. Women — respectable country-women, anyway — did not spend nights unescorted in hotels, even if they had the wherewithal. So while Dad worried himself nearly to death, and we chuntered about her, she, who panicked at the slightest domestic crisis, calmly dealt with her own predicament. A hotel manager believed her tale, and treated her to a meal and a night's accommodation on trust. Then she asked to be called in time to catch a

247

train at 6.00 a.m. Impossible, said the manager. She explained our anxiety — upon which he gave her the front door key, to let herself out next morning; but she had no means of telling the time — so he left her his 18 carat gold watch and chain to have by her bedside!

She used to tell that tale with her gift of mimicry at its very best, playing both parts to perfection.

'He must have seen that I was honest' she would conclude, with an air of intense self-satisfaction. Maybe he wouldn't have been quite so sanguine if he had been aware that she was her father's daughter.

She was *always* falling down, usually in some ludicrous situation or other, especially when her knees gave out under her seventeen stones odd. Very rarely were there serious consequences, though once she broke her spectacles and cut an artery, and once cracked a china teapot on the wall above her head, and badly scalded herself. When she felt herself falling, she always threw out her arms in a grand operatic gesture. That was what caused the teapot to be above her head as she fell backwards on to one of her cherished antiques — an eighteenth-century carved smoking-table with a tripod leg. It was unequal to the task of supporting her, and crumbled into matchwood. She grieved much more about that and her lovely china tea pot than she did about the blisters hanging like grapes from her nose and chin.

China was irreplaceable during the war, and she treasured a complete tea set of bone china.

What on earth possessed her to try to carry the whole lot of it on one tray up the step at the foot of the stairs we never knew: but she fell, threw up her arms, and it snowed fragments of china as far as the front door and halfway up the stairs. When Dad helped her up, she was still clutching the empty tray — the sight of which was too much for either of them. The completeness of the demolition job she had achieved without letting go of the tray caught both funny-bones, though it produced the opposite effect on my toddler daughter, who rushed to hide from the sight, peeping out of the door again and again to take another look, and bursting again into tears at such wholesale destruction.

Another time, attempting to throw away a bowl of dirty dishwater (we had no take away at my schoolhouse sink), she got too close to the thorn hedge before throwing. Next minute, we were treated to the sight of her with her head stuck firmly in the hedge, and her huge behind with one leg vaguely waving about, presented to us. We waited, on yet another occasion, for the hired decorator to put the finishing touches to our pristine kitchen before we could have our lunch. Mam prepared it on our Valor oil cooker — liver and bacon with thick rich gravy in a frying pan, and fresh green peas from the garden in a colander. She turned from the stove with one in either hand — staggered — performed her usual diva's gesture — and our gorgeous white ceiling was decorated afresh with slices of liver, splodges of gravy, and a lace-work of green peas. We sat down to bread and cheese, struggling for Mam's sake to hold down our mirth, although her own eyes told us that she was regretting the lost lunch rather than the spoiled decoration. About halfway through lunch my teenage daughter suddenly pointed her finger at Mam, and choked on her mouthful. We followed the pointing finger, and there, on Mam's broad left shoulder, exactly like a plaid-brooch, lay a slice of liver edged with a circle of peas. Then laughter got the better of us all, and eating became quite impossible.

I'm sorry if by this time you think the whole boiling of us was quite mad. Grandmother, in her day, certainly thought we were. 'There's some folks,' she once said tartly. 'There's some folks as I know that 'ould laugh to see a pudden crawl.'

To Dad, and Mam, and the rest of us down to the third and fourth generation, praise be, it was and is a saving grace. As Callisthenes wrote 'Laughter is a man's declaration of freedom. It is his refusal to go into bondage to his troubles.'

So I hope you are not too weary to enjoy the best ever of Mam's hilarious falls. It happened one evening in the late 1940s, when Mam and Dad had, at great cost to their own comfort, come to help me through a very sticky patch in my personal life by giving up their own home and coming to care for my baby daughter while I was at school. There they stopped till Dad died, never being able to return 'home' to the fen again.

I had gone to a WI meeting in the school next door. It was around 9.00 p.m. when Mam fancied a cup of tea, and went into the kitchen to make one. The conditions in my little Cambridgeshire school house c.1946 were as primitive as any we had left behind in the fens; in our own particular case, considerably worse than we had had down in Lotting Fen. With no take-away from our sink, and no refuse collection, we threw such things as tea-leaves into the bottom of the hedge. There was a stone step from the kitchen to a sloping, dark-blue-and-red-tiled doorway, down which Mam stepped on her way to the hedge. All our china teapots having gone west in her previous falls, Mam was emptying an aluminium one with a bakelite handle, the only replacement available at that time of austerity.

Mam stepped down on to the doorway, and fell down — for once, flat on her face and without her operatic flinging wide of arms. She got to her knees, but could get no further. Dad was reading in his chair in the little room at the foot of the stairs, but her cries for help reached him, and he staggered out as fast as he could. He was by this time approaching eighty, and both his ankles and wrists were swollen and set stiff with gout. There was no way he could lift her, or give the assistance she needed. There was, however, an old, wide, wooden water-butt in the angle of wall by the kitchen door. Dad wedged himself against the water-butt and the wall, within reach of Mam's hands.

'Pull yourself up on me' he told her. She obeyed, kneeling in front of him, and, using his trouser legs as hand holds, began to straighten

251

up. Maybe the experiment might have worked, if Dad had been wearing his best braces. As it was, the pair that held up his 'working trousers' were pre-war, and had lost all the elasticity they had ever had. They stretched well enough, but had no strength left to recover.

The more Mam pulled, the longer the braces stretched, and as his old baggy trousers were far too big for him, they descended inch by inch as well. They had, in fact, got to mid-thigh when I appeared round the corner, my meeting finished. The setting sun was bathing the whole scene with the most wonderful warm, rosy light, and I had been looking at the sunset until I turned the corner, and saw both my parents as I shall never, never forget them. With Dad's trousers at half-mast, the braces had reached the limit of their stretch. His shirt had escaped from the top of his trousers and that had been the last straw. Both had collapsed into absolute helplessness with laughter. Mam had her hands in the top of his trousers, and kneeling upright, had laid her head against his diaphragm. He was bracing himself against the water butt, so as to have his arms free, and had placed both gouty old hands on Mam's head, holding her to him, while peal after peal of laughter rang out in a duet towards the glorious sky.

I fetched a strong chair, and with its help we got Mam up, not in the least hurt, though a bit enfeebled with laughter. While she got her breath back, Dad 'made himself respectable again'. It was too lovely an evening to go in. Then Mam said 'But I should still like a cup of tea! Where's the teapot?'

What was left of it was at my feet, and I picked it up. She had fallen on it, spout downwards, and it was now a flat aluminium disc with a telescoped protrusion where the spout had been, and a bakelite handle, still intact, to hold it by.

One glance at it was enough to set both of them off again, only this time I made it into a trio. They were still wiping tears of mirth away when I finally took them tea made in a coffee pot. We had no teapots left.

Besides her gift of mimickry, and her readiness to laugh in the face of disaster, she also possessed a pithy wit and a gift for terse repartee that delighted us then, and is passed down as aphorisms to descendants who never even saw her in the flesh. Any peculiarity in our neighbours never missed her eagle eye, so were nicknamed accordingly. A great, raw-boned fen woman she christened 'Fosdyke' — I never knew why, though we always referred to her as 'Fozz'. Another, very 'holy', was 'Black Bess': a tall one, 'Long Tom': one with a decided moustache, 'Hairy Mary' and so on. When at last the Education Committee saw fit to build us a bathroom and flush toilet, they made it as clinical as possible by everything being plain white except the floor, which was black. Mam promptly christened it 'The White Sitty' or 'the penny pool' — and so on, and so on.

She grew larger and larger, and was confined to a wheelchair. I had to buy such new clothes as she had, when and where I could find anything 64 inches round the hips, 54 inches round the bust. She would not, and did not, admit to being that size. I had to cut out the size labels before showing them to her, or she would not have deigned to try them on. On one occasion, I missed the size-tag because it was sewn into the seam of the skirt. She had got the dress on for the first time, ready for me to push her to a village function. She complained of being cold. Not knowing she had made the fatal discovery, I wondered what could be agitating her so much. Her eyes were showing red flashes, and she was rubbing thumbs against forefingers on both hands, always a sign of a tempest about to break.

'Cold?' I said, unguardedly 'I thought that new frock would be warm. Isn't it?'

'I don't know!' she countered. 'How could I? It don't touch me anywhere. I might as well take shelter in a ten-acre field!'

Perhaps her best effort was to our butcher, in war time. She felt the deprivation of rationing very much, but in spite of it she grew bigger and bigger, lost all interest in keeping any shape, and was a problem to keep clean. There she sat, a shapeless mountain of flesh, helpless in her wheelchair and extremely deaf — but still vibrant with mental and emotional energy: dominating and domineering and unwilling to forego any single strand of her command over me and my household; at war with grocers and butchers and coal-merchants, and extremely vociferous about how she would conduct the war if they'd only let her. It was 10.30 p.m. on Saturday nights before we received our meagre weekly meat ration, and she was watching the clock one Saturday as the

254

hands crept towards 11.00 p.m. and the butcher had not arrived. When at last he opened the door, weary to the bone himself, she was waiting for him like a cat at a mousehole. He knew her well enough to read the danger signs, and was conciliatory.

'There, Mrs Edwards' he said. 'I've managed to get you a lovely little round of beef this week' — and laid it before her. Her experienced eye noted the number of skewers and she deftly whipped them out, revealing the 'round' of beef to be a rolled up strip of fat and gristle about 3 inches wide, and some 20 inches long. She picked it up between thumb and finger as if it had been something nasty the cat had brought in, and held it dangling at arm's length.

'You can take this back!' she said. 'And you can tell your boss from me THAT WHEN I WANT A SKIPPING-ROPE, I'LL BUY ONE.'

She then picked up the six steel skewers in her other hand, and said 'Take these as well. I've got enough of these now from his shop to make new railings right round Buckingham Palace!' (The Palace railings had been sacrificed to the war effort.)

O — I don't know though! There are so many gems to take one's pick from! Having talked to a woman recently widowed, she gave us a demonstration of the widow overdoing her grief enough to make it suspect.

'Cried enough tears to bath a cow in' said Mam.

She grew ever more domineering and demanding as time went by, her apparent

255

ingratitude and infuriating obstinacy (especially in the matter of getting her own way) driving us all near to the brink of insanity. I got the brunt of it because she lived in my house during the time I was a village school-marm supporting myself and a teenage daughter as well as helping to support Mam herself. Only very occasionally did she visit my sister or my brother.

There was very little respite for me from her overpowering presence. The more dependent she became, the more she tyrannised everyone in her orbit.

And still it was made just bearable because of her sense of fun, and her courage in the face of the loss of everything that had once made her the 'flaunting extravagant queen' of the fens. Even her deliberate 'awk'ardness' contained just enough humour to prevent us from either going mad ourselves, or murdering her.

My school coming under threat of closure, I took steps to save myself from the complete oblivion of becoming, as those of the Education Office proposed that I should, a peripatetic supply head-teacher till my retirement, 'fifteen years away only' as the staffing official put it. First of all I tried to obtain a place on a child-psychology course. I got the place, but when I asked for secondment for a year, I was told that it was 'not the type of course for a middle-aged countrywoman to be attempting'. I tried again. At the Bassingbourn literature course I had heard of the bursary given annually by the Cambridge Extra Mural Board to a mature student who had missed university at the normal age. Stung by the 'middle-age country-woman taunt,' encouraged by Uncle Harry's remark that 'Strettons could do anything', and upheld by 'my ol' fen pride', I submitted an essay on 'The Decline of Rural Idiom and its Effect on Modern Literature' and sent in my application form. I won the bursary, and a place at New Hall to go with it. I was certainly a 'mature student': very mature, because I was already forty-seven. The full three years normally taken for the English Tripos meant that by the time I had a degree, I should have passed the dreaded milestone of my half-century. Dare I risk getting a job again at fifty-plus? When it was suggested that my continued attendance at Bassingbourn for an unbroken period of six years could, if I was prepared to put the extra work in, allow me to take Part II after two years instead of three, I jumped at it, and accepted. The Bursary gave me all my tuition fees, and £350 per annum. Not enough to live on, keep a roof over Mam's head, and subsidise a daughter at college. I ransacked the pamphlet giving the names of all possible sponsors, and came up with an outright grant of £50 from Typhoo tea, and an annual grant from the Convenanters (on whom be blessings poured for ever!). I still had to borrow from anyone who would lend, and I still had to earn ten shillings by doing a talk for a WI, or a lecture to an educational institution whenever chance occurred. I had been, before the closure of my little school, a fairly popular if unqualified lecturer on children's creative work. My need to go on earning while a student at

Cambridge must have placed me into a category made up of very few souls. For two terms out of the six that my Tripos took, I used to run down the steps of the Mill Lane lecture rooms at 5.00 p.m. once a week, clawing off my undergraduate gown as I ran to where I had, with the motor-sub-proctor's permission, left my green Austin A35 van. Then I drove like the devil in order to be on the lecturer's dais at 7.30 p.m. — in Oxford!

I had also been granted permission to go on living at the School House while at Cambridge, in order to continue to look after Mam. My domestic help did extra hours, for which she was paid meagrely enough, considering what she had to put up with from my extremely disgruntled mother. A dear old neighbour often endured the evenings that I was out trying to keep my head reasonably above water financially. On the days when neither could, or would, go in and out to give Mam her meals, I had to hare the eight miles home between lectures to get Mam a meal and take her to the lavatory. With three years' work to put into two, the need to earn, the extra journeys and Mam herself to deal with, I must have been mad to attempt it. Suffice it to say that I did, leaving Cambridge with a 2:1 English Honours degree, and the New Hall English prize in my pocket.

Now Mam had, all our lives, done her utmost to drive us towards education, even more so, if anything, than Dad. But University education was out of her ken — or, at least, she chose to make it so because my chance to get the degree I had always craved for threatened to upset her own personal applecart. My studies took me away from her. I was no longer just the other side of the wall if she took it into her head to want me, or flew into a Rattles-like rage at being baulked in any way by our daily help. She regarded my initiative as a complete dereliction of duty, and set herself resolutely to make everything as difficult for me as she possibly could.

It would be better not to inquire what my prosperous brother and sister did to help me. They didn't approve of my adventure either, both being afraid that any success on my part would, or might, mean that they would have to take their share of looking after our increasingly 'awk'ard' parent. My situation was made even more difficult by the fact that my greatest support, my daughter, started her teacher-training course at the Fröebel Educational Insitute in Roehampton one week before I went up to New Hall. So, when I got home at 11.30 p.m. from Oxford, or from talking to a WI Group meeting in Norfolk, I still had to face all the end-of-the-day chores of seeing to Mam.

Often she would not talk to me at all, showing her disapproval of me and my outlandish desire for 'Eng. Lit.' by sullen sulking of the 'Thetis' or 'Hindenburg' variety. At other times she launched into voluble tirades of abuse, at my neglect of her, declaring 'I WILL NOT BE LEFT'; or, tearful, tell me yet again what she had sacrificed for her mother.

Until she was in bed, there was no chance

whatever for me to tackle my university course work — she saw to that. Getting her to bed, however, required the wiles of Odysseus as well as the strength of Heracles. This was due mostly to the design to which a great many village school houses were built. They were joined to the school room, and the narrow, steep stairs were on one side of the party-wall. As the tiny landing at the top led to a bedroom over hall and stairs, there could be no handrail for the three top steps on the hall side, while the narrow width made it impossible to put one on the wall.

The time came, just as I began my university course, when, for the first time I was left to cope with Mam all by myself. There was no one but me to help get her to bed. As I have said, she was by this time an inert mass of approximately twenty stone who spent her days in a wheelchair — but nothing and nobody could persuade her to have her bed downstairs. Like Grandmother, she was going to have her own way if it killed her — which in the end it did help to do. She *would* go upstairs, and I alone was there to assist her.

Having undressed her, washed as much as she would let me, taken down her hair and re-braided the thick plait, I heaved her out of her chair at the bottom of the stairs, and preceded her up them. She managed, slowly, to crawl up by leaning forward and taking her own weight on her hands, clutching at the bannister if she felt need. But when the third step from the top was reached, she had to straighten up and trust her knees and me. This is why I had to go up in front of her. I carried up her walking stick, which she then used to keep her balance while I took the strain and literally hauled her great bulk up the top three steps. I braced myself as well as I could against the landing wall, but it was poor security, and it is nothing short of a miracle that somebody did not find us both dead in a crumpled heap on the hall floor. In order to reach her and to take her weight, I had to stand close to the top of the stairs, planting both my feet firmly where I could, at the same time, bracing my right shoulder against the wall. Night after night, when she was on the top stair, she would either poke my feet, push them aside, or actually place her walking stick (and her weight) on my toe.

'Move your feet, can't you? Can't you see that's just where I want to put mine!'

On the rare, but much looked forward to occasions when Lois came to spend the night with us, Mam expected her to take part in the bed-time drill. Had she but realised it, this was tantamount to flying in the face of a so far patient Providence. To get her up those top three steps required every ounce of strength as well as complete self-possession and quick reaction by the person on the landing. When there was a second assistant, Mam ordered that she followed her up the stairs, in order to 'steady her from behind'. Much good it would have done if Mam had ever fallen backwards!

The added danger lay in the chance that as I was looking down the stairs, and Lois looking up, or vice-versa, we might catch each other's eye, and lose both strength and presence of mind

261

in hopeless attempts to smother mirth made almost hysterical by genuine fear.

On one such occasion, Mam ordered Lois to take the upper stand on the landing, while I ascended one step behind her enormous posterior. Lois planted her feet and prepared to heave — but Mam struck her sharply on her ankle with the walking-stick, saying 'Stand aside!' exactly like Dame Flora Robson playing Lady Catherine de Burgh in *Pride and Prejudice*.

Mam certainly lost another of her ninety-nine lives that night, as Lois looked down and caught my eye!

Her unremitting opposition to my university course set her 'wizening' very Rattles-like, to think up any ploy that would set yet another obstacle in my way. Her witty if embittered intelligence hit upon a very clever one.

Her legs truly did pain her a lot. She spent hours massaging her knees, and I rubbed them often with 'hoss'ile' (embrocation). She declared that they hurt her most when in bed, and nobody disbelieved her; but when she made it the excuse for going later and later and later to bed, I simply had to protest because I often had an essay to write after she had gone to sleep.

She tumbled to this, and understood that her reason for keeping me up half the night was a bit weak, because her legs hurt her anyway, even sitting in her chair. She had to find another reason.

She had not bothered about corseting her figure properly for years, but she surprised me when I came home one day by telling me she had had a visit from 'the Spirella lady' and had ordered a pair of properly fitted corsets and a garment she called 'a brazzia' to go with them. It took my breath away because I knew the cost of such garments, though I doubted if she'd even bothered to ask. They came — bright pink contraptions with laces and busks, with under-belts beneath and 'body belts' over the top, and a chandelier of suspenders dangling round their huge lower circumference. The cost took all that I had been saving towards my first new coat for ten years. (I was not without coats, because I was occasionally able to get into one of Lois's cast-offs.)

'The Spirella Lady' had told her she must put the corsets on, and take them off, while lying flat on her bed. There was no way in which she could achieve such a feat unaided. I had to leave her in bed till our long-suffering daily help came and helped her into the corsets. When it was time to take them off, there was no help but my own. Until she consented to be undressed, I was at her mercy. So there we sat, night after night, until midnight struck — then one o'clock, and two. While she was there, I was not allowed to give attention to anything but her. When heavy snores or sonorous snorts issued from her armchair, I would reach furtively for my briefcase, only to find her baleful eyes wide open as she growled 'I ain't asleep! I'm only mozing. I shan't go to bed yet.'

'What are you doing?' She snapped one night, opening her eyes to find me reading

263

'Working' I replied.

She snorted, for all the world like Job's warhorse saying 'Ha! Ha!' amid the trumpets. I wish there were words to describe the expression of cunning triumph on her face at her own powers of deception and detection.

'*Working?* Don't try to get over me with that sort of talk! Working — reading a book with a title like that?'

The title she had made out across the few feet that separated us was *The Romantic Agony* — a heavy and most erudite book of literary criticism. She obviously thought it was the second volume of *Lady Chatterley's Lover*. The average amount of sleep I got during my two years at Cambridge was less than five hours. Now and again I simply had to plead for somebody to give me a break for a few days. She had by this time convinced herself that wherever she was, her will was law. She would not to go bed until she was ready. Ironic as it was, it was this iron determination on her part that set the machinery of her death in motion.

She went to stay with Lois for a few days. Lois was a farmer's wife, as Mam had been, and nobody knew better than she did the need for rest in most farmer's households; but Dad had never grumbled at our late nights, and Lois, left to herself, would have been as much wax in Mam's hands as I. (None of us dared gainsay her, if the truth be told.) Lois, however, was not a free agent, as I was. She was caught between the hammer of Mam's will and the adamant anvil of her husband's. Mam would not go to bed; he would not allow Lois to sit up with her, because that disturbed his rest. A compromise had to be reached. It was decreed that she should be undressed and put into her nightdress at 10.00 p.m., and wheeled to the side of her bed. Then, when she was ready, she could manage to pull herself out of her chair and get her bottom on to the low divan bed. The ensuing sulks were Thetis and Hindenburg combined, but she had met her match in my brother-in-law. For two or three nights, the plan worked. Next night, everybody was awakened by an almighty crash, and Mam was found lying on the floor.

Before getting herself to the bedside, she had had to release the brake of her wheelchair. It was only 11.00 p.m., but she had decided to get into bed — who would ever know? So she took off the brake, and promptly fell asleep in the chair. Her heavy body sagged forward till the released wheels shot out backwards, and catapulted her on to the bedside rug. She was rushed to hospital, where it was stated that she was 'only bruised'. Technically, it may have been so, but trust our Mam to do everything to the last possible degree of exaggeration. She seemed to have received a shower of purplish-blue ink tinted with pink from some Zeus-like god above. Apart from the colour, she was, it seems, not hurt; yet the incident was, in fact, the beginning of the tragedy of her end. After all those years of teetering dangerously on the brink of eternity at the top of my stairs, she herself set going the machinery that brought about her end by falling out of her chair — in a bungalow!

She lived another six unhappy years — unhappy for us all, but worst of all for herself. I regret that I was often impatient and unkind to her, but it was not the fault of any of us that we could no longer satisfy or appease her, do what we might. Indeed, if the Archangel Gabriel himself had been seeking a situation, I doubt if he could have suited Mam. I certainly didn't. For one thing, all her worse fears had been realised. From being an overworked village schoolteacher of no account to anybody, I had been translated to university lecturer in education. Alas, the job was in the one town she held in contempt — Sheffield. Dad's sister Eva lived there, among the steel works in the Rother Valley. Mam had once visited her there, and once had been enough. It made no difference to Mam's objection that I mortgaged practically all of my new salary to build a bungalow precisely designed for her needs in the glorious Hope Valley of Derbyshire. My work was in Sheffield. Ergo, we lived in Tinsley. SHE WOULD NOT STOP. The surrounding hills terrified her. She was convinced they would fall on her. Worst of all, there was once again a man in my life.

Poor old Mam. I know she loved me. She liked him. She wanted us both to be happy — but not if it threatened her complete domination over me and my life. My Sir Galahad did everything he could to lessen the burden on me; but for his advent, my health and my sanity must have gone under, but her demands increased in proportion to the help available. Two satisfied her no better than one.

Help also included a daily 'housekeeper' and a gardener who played endless games of dominoes with her. (She actually admitted to liking the gardener!)

It is practically impossible to put into words the tragi-comedy of that period. As her physical condition worsened, her spirit and determination never to be anything but head of the household grew. Her wit, her tongue and her 'wisening' to get her own way were sharp and clear as ever. She was a living force.

Yet much of it was comedy, and she knew it. Take, for example, the ceremony of 'putting Nanny to bed' (new version).

We wheeled her chair to the side of a low double divan in the very pleasant room that had been designed as my study. She insisted on having this room because from there, even from the bed, she could observe the goings and comings of everyone in the main part of the bungalow. Once into her room, the ritual began. Brush the long hair, and replait it: anoint her back with witch-hazel 'in case it itched': rub her knees with embrocation, her arms with adrenalin cream, her heels with surgical spirit. Supply two clean handkerchiefs: arrange her nine pillows to suit her — three under her head, one under each knee, one under each arm, one under her feet, and a spare 'just in case'.

Wheel up her cantilever bedside table, and arrange it as she decreed with all her needs for the night. Her alarm clock, placed at just the correct angle: my large old school bell, which she clanged to summon me the moment she opened her eyes, sometimes five times a night: a glass of water: a bottle of aspirin, with two tablets extracted and ready to hand: a peeled orange, segments separated: a banana, peeled half-way: (neither fruit was ever eaten, though she did mangle the banana to a sticky mush occasionally). Then there was her Bible and a prayer-book. The print of the Bible was too small for my eyes, let alone hers, and the Book of Common Prayer completely inexplicable, as she had been 'chapel' all her life. Besides, its print was even smaller than her Bible's.

Even more inexplicable were the two books we had to place just within her reach every single night for years. One was *Culpepper's Herbal*, and the other *Little Women*. She was never known to open either, so what they signified is as much a mystery to me as it is to anybody. If all this sounds unbelievable, I can only say that I should doubt my own veracity of such incredible detail if I did not have the witness of my family and friends to assure me that I have not exaggerated.

That clanging handbell must have roused the entire neighbourhood, and I became as well trained to its sound as one of Pavlov's dogs. I was out of bed and along the passage to her room while still asleep!

Two willing (no, subservient) ministering angels suited her no better than one had done. She made up her mind to leave and go into an old folks' home. She would have her own way, and got it — but she still wanted it when she was installed there, setting her at odds with staff and other residents alike. We expected her back, and twice she came. Then, in the third home where she could have been happy, she threw a tantrum. Lois was there and heard the Matron tell her that if she put herself into such a state, she would have 'a seizure'. Lois had barely left when she did suffer a minor stroke that took the use entirely from one leg. They could no longer keep her. She had to be transferred to a long-stay geriatric hospital. It would have stood comparison with Bedlam. Let those who now bemoan the falling off of NHS standards be prepared to discover from what standards it has 'fallen'. The curtain is about to go up on the last tragic act of Mam's dramatic life.

The terrible force of her personality had landed her into the hands of people who did not know her and love her as we did. Because my own experience of the medical profession from the age of seven to the present has been nothing short of wonderful, it grieves me to have to report what happened to Mam at the hands of the proverbial one bad apple in the crop.

While in the residential home, Mam had lost some weight, no doubt as a result of a carefully balanced diet over which she had no direct control (as she had in my house). All the same, she was still an enormously fat and heavy patient to deal with; but she was eighty-eight years old, in constant pain from her arthritic hips and knees, very deaf, with cataracts on both her eyes. In spite of all that, her mind was keen, her spirits high, and her courage indomitable — at first.

They crash-dieted her, on the grounds that

269

they could not lift her. She was not 'a bed patient', but they kept her in bed though it increased her pain and boredom. She was not allowed out of bed even on to the commode. When we visited, we found her crying not only with pain, but with hunger, and worst of all, with thirst. (Where liquid is not given, urination is less frequent). From the mountain of flesh she had been, she was brought down in record time to about ten stones. Her wits began to fail. Lack of food resulted in senility.

Agonized as we were, we were helpless against unfeeling authority. We were beaten because we could not care for her ourselves — but the treatment she was getting was cruel in every meaning of the word. Every complaint or request I made on her behalf was always greeted with the same riposte . . . 'If you are not satisfied with our treatment of your mother, you must take her home and look after her yourself.'

I cannot begin to detail the horrendous misery she (and we) endured for the next six months or so.

Then she staged, as we might have anticipated she would, the last dramatic scene of her life.

She had been told that on a particular Saturday none of the three of us would be able to visit her. I was conducting a teachers' course in Cardiff: Gerald was house-hunting in Wales, pending his own retirement: and Lois had been invited to a wedding. Mam chose that day to become violently ill. Not one of us was available to answer the telephone, when the home tried to inform us — but by chance one of Lois's

270

married daughters had called at her mother's house, heard the telephone ringing and let herself in to answer it. It was therefore one of Mam's granddaughters who bore the brunt of that day.

Still vomiting, she was taken by ambulance to the general hospital, with Julie, my niece, in attendance, standing in for all three of Mam's absentee children. Not that anything we could have done would have made any difference. There was nothing Julie could do.

She sat, hour after hour, in the general hospital's waiting room, while Mam lay waiting for examination by the on-call specialist that had been sent for. He, too, was having an unusually busy day, and it was 10.00 p.m. before he arrived. Lois had still not returned home — after the wedding reception was over, a party of old friends had decided to 'make a day of it', ending with dinner at a hotel, all done on the spur of the moment, and therefore without letting anyone know.

The specialist, having been to see Mam, came brusquely into the waiting room just as Lois arrived to join Julie.

'Who is with Mrs Edwards?' His tone told both of them that he was in no good mood, but they were not prepared for what followed.

'Who has allowed an old lady of her age to get into this state? Have you let her go on living alone, unable even to get herself a meal or a drink? She has an enormous gallstone which must be removed, but surgery is impossible. She is completely starved and dehydrated. I cannot,

271

and will not, put a knife into such flesh! Luckily, she will not last the night. I have ordered a drip-feed, and if she does survive till morning, I will see her again, and re-consider.'

He swept out, giving them no chance to explain that those responsible were his colleagues in a hospital under the same management as his own. (He found out later.)

Not only was Mam alive next morning; she was alive three weeks later, and gradually gaining strength, so the surgeon decided to operate. Food had restored her to her old self.

They were dreadful weeks for us all. Suppose she recovered? We could *not* let her go back to where she had come from, yet none of us was in a position to take her home with us. I, because I had to keep my job, the other two for domestic reasons. The best we could hope for was that if all three of us could contribute, we might be able to pay for private care for her — but that was a bleak prospect. I was, still, a free agent. The other two were not. It was not voiced among us, but I think we all hoped she would die under the anaesthetic. Lois rang me up on the evening of the operation. Both of us were emotionally charged to the full.

'Well?' I said, as soon as I heard her voice.

'No' she replied. 'The news is bad.'

My heart surged with a great wave of relief.

'She's gone!' I said.

'No' said Lois. 'I told you the news was bad! The operation was a complete success. She's come round, she's cheerful, and asking how long it will be before she can go home.'

272

But the surgeon's first diagnosis had been the correct one. The cells had gone too far towards starvation, and could not regenerate. The incision would not heal, and to put it quite bluntly, she began to decompose while still alive and quite conscious. For three whole weeks my ever-recurring nightmare became actuality. I had to deal with a decomposing body, which was that of my still living, still conscious mother — the only one whom in my dreams I had never had to bury.

She wanted us beside her, but though our handkerchiefs contained disinfectant sachets and the nursing staff did all they could to help, it was only by sheer will-power that one could endure to stay five minutes. The doctors increased the dose of morphia they prescribed as day after day she still lingered. Her great old heart would simply not give in. (So much for theories about cholesterol!)

Christmas came. I saw her on the afternoon of Christmas Eve.

'You're holding your own', I lied.

'Am I? I'm so old' she said. 'Talk to me' — but before I could think of anything to say, she had slipped off into a drugged sleep, and I crept away to make my long drive back to Sussex before it grew too dark, and the road conditions too bad. I never saw her again.

Julie visited her on Christmas day, in the afternoon. As she came out of Mam's room, she came face to face with the surgeon, in 'civvies', and with a bottle of whisky sticking out under his jacket. They recognised each other, and he took her by the hand and led her into the

273

ward-sister's 'duty room', conveniently unoccupied.

'I'm drunk' he said 'but not too drunk to know what I'm saying! I've been to five ward parties. And I'm not on duty till tonight, late.'

'And do you know why I'm drunk? Because of that courageous old woman in there! Because I want to forget what has happened to her at the hands of my profession.'

(And much, much more. It must have done him good to let go the feelings he had been bottling up for more than six weeks.)

'I will see her again when I come in tonight' he said.

He kept his word. She died in the very early hours of Boxing Day.

We all cried tears of tremendous relief at those 'tidings of comfort and joy'. At the funeral, it was Gerald who put into words what all of us were thinking.

'It can't be Mam in that box' he said. 'IT'S TOO SMALL!'

How like her, to be a paradox to the very end. Her huge person had indeed 'shrunk to this little measure', but she lives on with those of us left who knew her, as large and powerful a personality as ever.

I grieve often that I could not 'finish it largely' as I was once urged to do. I often lost my temper with her, stung into retaliation by her bitter taunts and her ingratitude — or what seemed like ingratitude — at what I tried to do. I think I understand now that one life was simply not enough for her huge personality: she wanted

274

mine as well, and that I could not give wholly to her. I had obligations to myself, and to others, as well as to her. She had enough ego and spirit to occupy several bodies.

And if I regret — as I often do — losing my patience with her when she was old and helpless, it was not all my fault. If she is now being cared for by the angels she so firmly believed in, I guess that at this very moment there must be one of them beating his wings in exasperated fury against the golden gateposts, having failed to satisfy her or to escape her barbed though witty tongue.

Nobody could have had a more loving, generous, courageous, fun-loving and generally entertaining mother than we had; but it seems to me impossible that anyone could have had a more demanding, more provocative, more deliberately aggravating, wearing and infuriating one!

I knew all the time that she didn't mean to hurt me as she did. She just could not control the 'Rattles' side of herself. At her death, she left me a letter saying how sorry she was, and how grateful — to be read when she was gone.

It would not have been the same, I think, if she had not lost her support when Dad died. She outlived him by nineteen years. Some of her anger and reproach towards me was that I was not Dad. Once he had gone, she realised that she had won the heart and the hand of a prince among men, and occasionally broke into tears of guilt and remorse that she had taken him so much for granted. He had treated her always as a cherished only child, to be indulged if it were possible. He 'spoiled' her all his life, and such spoilt children tend to be desperate if deprivation comes to them. Perhaps it is Dad we ought to blame, not Mam herself.

I find it very difficult to forgive the self-satisfied medico who controlled that geriatric hospital, and the treatment meted out to my mother just because she was, in his terms 'grossly obese'. That perjorative term was applied to me, more than once, before my clever GP found my thyroid deficiency: it was likewise applied to Lois when she was dying of an undiagnosed cancer of the pancreas and had eaten nothing to speak of for three months. Her consultant wrote 'grossly obese' on his report, and told her to go home and lose twenty-eight pounds. She went home to die, but the last time I held her hand she cried, not because she knew we should never be together again, but because of the indignity that 'specialist' had heaped upon her. Obesity is considered a self-inflicted disease, for which, unlike lung cancer or Aids, there can be no sympathy. It is the one physical disability not protected by law from ridicule from comedians, for instance, or cartoonists, or the purveyors of sea-side postcards.

And how is it that an age which can set a man's foot on the moon, and contrive for us to sit by our own firesides and watch it happen: which can produce explosions that could wreck civilisation at the touch of a button: that has invented an even more terrifying threat in the prospect of artificial intelligence — *how* is it that it seems beyond the ingenuity of scientist or engineer to concoct a gadget to help lift or move a heavy patient in bed?

My Mam died in 1968. Nine hundred years before, in 1069, Sancho-the-Fat of Léon, who could only walk when supported by minions on each side, was deposed by his own nobles who wanted a more energetic king. They staged a successful coup, and poor Fat Sancho had to find refuge somewhere. He fled to Cordoba, where, as by lucky chance it happened, a famous Jewish physician named Maomonides was living. Poor deposed Fat Sancho called on him for help. A year later, Sancho, now slim, lithe, trim and very fit gathered together an army of other loyal exiles and led it personally, and victoriously, to claim his throne again.

If Maomonides could deal with obesity then, why can't our doctors do it now? Maybe he did put Sancho on a diet — but he left a soldier fit in body and mind at the end of his treatment, not a man starved of energy, wit or willpower, as Mam was and as I might have been had I not learned from the lesson that Mam's end taught me. How lucky we were to have had such a pair of extraordinary characters as Mam and Dad for parents!

Dad has been dead forty years, but he has never left me. I think of him, quote him, and enjoy him every day of my life, and especially at night. Just outside my bedroom door stands the cottage long-case clock that once belonged to the Welsh blacksmith. It was one of Dad's greatest treasures. He wound it every night, and as his gouty old hands raised the heavy, misshapen lead weight, it pleased him to think that he was going through exactly the same motions as those of at least four generations of 'Etherdses' before him. And when the weight was as high as it would go, he would close the door and secure it with the bent hairpin that served as a catch (and still does). Then he would pat the clock on its head and say 'Goo right, ol' gal' — just as he had heard his father and grandfather before. After which he would start up the stairs, placing his swollen feet sideways on the treads to help keep his balance; and as he went, he recited aloud 'Surely, goodness and mercy have followed me all the days of my life.'

(Gerald, in his manuscript, tells the same tale, but adds 'I reckon Dad got that right, for as far as I remember, they never catched up with him!')

But I want to leave Mam and Dad together. When Aunt Lizzie's so-detested lodger died, Mam felt obliged to pay her sister a visit. When she returned, she treated us to a vivid impression of Aunt Lizzie mourning, mouth turned down, eyes cast up, and an expression of resignation, like Patience on the monument, smiling at grief. Mam's figure sagged, her arms hung loose, though she brought up a hand clutching a large handkerchief now and then to wipe away a silent tear. Like the good actress she was, Mam kept up her impersonation just long enough before suddenly straightening up to deliver her exit line.

'Well!' Mam snorted. 'That's exactly how she looked! One more feather, and she'd have been gone to George!'

Dad's bellow of laughter has surely never really

died away. I hear its echo every time I meet one of the few real old fen tigers of our tribe still alive.

And Mam? I hope she is now in the sort of heaven she always imagined — a garden full of roses such as she used to grow with such success in New Fen. And I hope too that in that garden a table is spread before her laden with huge sirloins of beef and home-cured hams. There must be loaves of crusty bread, and right in front of her a crystal dish of yellow rosebuds arranged among their dark shining leaves — rosebuds made of butter lurking among the real ones, just as her clever fingers used to contrive out of her own matchless golden butter every churning day. Oh, and of course, there must be a china bowl full of Jersey cream so thick it needs a knife to cut it — despatched for her daily from the cows' heaven nearby where our darling pedigree Jersey, Golden Fairy, grazes eternally on asphodel.

My dream of Mam in Paradise would be completely satisfying to me if I could also imagine her being waited on by a certain doctor, himself suffering the torture of Tantalus, starving as he starved her in that terrible geriatric hospital; and by the matron who carried out his orders, leather-tongued with thirst as she pours Mam cup after cup of tea from the sort of delicate porcelain teapot Mam so loved to handle. Perhaps both doctor and nurse would that way learn the virtue of compassion.

So there I leave Mam — except for a sneaking feeling that Dad may be there too, and that she is probably giving him a vivid impression of Rattles tricking St Peter into letting him in through the

Pearly Gates at last.

And if Dad is there, why not Gerald and Lois too? Maybe it has happened just as Mam predicted.

It was during the best of times, when Mam was at her most powerful, forceful self, larger than life in every way. A party was toward, and she and Lois were transferring a gargantuan meal prepared in advance from the pantry to the large mahogany table in the house-place, through a door of slightly narrower dimensions than is normal. Mam's voice, raised a tone or two in good humoured irritation, was suddenly heard to exclaim 'Dear-oh-dear, Lois! I swear that when I meet you in heaven, it'll be in a doorway!'

Well — one can but hope!

8

The Etherdses--Mainly

If I had to sum up the difference in our relationships with the two sides of our family, I should say that it was coloured entirely by the difference in character and personality of our grandmothers. Our relationship with Grammam was shaped by love; that with Grandmother, by duty.

Why was it, for instance, that Grandmother challenged the truth of my statement about remembering waking up in my cradle? Surely, she knew perfectly well what the situation in our house was? The fact is that she didn't — I cannot recall her ever visiting us while I lived down the drove (that is, for the first four years of my life). On the other hand, we visited her quite a lot during the last year or two she was at the farm, and after we had moved into her house, she lived next door with Aunt Harriet, and occasionally paid us a stately visit, sitting upright in Dad's chair with her hands clasped over the handle of her walking stick, and her sparse hair covered by a crisp, starched mob-cap. I was in great awe of her and didn't really like her any more than she liked me. All the same, I was sent to pay her a duty visit once a week, where she sat in the front room of Aunt Harriet's house. She had taken with her from the farm side of the house the few pieces of furniture she deigned to care for, the best being a beautiful red mahogany bow-fronted chiffonier with an intricate oval pattern of raised carving on each door. My duty was to dust the carvings, and for pay she left me a couple of spoonfuls of her dockey-time basin of nut-megged arrowroot. I seemed to have a passion for trying or finishing up other people's curious meals — I must have been in my teens before the custom of Dad leaving me the last few spoonfuls of his bedtime bread-and-milk was dropped, at Lois's insistence. Other people had sugar, or sugar and cream, in their bread-and-milk (which I still love, except for its calorific value); but in his, Dad had salt and pepper, with a knob of butter added, and to me it was ambrosia. Lois ridiculed me into giving up the ritual — probably through jealousy, because it smacked of a special concession to the baby of the family.

Why Grandmother didn't like me very much, as I was well aware, was that I was at that time weak and sickly, which I had no right to be, being one of her tough breed. That was a poor excuse, seeing that Vernon was also her grandchild, and she had three others beside him who were not the best of physical specimens. Her real reason, of course, was that I was Mam's daughter, and Mam had never been accepted by Dad's mother or his oldest sister, Harriet. My Uncle Jim, was well blessed with a sense of humour: and it has to be recorded that Uncle John, Aunt Harriet's husband, was Dad's greatest ally in helping to keep the sunny side up, especially in the matter of practical jokes.

If I keep on stressing this particular characteristic of so many people bred in our fen, it is to counter the popular idea that all East Anglians are or at least, were, dour, as well as dumb and half-witted. Any true fen man will talk the leg off an iron pot, and lace his conversation with imagery and wit, the humour more often than not directed at himself and his peers. If the men outdid the women in this respect, it was probably because men met together more often than women did, and the consequence was that their conversation needed editing a little when women were present.

Women, too, seemed to feel the restrictive side of religion more than men — particularly the chapel-goers among them.

Dad's immediate family were divided into two distinct groups by this particular issue. His mother and his eldest sister (Aunt Harriet) were of the group which believed that their Christianity required them to be soberly strait-laced at all times. I truly do not remember ever seeing Grandmother smile, let alone laugh. Aunt Harriet did occasionally chuckle, but she always did it in a way that suggested she had ventured further than she ought to have done. Luckily, they did not affect the spirit of the whole congregation, because an overall atmosphere of joy, and of delight in the poetry and music of the service, is the impression left on me and my contemporaries. Sunday was 'a day of rest and gladness'. For Grandmother's little coterie, the flames of the Bottomless Pit scorched the spirit of joy, and Sabbath Puritanism lingered across the weekdays in between.

The present chapel was built in 1871 — but was never big enough from the start to hold the eager worshippers, and in 1906, a gallery was added to accommodate the overflow. Still, according to some reports, on special occasions like anniversaries there would be as many as fifty folks who couldn't get inside.

Grandmother must have been a fairly important member of the congregation both in the old and the new building, because when in 1971 a commemorative booklet was produced, she is remembered among the few named, as 'Old Rachael' (sic).

The chapel was enlarged again in 1929, when another building was added, side by side with the existing chapel, and connected to it by a passage and a door that opened right at the end of the Etherdses pew — thereby curing Dad's claustrophobia and making it less of an ordeal for him to sit through a service.

The new building came about because of a link with the brickyards. I have already mentioned how a brickmaker took his invention to the USA, and made a fortune. His daughter (née Ginn) when a girl, had been the sweetheart of 'Old Henry' Edwards. She had married one Samuel Austin, of Orton Waterville, near Peterborough, out in the States. (I am not absolutely certain whether it was her father, or her husband's father, who actually invented the brick-mould, though I always understood from Dad that it originated in one of The Heights brickyards.)

Bereft of her attentions, Henry courted and married another, whose baptismal name was Frances. He always referred to her as 'my pairtner', though there is no way of suggesting in print the true sound of the fenland 'air' or 'eir'.

When, in 1929, the extremely wealthy Austin family visited England, Mrs Austin wanted to see her native village, and the whole of The Heights was put *en fête* for their visit (though I have a feeling that they came more than once). However, I remember their arrival, in a huge, black, shiny limousine with a uniformed chauffeur at the wheel. The elders of the chapel had us all arranged *en bloc* outside the chapel, each side of the door, while in the doorway itself stood Old Henry, bent double on his two sticks, to be the first to greet them. He must, at this time, have been at least eighty years old — probably more.

The car drew up, the door opened, and Mrs Austin was helped out. Henry stepped forward, and she recognised him at once. Overcome, the elegantly dressed old lady bent her head, and kissed him.

The rest of the visit was a great success, and before they left, Mrs Aushtin, as Old Henry always pronounced it, had donated the bulk of the money needed to build the Sunday School and very much needed 'offices'.

So everything passed off well — except for that kiss. 'My pairtner', Frances, was very put out about it, and declared to all and sundry that 'It wasn't right. It wasn't proper, and she ha'n't ought to ha' done it.' O *tempora! O mores!*

When the foundation stone of the new building was laid, it was Old Henry who laid it, and after him we all laid ours with our initials carved on the side — still to be seen. W. H. and K. M. E. (Dad and Mam): G. E.: L. M. E.: S. M. E. (me) and by my side J. H. S. (Joyce, whose father had given the land) and then aunts, uncles, cousins and friends — now a memorial both to us and to a vanished way of life. My most vivid memory of that occasion was of its ending. A stone-laying ceremony has to be held outside, and there, standing between the old building and the new, I last saw Old Henry perform his balancing trick as he laid aside his sticks and sought to keep his balance without them to lead us with his concertina in singing:

Praise God from whom all blessings flow,
Praise Him all creatures here below.
Praise Him above, ye heavenly host,
Praise Father, Son and Holy Ghost.

Old Henry was, of course, one of 'the Etherdses', and first cousin to my grandfather. The 'Etherdses' were all descended from the drunken Welsh blacksmith. My great grandfather, leaving Ramsey to escape the cholera, built up a big enough holding of land to be given a vote — the only man of his time so distinguished. My great-grandmother, like Grandmother, was an Upwood girl, and seems to be remembered mostly for her meanness. They had four sons and one daughter. My grandfather, John, was born to them in 1837, and at the age of twenty he, too, married an Upwood girl.

She brought her religion ready-made with her. She would have been a tough enough character without it, but supported by it, she was like a rock — a fine, strong, determined, stern woman. One to inspire respect, admiration and awe, but not a great deal of love.

Someone wrote of Oliver Cromwell that he would have been all right if he hadn't let his religion get on top of him. Grandmother seems to have had the same Cromwellian streak. Perhaps that was no great wonder, because we were right in his family's home ground, after all. He often visited Biggin Malten, which was no more than a mile from where Grandmother first drew breath.

Puritanism had a firm hold on the district when, only a century or so later, the Evangelical revival also made a great impact. My guess is that both were grafted on to a healthy rootstock of Celtic paganism. Wesleyan Methodism, as I knew it, appeared to be a strange mixture of Puritan hellfire and John Wesley's 'glo'ry'.

My Grandad Etherds died in 1906, before my advent; but Dad talked a lot about him, and I always felt I knew him better than I did Grandmother. He was by all accounts, a shy, humble, uncomplicated man content to be led by the nose after his more domineering wife. She was a good scholar, and a hard worker, making tiles in the brickyards to supplement the income from their smallholding, in the early years of their marriage.

Aunt Harriet was their first child, born in

287

1860. Then came the ten-year gap caused by the deaths of the two infant Samuels. Although infant mortality was high everywhere, it seems a bit odd that Grandmother didn't simply produce healthy babies in her stride! One can't help wondering if her dedication to hard work and her notion of bettering themselves was what robbed Dad of his two elder brothers.

The gap meant that Aunt Harriet was almost of a different generation from Dad and his other two sisters. She was nearer to being Grandmother's contemporary than theirs. Aunt Harriet was very much like Grandmother, in every way, and lacked entirely the saving grace of humour that Dad and his youngest sister possessed in such abundance.

Nevertheless, I must accord thanks to Aunt Harriet where due. She was no great shakes as a cook, and not what anyone could describe as house-proud. The main reason for these failings was that she could never bear to be without a piece of creative handwork — knitting, crocheting, embroidering, tatting, netting and the like, in her fingers. At 10 a.m., by which time most of the fen women would have 'foed-out' their houses, got their children off to school, and prepared their men's dockey (often taking it to him wherever he was at work) — she could be found sitting in her house-place surrounded by dirty dishes near a hearth so choked with ashes that fresh turves thrown on wouldn't burn, 'jest turning the corner o' this crochet tablecloth edging' or 'jest finishing the scalloping along the top o' this sheet'.

It seems that both Lois and I inherited from her a similar craving for such employment. We certainly did not 'heir' it from Mam or her side of the family. Mam didn't mind getting out her sewing machine if she really had to, but my sister and I were very young when the task of mending Dad's stockings or sewing on Gerald's buttons devolved upon us. We didn't mind at all, because we both already had an affinity with any sort of needle, pin, or hook.

Grandad Edwards, urged on by Grandmother, became the miller when the first drainage mill was erected in Lotting Fen. The extra money, combined with Grandmother's earnings in the brickyard and saved by her frugal ways, helped them to accumulate enough capital to make a bid for the tenancy of some farm-land in New Fen when its owner decided to let it. He was a grand 'gentleman' who lived some distance away, and he was a devout Wesleyan — and so was Grandmother. It stood her in good stead, because Grandad's application was looked on with favour, and he was the tenant provisionally chosen. However, by this time Aunt Harriet was almost as prominent, chapel-wise, as her mother. She and John wanted to go up a notch as well — so she became Cassandra again, and prophesied woe to Grandad's venture unless she and John were allowed to take on half the farm that was to be let. I am pretty sure, because of all that happened afterwards, that Grandmother connived at this, and the result was that the land was cut into two lots, ours only being slightly the larger. The real trouble lay in the fact that the house had been built for one family's occupation, not two. It was hastily converted, and bits added at the back. But it was never a proper farmhouse — only two semi-detached cottages. The consequences of this bit of skullduggery on the part of Aunt Harriet continued till the day of her death, and after. Dad made several gallant attempts to buy the rest of the land, and the house, so as to re-unite them as had been first intended; but Aunt Harriet was too much for him, and he never succeeded. As she and Uncle John were childless, her fight was to retain it for the use of Uncle John's family, though they remained only tenant farmers to the end. As far as I know, Aunt Harriet had no particular love for her in-laws. My guess is that her reasons were negative rather than positive. She didn't care to get it for her in-laws, but she did care to stop Rattles' daughter from climbing higher still up the social scale.

Becoming a farmer, even a tenant farmer, was a bit of an ordeal for Grandad Etherds. He didn't understand business. However, in those Victorian days, the man was expected to be the boss, even if he wasn't, so of course all the business had to be done in his name. Consequently, in their first year up in New Fen, a cheque arrived made out to him. It was the first he had ever encountered. Grandmother had difficulty in making him believe that if he took the bit of paper to the bank in Ramsey, they would actually give him gold sovereigns in exchange for it. So it was with great diffidence that in dreadful embarrassment he pushed the cheque across the counter to the cashier, who, of course, didn't know him from Adam.

'What is your name?' asked the cashier.

Grandad was in a quandary. He had never, in his whole life so far, declared himself to be John Edwards. He was, to everybody except Grandmother, just 'Prooshia Etherds' (because he obstinately took the Prussian side in the Franco-Prussian dispute). It was, he felt, altogether too 'ikey' (stuck-up) to pronounce aloud his name as it was spelled. In a sort of desperation, he muttered 'John Edduds' through his whiskers. This seemed to give the rather supercilious cashier doubts.

'Ah!' said that worthy. 'And can you identify yourself, Mr — ah — Edduds? Can you prove that you are the man this cheque is made payable to?'

This sort of language only served to confuse Grandad more.

'We can't change this cheque unless you can find somebody to prove you are the man named on it' said the smoothy behind the counter, who nevertheless kept the cheque in his hands.

Here was a facer! His difficulty, combined with a suspicion that the other chap was 'laughing in his guts' at his predicament, overcame Grandad's habitual humility.

'I reckon as you're 'nation pertickerly!' he said.

'Ah, my good fellow. We have to be 'nation pertickerly in our business' said the clerk.

That riled Grandad, whose meek exterior only thinly covered the usual amount of fen-tiger

291

pride. He stalked out of the bank, determined to find somebody to prove his identity if it took him the rest of the day. Luckily, he came almost immediately face to face with the proprietor of the shop that supplied the grease, etc., for his windmill.

He was still put out when he got home, and recounted the tale.

'Do you mean to say you swore at him?' Grandmother demanded.

'No. I on'y told 'im 'e were 'nation pertickerly.'

'You did swear!' she snapped. 'What you meant was 'damnation', and that is swearing. I won't have swearing in this house!'

And as far as I know, there never was a time when her decree was broken. Dad never swore — and if the other men attached to the family ever did, they didn't do it indoors; but in general, this seemed to be accepted as a courtesy towards Dad, who really did dislike bad language or 'smutty talk'. But 'by Goles' as Aunt Harriet would have said, he was no saint! He was always up to tricks among his cronies, and I rarely meet any of my fenland peers but they still tell me a new tale about him, his tricks, and/or his anecdotes — by no means all suitable for polite company like Grandmother or Aunt Harriet!

Dad used to tell the tale about Grandad and the cheque with great delight, and the bit about the prohibition on swearing.

'Nation pertickerly' was in our family vocabulary, like a lot of other inside phrases. The irony, which amused Dad, was that Grandad got away with calling anybody who had annoyed him, or any difficult situation, or a too-frisky horse 'a horsbud'.

It seems that Grandmother never objected. Dad could only conclude that she had no idea of its origin as 'whore's bird', because if she had, it would have been anathema. Damnation, even unto the Bottomless Pit, would have faded like dew against the sun in the face of any expression even vaguely connected with sex!

Sex was the other name for the Devil. It was utterly taboo, the worst sin of all, far greater than any other in the decalogue. Not just the seventh commandment about adultery, but sex in its own right. For an unmarried girl to become pregnant was Sin. Yet in all rural societies such sin had always been a common one — as Dad said, Grandmother's own mother had produced an illegitimate child, and so had two of her seven sisters. He subscribed to the taboo as far as we were concerned while we were young — but in his old age, he often discussed it with me, and showed his true feelings about such things. For one thing, he failed to see why the poor old Devil should get all the blame for what Grandmother's puritanical God had set up — 'male and female created He them', didn't he? Dad also considered the attitude of women on this matter utter hypocrisy — men were much more honest about it. I think they probably had good reason for their outward attitude towards sex between the young. As one woman who used to 'do domestic' for us once said to me, regarding a youngster in trouble. 'She ain't the first, and won't be the last. If God ever made anything better, 'e kep' it for hisself.' There was a tolerance even among the women for their fallen sisters. Their outward intolerance of illegitimacy was probably shaped by economic and practical considerations in the first place, until it became a social stigma as well.

If one of the daughters of a large family produced a fatherless baby, it often fell to the girl's mother to bring the child up, along with her own youngest. That meant one more mouth to feed, and for a short time it also deprived the household of one provider.

At such a time, and in such an isolated place where contraception via old wives' tales was a hit-and-miss affair at the best, and abortion fraught with terrible dangers, the most sensible prevention was to make sex a religious sin and a social crime — to yield to such immoral temptation was to bring disgrace on the entire family. The only precaution a mother could arm a nubile daughter with was the fear of hell-fire, social disgrace, and the chance that her father would 'show her the door'. It did occasionally happen that way, and the poor girl then landed in the local workhouse completely ostracised by her Christian relatives. Not very often, though, I'm glad to report. I hold no brief whatsoever for late twentieth-century permissiveness, but I'm glad there were not too many fathers unloving enough to punish their daughters for such a natural sin. Usually, distressed though they may have been, they stood by their erring daughters, and welcomed the little newcomer. 'Every baby brings its own love with it' was a saying proved true over and over again. As one such unlawful grandfather once said to Dad, 'Bootiful blue eyes when yew com 'um at night.'

Early marriage and large families were the inevitable result of this socio-religious ban on any youthful sexual activity. With Grandmother and Aunt Harriet, the taboo was so strong that it boded ill for any girl over whom they had any influence, since the ultimate in prevention against such disaster was to make sure that a girl never had any social contact with a member of the opposite sex unsupervised. Fortunately for us, both Mam and Dad saw to it that their prohibition stopped short at our gate, though Grandmother and Aunt Harriet made no secret about their opinion of our free, though innocent 'goings on'.

Back, however, to Grandad and his farm. In spite of the fact that she had got her own way, Aunt Harriet's prediction of trouble was only too correct.

The farm did eventually do fairly well, as was proved when Grandmother died, but she kept Grandad in a constant state of anxiety — which, to some extent, Dad inherited. Farming is a risky occupation, and was much more so then than it is now.

Apart from the vagaries of the weather and the possibility of 'fen blows', floods and the like, it was then very much dependent upon animals: and as Dad used to say 'Never put your trust in anything that has a life to lose'. Grandad's greatest asset were his three heavy horses. One

295

Sunday, he came home from the morning service at chapel to find the barn door open, and all three of his horses helping themselves to new wheat from an uncovered tub of it just inside the door — left there to be as near at hand as possible when Grandad himself had to 'bait' the horses morning and night. He had no idea how much wheat they had eaten, nor whether they had taken a drink from the horse-trough that stood just outside the barn door. What he did know was that a pint of wheat could kill the strongest horse, and that if after eating some they had been at the water, there was little hope for them. How the barn door came to be open, no one ever discovered. Perhaps Grandad blamed himself, but that is something we shall never know. What he found that Sunday morning predicted ruin; if his horses all died, bankruptcy stared him in the face. The shock to him was beyond description.

The nearest vet lived at Wistow, about seven miles away. There were no telephones, nor even cycles. The only recourse he had was to go to fetch the vet himself. Luckily, the slow, fat old pony kept to draw the buggy was not in the same yard as the horses, so he hastily harnessed her up, and set out. In his haste and distress, he failed to provide himself with warm clothing, rugs, or a gig umbrella. Before he reached Wistow it had begun to rain, a cold, insistent rain that soon soaked him through.

The vet followed him home, and pronounced the horses to be in no danger. They had only just discovered the wheat, and had not taken a drink.

They did not die — but Grandad did. The shock, combined with his long cold ride wet through brought on pneumonia, and finished him off within the week.

Then Grandmother became in name what she has always been in fact, the boss. Dad gave up his various activities to become her horsekeeper, and a very hard taskmaster she was. He had already taken over the job of running the mill from his father, and had a smallholding of his own. In effect, he ran Grandmother's farm for her, but was paid no more than an ordinary labourer. It was no wonder Mam did not get on too well with her mother-in-law!

He was thirty-six when his father died, had been married five years, and my brother and sister had been born; but such was Grandmother's strength of character that he was still scared of her, and very much under her thumb. That, above all else, was what infuriated Mam — especially as Aunt Harriet, Grandmother's confidante and ally, who lived in the other part of Grandmother's house, constantly interfered.

To all intents and purposes, Dad became just another farm labourer, and this Mam found very hard to stomach. Even Dad admitted that his mother was a hard woman who could saw your leg off without flinching if she considered it warranted. A small proof is that it was to her that other women went to to get their ears pierced. Now Grandmother didn't have a great deal of sympathy with vanity or what she would have called 'bedizenment'; but it was firmly believed that piercing the ears was a cure for sore eyes, and on such grounds she was willing to oblige. She kept a darning needle mounted in a cork for the purpose, and had another cork ready to place behind the ear. Then she heated the piercing needle to red-hot in a candle-flame, allowed it to cool enough to be wiped clean on a bit of rag, and having marked the spot on the ear-lobe, plunged the still hot needle through and into the other cork.

After Grandad's early death, she went through a bad time financially, and it was perhaps this experience, added to a naturally more than frugal nature, that gave her her reputation for meanness. In the parlance of the fens, she was one who 'would skin a fart for its stink'. There are plenty of tales about her to prove this side of her character, but there is quite a lot to be said for her on the other. Her production of socks for the troops in the Great War was so remarkable that her photograph appeared in the local paper, aged eighty, with her mob cap seated firmly on her sparse hair above the stern old face, her bone knitting sheath secured firmly at the waist, and her hands busy on a sock. She could, they say, turn the heel without even bothering to glance downward at the knitting. Report has it that at eighty she could still crack a nut with her own teeth, but later had difficulty because she began to grow a third set.

Her firm control of everything and everybody is illustrated by a tale of an incident when she was having a corn-stack threshed by Jackson's team. She went round to see how the corn was coming through (that is, to check the yield). She found two labourers leaning against the drum, which had been temporarily stopped, and from which two three-part-full sacks of wheat still hung.

'What are you men idling about for', she demanded. 'Wasting my time!'

'Old yew 'ard, Missus' one of them replied. 'Carryin' corn's a 'ard ol' job, yer know!'

'You're being paid for it, ain't you? If you can't do it, get out o' the way and let me.' And to their chagrin, she released a sack from its hooks, manoeuvred it to the sack barrow, and strode off with it. (By my calculation, she must then have been well past seventy.) I, of course, only heard all these tales at second hand, but the fact that they exist at all proves that she was no shrinking violet, in spite of her inhibitions about the devil and his sexual proclivities. I connected her more with chapel than with the business of ordinary living.

With or without Grandmother, chapel played a great part in our lives, at least in our early years. The smell of a paraffin lamp still transports me back across the decades to that Sunday evening atmosphere as we walked in single file down the aisle in the pre-service hush to the very front. Mam sat in the first pew, where she had always sat as a child with Grammam, and I sat with her. It served her purpose because of her deafness; but in any case, even as Dad's wife, I doubt if she would have been allowed in to the Etherds' pew just behind us. It was full, even after Grandmother had departed, with Aunt Harriet, Uncle John, Dad, Aunt Loll and Uncle Jim.

Their presence so close behind was uncomfortable for me. The least whisper or wriggle on my part resulted in a sharp poke in the back from Aunt Harriet and a 'sh' that made far more of a disturbance than I had done.

After I had reached the age of reason, I did a lot of thinking sitting in that front pew at chapel, mostly about chapel matters. Sometimes I couldn't stay the course, and fell asleep with my head against Mam's plump, well-cushioned arm; but mostly I listened, and tried to puzzle out for myself what it was all about. A lot of what I heard made no sense at all, but — as all children do — I made sense out of much of it by fitting it with childlike logic into such experience as I had already gained. Not all of it was amenable to such logic, but our preachers were nothing if not histrionic, and wonderful phrases such as 'Sodom and Gomorrah' fell frequently and delightfully on my word-conscious ears.

I really did try to understand, taking words and phrases at their face value when I did know what they meant in other contexts. But I was often in a great puggatery to make two and two come to four.

There was the preacher before me in the pulpit. If he was dull and colourless, I forgot him and either went to sleep or found other surreptitious amusements. Most of the preachers, however, were too dramatic to ignore. So there he would be, ranting and roaring, pleading or sobbing, till he leaned across the top of the pulpit towards me and dropped his voice to a thrilling whisper as he exhorted his congreation

300

to beware the lure of the Whore of Babylon (?) and to shun 'The Evil One' (? Rattles?). No, this Evil One was, apparently, always prowling about looking for the unwary sinner, to drag him down into the flames of the Bottomless Pit, just as the Hooky Man was always where there was water to drag us children to a watery death. And once into the Bottomless Pit . . . the preacher would often go on to describe the horrors of hell in such vivid detail that it seemed he must only have recently returned from a prolonged visit there. So it was all the more puzzling when this fascinating if terrifying peroration came suddenly to a stop, and everybody with one accord leaned forward, hand over eyes, as he said 'May God bless to us the reading and study of His word' — and we all sat up again to hear him announce the final hymn. I loved the hymns — but as with the Bible readings or the sermons, I sought meaning for their words. After such a sermon as I have just described, it was a bit disconcerting to hear the same preacher in front of me, as well as the whole congregation behind me, belting out:

Whosoever will may come!
Whosoever will may come!
Whosoever will
Whosoever will
Whosoever will may come.

(My mind was still in the sulphurous region of the BP and Hell. Was it there we could all go at will?)

301

Sankey and Moody hymns were not often used during the evening service, but some were such great favourites that they intruded now and then. The Methodist hymn book provided hymns just as bewildering. My ear for words was accompanied by an extremely active visual imagination. Some of the visions the hymn words produced were glorious: others were just plain ridiculous.

His chariots of wrath the deep thunder-
  clouds form,
And dark is His path on the wings of the
  storm.

I still thrill to the words, and I can still see the picture they conjured up for me then . . . of God careering across our wide fenland sky in a sort of chariot drawn by four white horses all rearing and cavorting and/or galloping like cart horses bolting, their hooves striking lightning-flashes just like a runaway cart horse struck sparks from the lumps of granite on the road in front of our farm. Then, when God leaned forward and cracked his Aweful whip, the Heavens were rent with the roll and clap of thunder.

Wonderful! Marvellous! King of kings, and Lord of Lords!

But what about all those inexplicable references to 'the lamb'?

As far as I was aware, lambs were baby sheep with curly coats and adorable faces, with short tails that moved at incredible speed, and tiny, delicate black hooves. We didn't see lambs in our fen, but we did when we walked to Ramsey across Biggin Fields, and oh the joy of it! Especially when a group of them played together, chasing each other, and every now and then one of them leapt straight up into the air with all four little black-hoofed legs straight and rigid.

This being my internal picture connected with 'lambs', what was I to make of

> Crown him with many crowns,
> The lamb upon his throne.

What throne? A gold throne, of course, as in all good fairy tales. So there he sat on this golden throne, a dear little black-faced lamb with a jewelled crown over each little black ear, bracelets of similar crowns round each woolly foreleg, and still more dangling like anklets along each stiff, protruding little hindleg. The hymn specifically said 'Crown *him with many crowns.*'

> Hark how the heavenly anthem drowns
> All music but its own

The heavenly anthem was what the heavenly host sang at the first Christmas. So standing behind my many-crowned lamb was a host of white-winged angels all bellowing as loud as they could to drown some other sound. What could that be but the 'baa-ing' of the lamb?

(While I remember, I must interpolate here a tiny bit of agricultural history. Sheep had been run on 'summer lands' as late as Dad's early childhood, and he had minded sheep even on The Heights. He used to make me envious with tales of his cade lamb, brought up on a bottle and kept till it was a lusty sheep, when it had to be killed not because of its value for the pot, but because it had never grown out of its playful habit of lowering its head and charging unsuspecting grown-ups. After having leapt into the laps of several lady visitors, and butted several male ones flat on to their backs in the dust, it had to go.)

Dad also told the story of another boy shepherd who, not having been to school, could not count. He therefore used the age-old method of other parts of the country, of tallying his sheep back into the fold my means of a well-remembered 'counting rhyme' or 'sheep-tally'. Except, in this case, there was no such rhyme traditionally in use. The usual jingles tallied the sheep in twenties: so did the fenland shepherd, but he used what he knew best, the Lord's Prayer:

Our father/chartineaven/hallow-edbe/Thy/
   Name (5)
Kingdomcome/willbedone/earthastis/in/
   Heaven (10)
Giveusday/daily bread/giveus tresspass/
   weefgive/trespassgenstus/ (15)
Temstation/liverusevil/thineskingdom/
poweranglory/everanever/a-MEN (20)

to count them as they went through a gap in the hurdles. When two sheep collided, 'th ol' bor' took one look and legged it as fast as he could to the owner, bawling 'Mairster! Mairster! Can yer come? Our Father's knocked Chartineaven's eye out!'

We accepted without question the Sunday ritual of Sunday School, afternoon service and evening service, plus hanging about while our elders finished the day with a prayer-meeting. For the adults, it was both duty and pleasure, providing as it did the chance of meeting friends and neighbours on a social footing. For the adolescents, it provided a chance to mix with the opposite sex, and

many a grand little wedding was planned
in the twi-twi-light outside the chapel door.

For the children it was law, chore, and boredom, for much of the year, excluding the 'anni' highlight.

Our Sunday School was run by men — it seems to me, almost the same team as ran Freddie Jackson's threshing tackle. Dad had ceased to be Sunday School superintendent by my time. The first superintendent I remember was 'Old Henry', who, bent double by his years of turf-turning, gave us his weekly homily leaning on two sticks. He always ended it with a hint of the pleasure in store for the next Sunday.

'And now my little ol' ducks, if I'm spore till next week, we shall be a-talkin' about little King

Josi-ay an' his little ol' shutknife.' (Or something of the kind.)

The grown-ups couldn't let it alone even after their prayer-meeting. They drifted off in groups to call at one or another's cottages to finish the day with hymn-singing, round the family musician on harmonium, organ, (piano, in our case) or concertina. The hymns were mostly those of Sankey and Moody. We took turns to choose the hymns and looking back, I realise how the favourites chosen fitted the personalities of the singers who asked for them. Aunt Harriet would always want ones that in my mind were connected with funerals — *Jesu, lover of my soul* or *Abide with me*. Aunt Loll, on the other hand, liked the hopeful ones. I always connect her with *O Beulah land, sweet Beulah land*. Dad loved *All hail the power of Jesu's name* sung to the rolling *Diadem* tune: Uncle John went for those he understood; such as *Bringing in the Shoaves* (sheaves) or *Where are the reapers?* Mam, always with Grammam in her thoughts, asked for *Come over the line* or *Shall we gather at the river?* Our last one was, by common consent, either *Count your blessings* or *God be with you till we meet again*.

To all of us children, the hymns were what made chapel bearable — a chance to move, stand up and take part between prayers and readings and more prayers. A relief, because there was still the long sermon to endure. Many, like me, learned to shut their ears to the dull if worthy preachers, pathetically fervent though their homelies were. After all, we got enough practice in Sunday School to learn how to endure through boring sermons. Besides, we had the same rituals as other children up and down the land had. Hymnbooks were above suspicion by those watching over us in rows as we sat in our Sunday School 'classes', and we all held one. Then, all looking as if butter wouldn't melt in our mouths, we opened them at the fly-page where in Roman capitals were the words CONTENTS and PREFACE. We elbow-jogged the next child and pointed with index-finger to each letter of 'CONTENTS' in turn. To him or her, the message read:

Cows Ought Not To Eat Nasty Turnip Stalks

Then he or she would turn to PREFACE and return the compliment, meaning:

Percy Roberts Eating Fish After Catching Eels

This last must, I think, have been indigenous, because Percy Roberts was a living neighbour.

Once I had truly recovered from my near-fatal illness, and had grabbed hold of life again with both hands, my powers of reasoning had also become unusually acute, and I looked at the chapel scene with a somewhat sceptical eye. Till then, I had accepted chapel and all it stood for as a trial ordained personally by God, though relayed to me by such as Grandmother, Aunt Harriet, Old Henry — even Dad. But it was Dad who began my process of reasoning for myself about it. Why was it that Dad never put on a 'chapel-face', solemn, strait-laced and grim? It came to me once like a gleam of sunshine that Dad did not take literally either the threats of our more pessimistic preachers, nor the word of the Lord, especially those obscure places where it blatantly contradicted itself.

He'd actually make jokes about the Holy Bible! I used to worry a bit about the salvation of his eternal soul, when, for example, after we had sat through a grave sermon on the dangers of breaking the third commandment 'Thou shalt not take the name of the Lord in vain', he would refer cheerfully next morning to his cheque-book as 'the Lamb's book of life'. (Aunt Harriet was offended often by his being so 'blastpheemious', and told him so.)

Then he was always using phrases from the Holy Word in ways for which they were never intended. A child discovered in mischief in our yard would be told that he'd be 'put on the Isle of Patmos' if he ever did it again. Making fun of St Paul! How dared he?

He had a lovely variety of threats that were never once put into action. His favourite was to threaten 'sixteen private lashes on the bare belly with a smooking hot pudden-bag'.

Mam, of course, had always had a keen eye for the idiosyncrasies of the various local preachers, and as soon as we reached home would put on impersonations of them, with Dad egging her on and supplying a running commentary of what they had said at places where her hearing had failed her.

It dawned on me gradually, that in contrast to

Grandmother and Aunt Harriet, Dad and Mam both dared to get pleasure, even fun, out of chapel and their religion.

Moreover, once Grandmother had died, the all-pervading disapproval of the full pew behind us seemed to lesson. Aunt Harriet, unsupported, had difficulty in keeping her volatile pewful of 'Etherdses' in order. Uncle John, sitting tight against the wall, gave us a wink, or made a rabbit out of his handkerchief to amuse us: Uncle Jim, at the other end of the pew, always had a smile and a twinkle if we turned and caught his eye. Dad — well, Dad was no different, wherever he was; and Aunt Loll, squeezed between Uncle Jim and Dad, often got infected with their light-hearted 'irreverence'. Her risible faculties always had to be held in on a tight rein, and protected from Aunt Harriet's immediate domination, they often broke loose and kicked over the traces.

She suffered from a persistent tickling cough, which she tried to keep in check at chapel by sucking large, flat, rectangular cough sweets with a considerable content of chlorodine (hot and smelly) in them. I loved them, and she knew it, so before the service started she always slipped one to me, and again during the moment before the sermon, when Aunt Harriet leaned forward with her head in her hands to issue her weekly demands of and commands to the Lord. On one occasion, the cough sweet nearly proved Aunt Loll's undoing.

The preacher that Sunday was one of our own community, a man whose appearance, language and behaviour during the week left a good deal to be desired in most people's eyes; but it was ungrudgingly acknowledged that he was a better preacher than most, and for his appearances in the pulpit he would have a good wash, comb his splendid crop of grizzled hair and his patriarchal beard, and don a dark suit, making himself look quite respectable and presentable. On this particular Sunday, his appearance was quite remarkable. He was sitting in the pulpit when we entered, and we could see that he was wearing a new black jacket (or, at least, one we had not seen before), accompanied by a stiff, starched, white winged collar. His beard hid the rest.

Aunt Loll issued her pre-service sweet to me, and popped one into her own mouth. Then the preacher stood up to begin the service, and all was revealed. The collar belonged to a starched dickey which was neither quite wide enough nor quite long enough for its present wearer. As he raised his arms wide for his first exhortation to worship, there was a loud pop, and the dickey front broke loose from his old trouser band, and stood boldly out before him, supporting his huge grizzled beard. Moreover, it had burst open the top button of his trouser flies, and let free an inch or two of protruding flannel shirt.

Aunt Loll gasped in her effort to suppress the giggle that rose spontaneously to her throat, and down went the cough lozenge, whole — where it stuck. Her whoops for air were at first mixed unmistakably with suppressed giggles, until at last somebody realised that she was actually *in extremis*. Then everybody clawed up and rushed to thump her on the back until, mercifully, the lozenge shot out of her mouth. I'd chewed mine up in fear and excitement, and my eyes were watering because of a smarting, stinging tongue as Aunt Harriet, severe and unsmiling, conducted her sister down the aisle and out into the fresh air. Unfortunately, the dignity of the exit was marred by Aunt Loll's stifled giggles, disguised as far as she could manage it, as coughs.

I was aware then, as I am now, of the fervency of belief of the preachers and others who put their all into acting as our leaders and teachers. However much fun we might get out of them at home (and we did!), Dad always made it quite plain that they were to be respected, even admired, for their courage in standing there in the pulpit at all; and that God would judge them by their intentions, not by what they achieved.

As far as I was concerned they didn't have much success in turning me into a True Believer of Aunt Harriet's variety. There were too many things that made me 'wonder-full' and even more curious than ever. There was, I thought, very great disparity between God-the-Father as pictured by them, and His colourless, drooping, sad and unsmiling Son. God was a huge, flamboyant, colourful character, a bit terrifying perhaps ('*the fear of the Lord is the beginning of wisdom*'), but at least dramatic enough to be interesting. Jesus had no such attractive attributes, as far as I could see. I knew all the stories about Him, and was constantly being reminded that it was my fault, and that of others like me, that such dreadful things had happened to Him.

We may not know, we cannot tell
What pains he had to bear.
Yet we believe it was for us
He hung and suffered there.

It made me uncomfortable, like Grandmother
had done, because I didn't feel guilty but dare
not say so. I hurried past all the pictures of
his limp, bleeding body being taken down
from the cross, until one day it struck me that
they were the only ones I had ever seen of
him with legs. At any rate legs made Him
more real. The pictures I saw of Him were in
The Life of Christ, the only book other than
the Bible we were allowed on Sundays, or
those in our Sunday School prizes, or the
cards occasionally awarded for good attendance. All showed the same sort of Man — if
He was a man? Mostly, they portrayed a man
such as I, at any rate, had never set eyes on.
His face, in those pictures — that countenance
which in Heaven we should spend our eternity
gazing upon, provided we ever got there
— would not have stood a one-in-a-million
chance in a contest of manliness against Dad
or any of my 'uncles', real or by courtesy.
They were all brown-faced and healthy,
exuding life and strength. He was long-faced,
thin, straggly-bearded, and pale to a degree, in
spite of all the New Testament stories of Him
being out and about over hills and even
deserts. He always kept His eyes half-closed,
and therefore seemed to be about to faint. If,
at that time, I had been as wordly-wise as I

am now, I should have unhesitatingly placed Him as a transvestite, because he was always robed in what I thought was a woman's 'bedgown', white, 'draggly', and too loose. Then, as one of my peers at school once asked, why did He always have a plate on His head with no visible indication of how He kept it from falling off?

Though His disciples were often shown with perfectly normal, strong hairy legs, He kept His own well out of sight under the bedgown — except for His feet, which were always bare. Moreover, they never touched the ground, but hovered about four inches above it, the toes pointing downwards at an angle impossible to all but the double-jointed. How did all this square up with the story of Him strolling through a cornfield (there's nothing much more uncomfortable than stubble) — or striding up and down mountains, through deserts and over stony paths while admonishing well-shod disciples?

Though I should have been wary of admitting such 'blastpheemious' thoughts for fear of Eternal Damnation, the awful truth is that I did not care very much for the wishy-washy Jesus of those pictures. He was too 'meek and mild': in fact, as I thought privately, a real ninny. Not at all the kind I desired as 'my master and my friend'. He never even smiled, let alone laughed. Didn't anything ever amuse Him?

I knew quite well that he cried. 'Jesus wept.' The shortest sentence in the whole Bible, as I was told, and a fat lot of good that knowledge was to me until, many years later, I found it useful as an example of subject and predicate, when teaching grammar. It did do me good to hear a strong, manly voice rolling out such phrases as 'Seek Him who made the seven stars and Orion' — but 'Jesus wept'? I didn't want to know. Why did He never laugh? The only conclusion I could reach was that Grandmother was right, after all. It must be a Sin to laugh, especially at chapel matters. In which case, I and all my family were thrice-doomed Sinners. It was a great consolation to know that Mam and Dad would be in Hell with me — and that Grandmother and Aunt Harriet wouldn't!

When I reached Grammar School age, I begged my parents not to make me go to Sunday School any more, but they would not relent. I'm afraid it was a sad misjudgement on their part. I was not old enough to appreciate the depth or sincerity of belief that my simple-minded teachers there possessed, or their courage and integrity. It also served to give me an inflated idea of my own cleverness, that I could pick logical holes in their tales and homilies — which in turn gave me an uneasy guilt that I was there at all, pretending to believe them when I didn't.

I think that if then I had explained my reasons to Dad, he would have understood, even if he had still decreed attendance. So I went until I was between twelve and thirteen, and then rebelled. I continued to go to chapel with Mam when I couldn't wriggle out of it till I was sixteen. Dad had ceased to go, because the worsening of his arrythmia caused him to be a bit claustrophobic. He was better after the new piece was added, because of the door at the end of the 'Etherds' pew. It may have been a bit of an excuse, though, because his keen intelligence needed stronger meat than the dwindling band of good local preachers could offer him. After the Great War, the uninhibited heartiness of worship began to fade, and by the end of World War II, it had practically disappeared. The new generation, though fewer and perhaps just as fervent, were better educated, more self-conscious and much more inhibited. The same applied to the congregation. The great old stalwarts of both sexes had 'one by one sunk silently to rest'. The zest had vanished, and though the better educated preachers touched the mind better, they no longer had the gift of tugging at the heart-strings.

We all became backsliders, one after the other, and I regret it, because we were only one family out of many. I can now appreciate how truly remarkable the local preacher system was, in its heyday. It still exists, of course, though only a shadow of what it once was. In any case congregations have dwindled to the point where many small chapels have had to close (though The Heights Chapel is still alive, and while there's life, there's hope).

In our home, Duty bade us go, but our family predilection for extracting humour out of everything rather took the edge off our 'righteousness'. Combined with Mam's gift for mimicry, anybody would have been justified in thinking we had been to a music-hall rather than

315

Divine Service when we sat down to Sunday supper.

I feel pretty sure that God — I don't know about 'the Lord' — had to take the good intentions of a lot of the local preachers, rather than their performance in the pulpits, as the measure of their worth. I hope, for our sakes, that God has enough sense of humour himself to forgive us our mirth at their expense.

The effort that many men put into their desire to 'preach God's word' was enormous. A man who had worked like distraction every hour of daylight for six days a week would set out on a Sunday morning to walk six or seven miles to the chapel he had been assigned to on 'the plan', preach two sermons and then walk home again. By my time, the bicycle had become their means of transport and things were that much easier. There was one fairly local man whose speech had a definite impediment, yet he was determined to become a local preacher. Too poor to buy a cycle, he began by walking to his work for God: then he got a better job, and bought a cycle — but before long he also met and married a wife. After that, he set out as before, with his wife in her Sunday clothes sitting side-saddle on his carrier. Nature took its course, and before long there was a baby. Not to be deterred, the baby in an old pram was towed along behind. After the advent of a second child, he had to abandon his family at home, and once more make his journey alone. Fenland roads, of course, are very flat, but even so there is a limit to one man's horse-power when propelling a weighted vehicle.

In the youth of Dad and Mam, many a local preacher lacked the skill to read the Bible from which he preached. It did not deter them. They had heard the passages and the psalms so often in their childhood that they had them off by heart, and pretended to be reading from the pulpit Bible. No doubt a lot of them did, in fact, learn to read by doing so, as a child in school will learn to read from a favourite story book when all systematic reading schemes have made little impression.

Then there was the question of their delivery of the sermon. The orthodox, good preachers rather bored us (I speak for nobody else!). What we loved were the ranters, who hung over the edge of the pulpit in tears of passion or raised hands eyes and voices beseeching forgiveness from 'Him Above' for all our sins besides their own. There were those who took their own sins as examples, and dwelt upon them with such fervour that one couldn't help wondering if they spent time between Sunday and Sunday deliberately adding to them, or at least fishing in an imaginary pool of sinfulness to hook out just one more tiddler of a sin to add. Those whose conversion had been sudden were so utterly genuine in their repentance that they made a lot of us feel uncomfortable about our own lack of it. Such a one was Potter Proud, who kept a cycle repair shop in Ramsey. After his sudden conversion he toured the villages, week after week standing in the pulpit holding himself up as the greatest sinner ever on his way to hell, until Grace Abounding caught him in his fall, and brought him safely Home.

Amazing grace! (How sweet the sound)
That saved a wretch like me!
I once was lost, but now am found,
Was blind, but now I see.

We did not amuse ourselves at Potter Proud's expense. After listening to his homely, direct, unvarnished confession and repentance, we were moved to emotions other than laughter. (The recent popularity of John Newton's hymn to its early American melody has revived for me the memory of Potter Proud. I think that John Bunyan could not have bettered him when he was in full swing; and even the most irreverent of us went home thoughtful.)

But the preachers, like the rest of us *'differed one from another like the stars in glory'*. Some of them simply enjoyed the distinction of being a public speaker with a captive audience. These were often the most uneducated, and the peculiarity of this particular group was general pomposity and showy self-esteem. This made them extra vulnerable to criticism, and if a breath of scandal ever touched them, they thundered denials from the pulpit, and denunciation of the liars who had started such bearing of false witness against their neighbours. One such incident put a catchword into our family vocabulary, still liable to be used three-quarters

318

of a century later as a heated denial of an untrue accusation.

Somehow, a tale had got about that one such lay preacher had been observed sneaking away to go fishing on the Sabbath. He was a small, spare man, so short that only his head and shoulders were visible above the lectern on the pulpit front — but on this occasion his damaged self-esteem and angry pride filled the chapel with its fury, as he related the rumour and railed against its calumny. Banging his fist on the pulpit, he roared in his high-pitched, rather squeaky voice — as Dad said 'like a sucking dove':

HOLMES NEVER WENT A-FISHING!

(We never were allowed to forget that. Mam could 'do' him to a T.)

We also had another favourite quote, especially if a gang of unexpected guests arrived during a meal, and we had to move round to make room for them at the table. This was from a completely humble, uneducated fenman who could never get through his sermon without his best-remembered 'text' from the Bible. Somehow or other, he would work it in, and deliver with full blast.

'*They shall come from the north, and from the south, and from the east, and from the west, and they shall SIDDOWN with Abraham, Isaac and Jacob.*'

Grandmother's illegitimate brother 'Ike' (long before my time) was a local preacher. He was also a farmer of considerable wealth, having married, at eighteen, the widow of his boss on the farm to which he had been sent as 'a farmer's boy'. The boss, it appeared, was such a skinflint that in spite of being quite well aware of the danger, he had insisted on going gault-digging all alone one Saturday afternoon. The gault-pit caved in on him, and smothered him, and Ike slipped into his shoes, and his bed.

Ike prospered until he was wealthy, important, and very busy: but not too busy to 'witness for the Lord' from the pulpit every Sunday. However, it seems to be the case that material concerns occupied him to such an extent during the week that he rarely had time to prepare a sermon, and gave his talks extempore. He got into our pulpit once, according to Dad, without the least idea of what he was going to say. Quite unabashed, he leaned towards his congregation, and began 'Now, my fren's, what shall we talk about? Let's talk about the hangels!'

(There is no way I can convey the fenland 'ow' or 'ou' sound: 'see-OW-and'.) There was another very local preacher of my own era whose delivery was most peculiar. He spoke in short sharp bursts with long pauses between. (We said he talked 'in stelches'.)

Dad's old friend Banker Bill was not much of a chapel-goer, but he had been persuaded by another ranter we called 'Jeremiah' to try it again. When we went to Banker's for a Sunday evening get-together after the 'stelcher' had been preaching, Banker remarked on his queer delivery. Then he added 'And as for 'is singin' — 'e sings just like 'e talks — like a pig a-piddling.'

Yet another preacher worthy of remembrance (because of Dad's aversion) was, believe it or not, female. She got Dad's back up as few other people ever did. Some of it, no doubt, was because to him it seemed as unseemly as the ordination of women does to many Anglicans at present. Or it may have been that she made the mistake of 'talking down' in a posh voice to her 'uneddicated' peasant congregation. Mostly, though, I believe it to be her deliberate theatricality. She always wore a dark, long dress with white gauzy sleeves to which drapes were attached, so that when she flung her arms wide to exhort sinners to step forward and repent, they spread out like wings or the sails of a ship. This bit of show-biz caught Dad on the raw. He sensed how phoney it all was, and he couldn't take it. As soon as the plan of preachers for the next quarter arrived, he would note when 'White Wings' was preaching, and stage himself a very bad attack of his extra-systole, so as to stay at home with his book. He did not confine himself to the Bible, either.

The sermon was usually based upon a biblical text, and the ingenuity of interpretation was wonderful in its own right. Unrelated texts from the Bible were part of our daily fare. We were not expected to understand them, only to learn and be able to repeat them. We were given the text one Sunday, to learn and be able to say on the next. Having been blessed with a photographic memory for print, I only had to read mine through twice. But that was not our only acquaintance with 'textes' (texties). (Every noun ending with 't' still had the Old English 'e' inserted in the plural, in our dialect; so ghost, ghostes; vest, vestes, and so on.)

We met such 'textes' everywhere, because most cottages had framed 'textes' hanging on their walls. Many were dark with age, and blackened by peatsmoke, though printed on shiny, creamy-yellow paper, and framed on wood in such a fashion as to form a wooden cross at each of the four corners. Very occasially, they had been executed with needle and thread, as samplers.

They served as wall decorations at a time when pictures were scarce and photographs, though popular, still beyond the purse of many cottagers. (Great was the penny-pinching that went on to achieve the status-symbol of a family group photograph.) The framed texts were very precious to their possessors.

Some of the reverence given to these browned and foxed bits of paper was religious — they were, after all, words from The Word of God. Some of it, I feel certain, was no more than superstition. The texts acted in the same way as 'hex' signs, a means of warding off evil.

In my youth, they were still treasured by many who could not read them, though their owners could usually tell you what they said, even if they sometimes mixed them up. Others, completely illiterate, actually had no idea what the words were, which sometimes led to strange situations. On the other hand, perfectly literate women such as Aunt Harriet seemed impervious to the irony they could create. Fixed to the inside of the door of her wooden privy at the bottom of the garden was such a text, which read 'Christ is the head of this house.' It wouldn't have been quite so ironic if 'the closet' or 'the petty' was not more often than not referred to (politely) as 'the little house'. A friend of mine told me that her aunt also had a text in the same place, facing the seat and the sitter. This one declared, 'Thou, God, seest me.'

Perhaps the funniest story of this nature I ever heard was one told to me by my gardener, a man well into his seventies, who, like me, had been brought up among fenland chapel-goers. It concerned two regular attenders at a chapel he knew well, both of whom were illiterate. In middle age, they married each other, and among their wedding presents were two texts, framed as usual. They hung them above the head of their double bed. Above her head, the text read, 'I need Thee every hour'; above his was 'Lord, give me strength.' Possibly, even probably, apochryphal; but it does illustrate the custom, and the sometimes strange results of the juxtaposition of texts. Another pair on the chimney breast of an old house were not actually from the Bible, but had the same superstitious significance and the same unconscious humour. On the left, the text asked 'What is home without a mother?' and the one on the right answered 'Peace, perfect peace'.

Though I can't bring myself to soften (much) the impression of Grandmother as a hard, proud woman of stern and unyielding nature. I think I may have done Aunt Harriet a bit of unjustice. After Grandmother's death she did, now and again, let up on her religiosity, and even let her back hair down — on, for example, the occasion of a family gathering, such as our annual round of Christmas parties.

For these occasions she would don her very best. She was a short, dumpy woman, with her bosom pushed sky high by her whalebone corset. She usually wore black bombazine for 'best', trimmed vertically down the front with tucks, lace and beading, in an effort to make herself look as much like Queen Victoria as she could. She succeeded, too, apart from the Queen's widow's weed headress. Uncle John only conferred the distinction of widowhood on her when she was well into her eighties.

She actually enjoyed these family parties, and would bake along with all the other women involved, with good will if dubious success. Cooking was definitely not her strong suit.

She was not as stern and sour as Grandmother could be: she was simply stolid, staid and straight-laced, and she did have soft spots if you could find the right place — like getting the milk out of a coconut.

She knew we made fun of her about one of her idiosyncrasies and joined us in our amusement when it happened. She only ever had three nephews 'by blood' as she would have said, and one of them had died. She was not likely to confuse the other two; but there were seven of us, her 'blood' nieces, and she was utterly incapable of hitting the name of the one she wanted without going through the whole litany chronologically. So she would begin 'Elsie

— lawks! Ivy — lawks! Doris — lawks! Lois — lawks! Phyllis — lawks! SYBIL! (The seventh was Ruby.) Once started on this chant there was no stopping her till she reached the name she wanted, by which time one of us would have begun to titter — especially as the habit was infuriating to her, so that she clicked her tongue quite loudly in frustration with every intervening 'lawks!'. She did sometimes break down, and chuckle with the rest of us. Names meant a lot to people of her generation, possibly because there were so few families that given names were more important than patronyms. As the oldest female in the family, she expected to be consulted about the choice of name when any new baby was expected. Mam had other ideas, and Aunt Harriet had no say whatsoever in naming Gerald, but when Mam's second child was expected, Aunt Harriet let Dad know that she expected to be allowed the choice of its name. Mam was considerably put out by this 'in-law' interference. The last thing she wanted was a Jeremiah John or a Hannah Lydia, which she might get when Aunt Harriet followed the age-old custom of inserting a knife into the Bible. For once, however, Mam held her tongue, determined, if the baby proved to be the girl she wanted, to call it Lois Mary. Lois because she liked the name, and Mary after Grammam. It was a girl and Aunt Harriet insisted on her rights. She pushed the thin end of the carving knife into the Bible — at the first chapter of St Paul's Second Epistle to Timothy:

When I call to remembrance the unfeigned
    faith that is in thee,
which dwelt first in thy grandmother Lois,
    and thy mother Eunice . . .

Faced with the choice between Lois and Eunice,
she chose the former; and all, as Dickens said,
was gas and gaiters. Dad went to register his new
daughter very relieved because of a family row so
providentially averted — but forgot (did he?)
what Mam had told him the second name was to
be. So he registered her as Lois Miriam. In the
general schemozzle of my birth, nobody cared
what I was called. Mam had once met a Lady
Sybil who was extremely beautiful, and said that
that would do — and as nobody else had been
named after Grammam, I got the Mary, too.
Miriam, of course, is only the Jewish version of
Mary anyway, and Mary as a second name is still
carried down the family. To be fair, so is Rachel
(sic), and it now looks as if there is likely to be a
line of Lois's, too. In rural districts, family names
still mean a great deal.

Back, though, to our family gatherings. After
tea, the evening was given up to playing
age-old games, most of them involving ritual
rhymes or sequences that had to be
remembered and repeated. Take, for instance,
any game at which a participant failed: he was
given 'a forfeit', and had to hand over some
article to the master (or mistress) of this
particular ceremony — a ring, his necktie, a
handkerchief, or whatever. When the time
came for the 'forfeits' to be paid, a male

member of the gathering was blindfolded and made to kneel before the MC, who took at random each article forfeited, and holding it above the blindfolded man's head, intoned:

Jack! Jack!
There's a very pretty thing hanging over
   thy back
A very pretty thing, and a good one, too
What do you command its owner to do?

The blindfolded one then issued a decree such as 'sing a song' or 'tell a tale', or 'turn out his pockets for all to see' or 'kiss four bare legs'. Bare legs? Were there such things — in Aunt Harriet's presence? The young would be most embarrassed by such a command, but there was a way out. If such a forfeit fell to Dad, he would solemnly insist on Uncle John baring his legs to be kissed, or something similar. If it fell to Aunt Harriet she would waddle to the middle of the room, pick up a simple wooden chair, and loudly plant a kiss on each of its bare legs.

There were round games which were nothing more than memory tests, and I regret enormously that I can remember but one in its entirety:

Ten old maids went out one day
To see if they could find a man that way.
Nine old rakes in a hay-field raking
Eight old bakes in a bake-house baking
   (bakers?)
Seven old crows in a crab-tree quaking

327

Six grey mares, all sharp, shodden and
   shorn
Tails and manes tied up and uniform;
Five green chimney pots,
Four running hares,
Three black weasels,
Two white does,
The old grey goose and
AWAY SHE GOES

One person quoted the first couplet, the next
sitting in the circle joined in, and so on till 'Five
green chimney pots' at which the whole circle
gave voice, speeding the tempo like 'The Sailor's
Hornpipe' at the Last Night of the Proms, till
AWAY SHE GOES was shouted.

I cannot help but wonder from what depths
of history and symbol the end of the rhyme
developed. It would take a chapter entire to
list and describe all the ritual games. Dad, of
course, excelled in the word games and was
never to be trusted not to change the message
completely to some witty but nonsensical
allusion to one of the gathering when playing
Russian Scandal. While the rest of us sucked
our pencils to make some sort of sense in a
'telegram', he'd have his finished in a
twinkling. One such stands out in my memory.
The word we had been given was HAPPINESS.
Dad, as always, was the first to finish, and at
the end of the timed three minutes, read out
'Have apples pears plums in now. Early
spinach stunted'. I don't know why it was
funny then, or why I can't write it all these

decades later without wanting to giggle. Maybe the psychologists would have theories about that?

We played a game called Robbing the Hen Roost. Each player was given a phrase from a story of a raid on the hen roost, which phrase only he was allowed to utter in answer to any question put to him by the MC in the middle of the ring. We always managed it so that Aunt Loll got the phrase, 'I carried the lantern', which enabled us to think up questions in advance, such as 'What part did you play in the procession at Queen Vicky's funeral?' or 'What do you remember about your wedding day?' Aunt Loll, bless her, never minded our deliberate fun at her expense. She would have been disappointed to have done anything else but 'carry the lantern'.

I was, however, thinking of Aunt Harriet when I began on this tack, and there was one game that required her tabu on getting any amusement out of religion to be broken. It was called 'Spots'. Each person in the ring had to name himself (or herself) after some character to be found in the Old Testament — Methuselah, Habbukuk, Nebuchadnezzar, Sennacherib etc. (They had to be male names.)

One person stood in the centre of the circle holding a saucer of flour. He pointed in turn to each, who gave his chosen biblical name only once — and everybody was expected to remember, a feat of memory that the whole game depended on. Then the MC would point solemnly to somebody, saying as he did do:

I, Hezekiah, of the tribe of Jehosophat, have no spots. But how many spots has thou, Daniel of the tribe of Mephibosheth?

Then whoever had been addressed had to remember not only who he was, and what tribe he had been allotted to, but everybody else's name and lineage as well, as in turn Daniel addressed Methuselah and gave him a tribe. If the wording was wrong, the name or tribe forgotten or muddled, the offender was marked by a spot of flour on his forehead. As one could not see one's own spots, it became harder and harder to recall how many spots one had collected, and this, too, was a fault for which another was added.

And there would be Aunt Harriet with flour trickling down her chin to drop off on to her bombazine finery, saying 'I, Melchizadek, being of the tribe of Magog, have seven spots. But how many spots hath thou Bill — I mean Tigath Pileser, of the tribe of Amalek?' Thereby, of course, earning her eighth 'spot'.

This was Uncle John's favourite of all the games, probably because he could only just make out three-letter-words, and liked mouthing the names he had heard so often from Aunt Harriet's supper-time Bible readings. He would end the game covered in flour, and his best, dark chapel suit would be as white down the front as his thick crop of snow-white hair. And through it all, Aunt Harriet never once put on her chapel face or mein, or turned a hair at this sending up of

330

'the Word of the Lord'. Let justice be done — she was no spoil-sport.

When the party was at our house, it was enlivened by tumblers-full of Mam's home-made orange wine, which in some years was very potent. There was little chance of anyone taking too much, because abstemiousness was a virtue trained into us, as well as being a habit acquired by necessity. Some never partook of it at all — I, for one, because from childhood I have disliked the taste of alcohol. Uncle Jim had 'taken the pledge' on oath in his youth and in all his life never broke it by accepting a glass of beer or a tot of brandy, even as a medicinal stimulant. But how he did enjoy a glass a Mam's home made wine!

Wine, by inference, was excluded from the prohibition, for does not the psalmist say: *'and wine, that maketh glad the heart of man'*?

Our hearts were glad enough, on such occasions, without alcohol to make them so. And as the storm lanterns were being lit to guide each party home through the snow, or down the sodden drove, Lois at the piano or Doris at the organ (or Elsie, if she happened to be visiting) would be playing 'God be with us till we meet again'.

There is a touch of nostalgic sentiment as I recall the sound of the singing, the smell of the lanterns, the sight of Uncle John's flour-spotted waistcoat. I know just how Walter de la Mare felt when he wrote *'Where's the Queen of Sheba? Where's King Solomon?'* Of all who ever attended our family parties only three are left — Elsie (now ninety-three), Ruby and Sybil. Except for the three of us, all the rest, like Bathsheba and Solomon, are *'Gone, gone, gone!'*

9

School Days

I know, because I have been told, that I started school when I was five, but I have no recollection whatsoever of it. I turned five a couple of weeks after the Armistice in November 1918, and I guess that everybody thought it sensible that I should make my debut there when school reopened after Christmas; but that coincided with Grammam's illness and death, which event traumatically overshadowed everything else for a long time. I seem to recall vaguely having a lot of headaches and colds and stomach upsets which prevented me from going to school. I suspect now that they were Mam's inventions far more than my own. With Grammam gone, Mam's life was disoriented: and, superstitious as she always was, her nerve had given out — witness the story, already told, of the handkerchief. Lois was at the grammar school, and had gone away all day: Gerald was working alongside Dad on the farm. I can quite see how Mam would have dreaded spending long days alone in the house. At least I was something else living, and a pair of good ears for her.

Dad must have understood her need, too, I believe, or he would have been worried that I was not keeping up, educationally, with other youngsters like Jess, for example. She had started school at four, and being one of a large and exceedingly clever family, was already able to read and 'sum', or so it was said. I have no reason to doubt it: I have known many children able to read fluently, with understanding, before the age of five.

Whatever the reason, my sporadic attendance tailed off until it became total absence, because the headaches, sore throats and general listlessness became real. By the time I was well enough to start going again, I was already seven-and-a-half years old.

No-one then could possibly have foreseen that the still pale, still 'backward' child I was would have somehow found her way in the end to Cambridge university, or have become quite a well-known name in the field of education: but thus it was, and after fifty years of teaching everything from infants to post-graduates, I'm afraid the 'educationist' in me is bound to pop up and have her say here and there.

Dad and Mam (ten years apart) had both attended the school endowed by the Fellowes family opposite St Mary's Church, controlled in all its doings by the Anglican church, and overlooked, quite literally, by the parson. But following the Balfour Education Act of 1902, new 'council' schools to cater for the whole age range from five to fourteen were built, one almost opposite to Grandmother's farm in New Fen, the Heights School, and one the other side of the river to serve the Herne and Daintree.

When Gerald and Lois trudged about a mile and a half up the drove and along the high road to the Heights School, it was still in its first few years of existence. By the time I began to attend regularly in 1920, all I had to do was to cross the road about a hundred yards from our front gate.

I suppose most children, even now, accept schooling as inevitable, either in patient endurance or pleasant resignation, as part of the life adults decree for them. I don't remember having any particular feelings towards it at all, except that one never knew what the day might bring, pleasant or unpleasant. I can't remember ever feeling that it was incumbent upon me to 'try hard' to do anything in particular. I knew that at ten some children 'got scholarships' to the grammar school, and that Jess would be one of them, because her family seemed to follow each other there like ducks to a pond. I believe I took it for granted that by some chance or other Joyce and I would be translated thither — but I had no consciousness at all of working towards it. Trying hard to recapture my feelings about school in general after sixty-five years, I am surprised to find how the three years I spent at the Heights School seemed just to have drifted by in a generally pleasant, but as far as I was concerned aimless, dream.

It did not begin that way, however. My first day back at school was not a pleasant one. I found myself, aged seven-and-a-half, still a bit pale and long rather than tunky (which I soon became), sitting at a very low table on a very tiny chair in the company of three other four-year-old entrants.

I will not be made to believe that I could not read by then. Indeed, I am quite sure that I could, because I do remember my puzzlement at an extraordinary bit of ritual that I was enjoined to take part in that first day. I stood with the rest of the babies before 'Old Granny' (our head-teacher's mother) who was holding up cards about nine inches square containing large red capital letters. She held up three at a time — or, at least, one at a time till she held three — and we were obliged to repeat after her whatever she said in her high-pitched, 'put-on', genteel voice. As she raised the cards, she squeaked R-A-T: Rat. C-A-T: Cat, and so on to S-A-T: Sat.

I didn't know what this game was supposed to be in aid of, though I quite enjoyed it. I can't be blamed for not connecting it with what I already understood as 'reading'. I know that I had not been taught to read, but I'm equally sure that I had already absorbed the skill from having been always in the company of books and readers, read to by Dad every single day, and born precociously word-conscious. (I know from experience how easily some children can do this without effort at all — they just read.)

On the other hand, I had only a very basic concept of number, and I suspect that it was this inadequacy on my part that led to the decision to place me among the four-year-old entrants.

The infant teacher was the younger, completely unqualified sister of Miss, our head teacher. As they both had the same surname, we called our infant 'supplementary teacher' (her grading in the teaching hierarchy, not her role) by her Christian name, Miss Mabel. It was their widowed mother, 'Old Granny', who was the real 'supplementary' teacher, called in to help in any emergency. (I wonder, now, if she got paid for her services?) She was certainly called in very often, in any part of the school, to 'teach' any subject. As I say, she strove to be 'superior' to all her local yokel neighbours, as I believe she regarded them. After all, was she not the widow of a station master?

All of us who endured her mode of teaching have memories of her — dropping off to sleep, for example, in front of the class, and making no effort to rouse herself. Lois never forgot the time when Granny was supervising a needlework class, and Lois had reached the crucial point at which the heel of a sock had to be turned. She approached the slight, black-clad figure sitting with closed eyes before the rows of desks, and asked for help and instruction.

Granny half-opened her eyes to see who it was, and then said reedily 'Lois, you are quate old enough to use your own jadgement.' Lois was approximately nine at the time.

Gerald, on the other hand, went home one day and told Dad about that morning's scripture lesson, conducted by Granny. Gerald was thirteen, and most of the other boys in the class ranged from ten upwards. The method employed by Granny was for the boys to read aloud from the Bible, taking a verse each from whatever passage their elderly teacher hit upon. I think she cannot have given much time or thought to the preparation of her lesson, because what she required them to read that day was whatever bit of the Old Testament it is that includes the phrase 'and every man that pisseth against the wall'. Well, according to Gerald, whichever 'ol' bor' it was who got to the dubious word refused to speak it, and stuck. I doubt if ever such wholehearted attention had been given to a scripture lesson by a gang of boys before, or for that matter, since, as they all held their breath to see what would happen. At last, opening her eyes and scanning the Bible on her knee, Granny put on her squeakiest voice, pursed her lips to a prunes and prisms shape, and in as ladylike a manner as possible, pushed the business on.

'Piss-eth,' she said. 'Next boy.'

This was too good a 'mo'sel' for Dad to keep to himself. I'm not at all sure whether it is a measure of our enlightenment or our basic crudity that it was henceforth added to the list of impersonations we were always asking Mam to do for us.

Now Miss Mabel was a frequent visitor to our house, and must have known my general state of intelligence; but her job was to teach me what I didn't know, and this no doubt accounts for the indignity I felt at being put down with 'the babies'.

She came up to me, and placed on the table in front of me a grubby little linen bag drawn up tightly at the neck. 'I want you to count out ten of these and put them in a straight line on your table,' she said.

Surely I must have been able to count up to ten already? However that may have been, I undid the bag as instructed, and plunged my hand in. When I took it out again, I held a fistful of small cowrie shells.

I was enchanted. I had never before seen or touched any inanimate objects so gloriously, satisfyingly, thrillingly exquisite. I examined them one by one with ecstatic delight, especially on the underside where the tiny-toothed, scalloped edge curled inward like a miniature wave on a fairyland beach as its warm creaminess disappeared into the mysterious darkness of the shell's interior. I picked them up one by one to rub their silkiness across my lips, the tactile pleasure of their smoothness attracting me almost as much as their shape and colour. They transported me to a world of sensual delight, and I was enraptured by it.

Miss Mabel returned. I had forgotten about putting ten shells out in a line. I had not obeyed her instruction. Now Miss Mabel was in general a rather timid, gentle soul, very much second-fiddle to her more important and forceful older sister; but she seemed to find my disobedience infuriating. She denounced me as a dunce, loudly proclaiming the disgrace of a girl of seven who had to sit with the babies because she couldn't count up to ten. I wriggled with embarrassment and humiliation, but my disgrace was not keen enough to neutralise my pleasure in the shells. I was consumed by desire. I wanted one of them for my very own. Surely, one would not be missed out of so many? All around me, infant tables were littered with them. I fought a moral battle, my desire against the sixth commandment, of which I was quite well aware;

and conscience won. I put every single shell reluctantly back into its linen bag and drew up the string. Sadly I dropped the bag into the box held out before me by that day's monitor. I saw them on other children's desks in the days that followed, but I was never given cowrie shells to count with again. Why?

I think I know. I believe Miss Mabel had observed my behaviour with those shells only too well, and too closely for her own prim comfort. She was already 'an old maid', never likely to marry. I cannot but conclude that she found my obvious sensual pleasure in those cowrie-shells far too close to a sexual one for her own peace of mind.

My love for cowrie shells has never diminished. I keep one, about the size of a pea, in my purse — a nest-egg for good luck. Others lie about where I can touch them as I pass. It is very strange that their brown-and-white circular patterns have no phobic effect on me whatsoever, though the school incident came a year or more after my butterfly nightmare.

I really did not intend to start on my recollections of school with a touch of professional criticism, though I shall have other professional reservations, no doubt, gained from hindsight; but all of them together cannot dull the astonishment I feel now when I survey from a distance of sixty odd years not what we did not learn, but what we did.

Let me make it quite clear. I was only at the Heights Elementary School for three years, leaving at Easter 1924 to become a fee-paying pupil at Ramsey Grammar School. But what a foundation I had been given at my first school for the second, equally good, to build on!

At the Heights School, our Miss taught in 'the big room' all the children from nine to fourteen. As she was the head-teacher, she had all the administration to cope with as well, completely unaided by any school secretary, or non-teaching helper or anything else of the kind. If the good Lord sent her a cripple or a mongol or a cretin or the village idiot (we dared call a spade a spade in those crude days) she had to take it, or them, in her stride. She had to cope at lunch times with those who came from the depths of the fens too far to go home, and therefore brought their dockey with them (often it consisted of a large potato, well scrubbed, to roast on top of the old Tortoise stove).

Fenland boys when they reached their teens were not exactly amenable to book-learning. They felt they should be out earning, and resented a law that kept them sitting at desks too small for them reading verses from the Bible, however interesting, to Old Granny's sleepy ears. A lot of both sexes escaped I think, once past the age of twelve, no doubt with the connivance of Miss. But some stayed on — Gerald, for example — to the age of thirteen plus. They cannot have been easy to discipline, yet somehow she managed. She had one thing on her side, of course — authority. Authority was handed down ultimately from God, so any kind of authority was respected. Parents — in general the natural enemies of school teachers in those days — might resent authority, but they rarely flouted it openly. Even Grandad Rattles had made sure his children went to school.

With hindsight, one could have forgiven Miss for keeping the school open and getting away with as little in the way of teaching as she could; but it was not so. Every subject now included in the 'new' National Curriculum was there on our timetable, except for Design and Technology, and Computer Studies — the latter for obvious reasons.

Having started late, I only had one year in the Junior room with Miss Ellie before reaching 'the big room' at the age of nine. At first we sat in long desks with no backs, designed to hold six of us because there were only six cracked, sticky inkwells, filled once a week with thin watery ink made from an evil-smelling powder and water. After a week the awful stuff corroded the pin-pointed steel nibs we were just trying to learn to use — but to get a new pen-nib out of Miss was like getting something from the treasure guarded by Fafnir the dragon. One simply dared not ask. In spite of there being six inkwells, the long backless seats held seven of us. Joyce and I sat together in the back row, and disgraced ouselves dreadfully in our first week there by getting a fit of the giggles. We had been asked to learn a bit of verse called *The Rainbow Fairies*, the first stanza of which was:

Two little clouds one summer's day
Went flying through the sky.
They went so fast, they bumped their
    heads
And both began to cry.

I don't know now what made it appear so hilariously funny to us, but when it came to our turn to stand up and say it, we couldn't. Being told, severely, to sit down till we could control ourselves, we did so, cracked out heads together, and found that two little woollen bobbles at the neck of Joyce's jumper had somehow become entangled round a button on my blouse. What a silly little incident, like 'Four ducks on a pond':

To remember for years,
To remember with tears.

During the second year in 'the big room', we progressed to iron-shod 'dual desks'. Miss took this opportunity of separating me from Joyce — no doubt lest we stimulated each other to laughter instead of work. Outside the classroom, we were still inseparable, as we remained till we were twenty and our ways inevitably parted.

I have no idea how Miss regarded my educational potential. I am sure I was not thought of as clever in the same way as Jess was, probably because, as far as I remember, I never had the least element of competitiveness in me. As long as I kept out of trouble for not doing anything wrong, I just floated along comfortably, for most of the time, enjoying all the mysteries of education.

Though still utterly uncomprehending of anything mathematical, I was bright enough to learn the tricks required to get my sums right. My sum book thus displaying at the end of each day the required number of blue ticks instead of kisses, my teacher had every reason to believe that I knew what I was doing. In truth, I had no more idea what it was all about than (to quote Dad) 'a cat knows about Holy Communion'. I had to wait until at around the age of fifteen a sudden understanding and consequent interest in algebra raised the curtain on arithmetic for me. Maybe the real difficulty was that practically every other subject was based on words, and where words were concerned, I soaked the matter up without effort, and with a good deal of pleasure. I was lucky. There was only one other subject besides arithmetic that I did not catch on to — ever, though I longed to with all my heart. I'll come back to that later.

Children who did not have my gift of absorbing words paid all ways round for their helpless inadequacy. Corporal punishment was freely applied as a corrector of incomprehension. Our Miss was not merely quite handy with the cane; she could be, and often was, positively vicious. I am in no position to judge her for its use as a keeper of some sort of discipline over boys bigger and stronger than she was, but I can't believe the cane has ever helped any child to understand anything. In our case, the cane was applied for any and every misdemeanour from talking in class or forgetting your handkerchief to saying words you did not know were forbidden, or being half a minute late.

The school day began by Miss appearing at the door to the girls' playground, lustily clanking a handbell. Miss Ellie performed the same duty at the boys' door. At the back of the school building, the playgrounds were divided by a high

344

brick wall, a row of back-to-back toilets, and a covered playground area each side in which to take shelter on wet days.

In the front, the paved yards were separated only by a row of red, spiked iron railings — through which it was forbidden, on pain of *really* getting the cane to converse or communicate in any way whatsoever with the opposite sex.

On the first sound of the bell, we froze like statues on the spot, though all raising our voices to top pitch to warn those 'round the back'. 'All in! All in!' we yelled. (I must have been well into my teens before I realised that 'All in' was not the magic equivalent to 'Open Sesame' or 'Hey Presto', but merely a union-like command of 'All in' instead of 'All out'.)

Miss commanded us to 'form lines', and with military-like precision we obeyed, until class by class we were admitted, edging one by one in front of the august personage in the doorway. Once we had been shepherded inside, Miss followed. We answered our names standing, and then 'hands together, eyes closed,' gabbled our morning prayer, and sat down to our daily ration of the scriptures. I use the plural deliberately, for what we had was not what was later known as 'Scripture' or the Scripture lesson. Miss knew quite well that all of us were well acquainted already with those stories from either of the Testaments that were sexually respectable, and she did not make the mistake of duplicating our religious knowledge, or of muddling us with a different version from Old Henry's, for example. Instead, she set us the task of learning yet another passage from the Bible by heart.

(Having been head of a village school, single-handed, for eighteen years myself, I know why Miss made us learn instead of teaching us what we already knew. She had a mountain of other bits and pieces to attend to first thing every morning.)

Perhaps the rest were not as consciously interested as I was; perhaps they were robbed of any pleasure in the task set them by the knowledge that failure to learn the passage might result in getting the cane; but whether they enjoyed it or not, they absorbed a lot of it, and I suppose some of this was because the clan as a whole had a predeliction for words.

If they suffered, I didn't. I only ever had to read a passage through twice, listen inwardly to my own voice repeating it, and I had got it.

We were learning by rote. Just fancy — being subjected to that terrible method against which all teachers who are anti-Baker and all his works are wearing out their voices vociferously denouncing at present. How can it be that any of my generation ever became imaginatively perceptive enough to come in out of the rain. O dear! I'm still restricted by Grandmother's adamant rules against swearing — but my instinctive reaction is what BLOODY NONSENSE all this hormpolodge against a bit of learning by rote is. It only means repeating from memory after all. What is more, children love doing it, and do it all the time with bits of their own lore you would sometimes prefer them not to air in public. How long does it take any child to memorise a rude rhyme? Such as, for example:

I ran a bug around a mill
I have his blood. He knows I will.

Absolutely respectable until you say it fast. How many children don't know:

Old Mother Riley bought a cow
She tried to milk it, but didn't know how
. . .

— or one of its many different versions?
How many children in cathedral, church or chapel choirs have not sung ribald words to Christmas carols?

O how drastic
Loose elastic
Giving all a perfect sight

(In most cases, far more lines of verse than the 1989 Act suggests they should memorise.)
What we learned was not the spurious verse or poetry (so-called) of today. It was either skilled poetry, or prose written when English was at its very peak of dignity and beauty, the seventeenth-century. Maybe for many it was at the time a difficult chore, but for a few of us, who learned them by heart, the words worked their own magic.
How, then or now, could I not thrill to such wonderful phrases and magic rhythms of:

The heavens declare the glory of God, and
the firmament showeth his handiwork.

Day unto day uttereth speech, and night
    unto night
Showeth knowledge.

and

Happy is the man that findeth wisdom, and
the man that getteth understanding: for the
merchandise of it is better than the merchandise
of silver, and the gain thereof than fine gold.

Other passages had an added appeal to me
because of my ability, already mentioned, to
visualise words into pictures in my mind's eye.
Take Psalm CIV, for example:

Bless the Lord, O my soul. O Lord my God,
thou art very great: thou art clothed with
honour and majesty. Who coverest thyself with
light as with a garment: who stretchest out the
heavens like a curtain: who maketh the clouds
his chariot: who walketh upon the wings of the
wind . . .

Sometimes, it was the perverse attraction of their
incomprehensibility that held me, and exercised
my mind. Psalm CI, for instance:

I will lift up mine eyes to the hills, from
whence cometh my help.

What hills? The only hills we had actual
experience of were Upwood Hill, Bury Hill, or
Shillow — places where Dad had to let our old

348

pony walk instead of trot. I knew, as fact quite unrelated to experience, about the Chiltern hills and the Cheviot hills; but I considered that if I had really needed help urgently, even Upwood Hill would have been too far away to be of much use. I have spent a lifetime investigating, and delighting in the nature of children's logic. It boils down, inevitably, to their valiant attempts to solve the unknown by means of known experience. Out of reach of any practical experience was the yet more astounding injunction of Chapter LV of Isaiah:

Ho, every one that thirsteth, come ye to the waters, and he that hath no money, come ye, buy and eat; yea, come, buy wine and milk, without money and without price.

That one really was a bit of a facer. But I stored it, along with the rest, at the bottom of my mind in the same way as a hamster stores food in his cheek, for later digestion. I can't say I ever got any religious solace from all this — and yet? If such words, or music, or art uplifts the human spirit, this surely brings it as near to whatever gods there be as anything can.

When I recall 'the big room' at school, I see in my mind's eye a bookcase on which the shelves bore piles of thin, cardboard-covered books, all uniformly of a dull, faded, grey-green colour. From them I discovered that the cover of a book is no guide to its contents, any more than the wrinkled brown skin of a russet apple is to the taste of it around Christmas time. Those

349

dreadful covers enclosed 'the old leg-ends of Greece' (as a child once read aloud).

Unfortunately, the editor of this particular series had striven to make his material more easily accessible to young readers by breaking up the words into syllables. It was a bit distracting to have to reconstitute sentences such as 'So he de-ci-ded to con-sult the o-rac-le of A-pol-lo at Del-phi', but one soon got accustomed to it. At least, I speak for myself, and it did not detract from the magic of the stories.

I was at this time in my tenth year, and already an avid reader, acquainted with many of the works of Dickens, Twain and Harrison Ainsworth, from having had them read aloud to me by Dad. I had a fair library of my own — my Christmas *Chatterbox* annuals side by side with bound volumes of the *Girls Own Paper* (rescued from the 'London Muck'). Lois, who would by this time be in her nineteenth year, favoured Ethel M. Dell and Florence Barclay, which I used to steal and read at bedtime by the light of a flickering candle — substituting one of my Sunday School prizes if footsteps sounded on the stairs. One could also be pretty sure that an unannounced visit to Aunt Harriet would find *East Lynne* or any other novel novel by Mrs Henry Wood lying open on the table among the dirty crocks and the crochet-cotton, so that if one got in quietly enough when she was having forty winks, there was time for a surreptitious read.

As food to a hungry boy, whatever sort of print it was, it all went the same way down as far as I was concerned. At about the age of thirteen

I discovered the Mars books of Edgar Rice Burroughs, the westerns of Zane Grey, and the romantic fiction of Jeffery Farnol. They provided a perfect balance to the classics of Jane Austen, Meredith, George Eliot and Thomas Hardy I was being encouraged to read at school. It turned me into the catholic reader I still am today.

We did English composition every day. I found this more frustrating than pleasurable, though I spent a lot of time doing it to please myself at home. There were all sorts of reasons for my frustration. We were allotted only half an hour for it, so there was never enough time to finish, or get down all the ideas one had. Those awful crossed pen nibs, corroded by the nasty-smelling ink, took any pleasure out of the activity of handwriting (such as I am enjoying at this very moment with pristine unlined paper and the bite of my fountain-pen's gold square italic nib).

We were taught a copperplate hand, which we practised every day and which can look beautiful; but it is related more nearly to a graving tool than a pen-nib, and quite unsuitable for young fingers. We learned how to do it by copying out a proverb or a wise saying each day:

Speech is silvern, but silence is golden.
Great oaks from little acorns grow.
Daylight peeps through very small win-
    dows.

— and so on. What a pity it is that such literary pithiness is now derided as cliché.

The subjects set for our compositions varied

widely, though it was not often we were given a title that inspired much creativity, the objective being that we should be able to construct intelligible sentences, not immortal prose. No doubt that Miss, surveying her class of thirty or more mixed tiger-cubs ranging in age from nine to fourteen, was justified in her assumption that most of us would eventually find occupation on the fenland fields, either traumpling along behind a cart or a plough, or crawling on hands and knees weeding onions or singling sugar-beet.

She probably believed that any of us who had enough sense to go into good service were the lucky ones. Be that as it may, she strove to instil into us such knowledge as might be useful to us as kitchenmaids, while at the same time doing her best to polish our use of language; so we were given a lesson on 'How to light a fire', or 'The proper order of washing up', and then commanded to write in a composition what we had learned. I don't know what the boys did while we wrote 'Wash glass first, then cutlery, then silver, then china. Leave all cooking utensils till last.' I can hardly credit that Miss took it upon herself to teach them how to draw a straight furrow, or the optimum depth to set potatoes and celery plants.

Another bee in the bonnet of our Miss was that we must all know how to write a letter of application for a job, concentrating on the rigid rules thereof. She was adamant that no letter, of whatever kind, should ever begin with the pronoun I, since this showed arrogance and self-conceit past all bearing. Though I cannot now see that it matters, I nevertheless still go to considerable trouble to avoid putting myself forward in such an unseemly manner when writing a letter. Just another example of the truth of the old adage that 'As the twig is bent, so shall the tree grow.'

I have in passing dealt with history, which I always found fascinating, even if any facts we learned were of dubious accuracy. Still, it was nice to know that:

> King Henry the Eighth to six spouses was
> wedded:
> One died, one survived, two divorced, two
> beheaded.

I imagine we did *know* the meaning of divorce? Not that we could have cared: those bloodily beheaded were the only truly interesting ones.

Geography consisted almost entirely of facts about the British Isles. With a map hanging over the blackboard in front of us, we learned facts of such number and in such a manner as to have satisfied even Mr Gradgrind![1]

I could, at the age of ten, have placed any range of mountains or hills correctly on a blank map of the British Isles, named the range, located and named its highest peak and given the height of it in feet (much good that ever did me). I could recite the names of the chief rivers, beginning Dee, Don, Spey, Tweed, Forth, Tay . . . , with a special warming of voice when in

---

[1] *Hard Times* by Charles Dickens.

unison we reached Witham, Welland, Nene and Great Ouse. I had actually been on a punt on the Great Ouse at St Ives, as well as hearing men grumbling about paying 'th'ol' Ousel' drainage rate.

Next were all the large industrial towns, and the chief products made there: Sheffield for knives and scissors; Middlesborough for railway engines; Manchester for cotton; Bradford for wool; Batley for shoddy; Macclesfield for silk; Redditch for needles; Hanley, Burslem, Turnstall, Stoke-on-Trent and Newcastle-under-Lyme for pottery; Yarmouth for herrings; Walsall, Wolverhampton and Wednesbury for locks and keys; and Birmingham — ah! Birmingham! — for everything, we were told, from a pin to a traction engine.

Now if there ever was any worse educational lumber than this, I should like to hear of it — yet it had, for me, an indescribable (and surely incomprehensible?) distant magic. Who could resist the enticing invitation of Walsall, Wolverhampton and Wednesbury? Or, for that matter, the equal enticement of sea-crossings? Larne to Stranraer; Dover to Calais; Harwich to the Hook of Holland; Milford Haven to Fishguard.

Dreams of impossible romance; but not dreams with much factual substance behind them. Just a mish-mash of half-understood words. If this were so to me, what must it have been to most of my contemporaries? Perhaps they understood better than I did, because maybe they listened while I went off chasing rainbows created by the sounds of words. Teaching was, of course, all done by talk and chalk. We had maps — but no geography books; if we had had such things, there would have been no pictures. I was a teacher myself before I saw a set of geography books with pictures of an Eskimo, a Tuareg with a camel, a Maori with a canoe and so on (all by that time on their way out of the past and into a new, twentieth-century, shrinking world).

I'm struck by my own ignorance of real hills — while at the same time knowing so many facts about the geography of the British Isles. I had seen pictures of hills and mountains in a biblical context; perhaps that is why I didn't make the connection that Jesus in his bedgown preaching his sermon on the mount had any remote relationship with geography. We sang 'From Greenland's Icy Mountains' and 'Hills of the North Rejoice', as well as being quite aware of the 'Green Hill Far Away' that was remarkable having no city wall round it. But *hills?* They were truly out of my ken. I knew, because Miss had said so, that the Wrekin sort of stood by itself. I had a mental picture of it — exactly like a giant version of one of the ubiquitous traffic-cones of today. Therefore 'a range of mountains' was a long line of enormous traffic-cones (surely I don't really have to say that there was no traffic then, so the traffic-cone belonged in my imagination only — a futuristic bit of science fiction).

Now if you don't believe that a reasonably intelligent child could possibly have had a store of such knowledge as the height of Ben Nevis or Scafell without knowing what a hill was, I can only suggest that you go as far as you can get down one of the droves that lead to Raveley Drain, and take a look all round you to where the horizon rests on the earth. That will teach you!

Of course, the educational point that it makes is no longer valid. Children now have access to the whole world, and know the surface of the moon by sight as well as they do their own back yard or street. We didn't. We didn't even have picture postcards sent by friends and relatives who had been away on holiday, because if anybody ever did leave the fen, they were not likely to spend money on a card or postage at a penny a time.

Our Miss used to go away, with Granny and Miss Mabel, for about two weeks each summer holiday. While she had gone, Aunt Harriet had the key of the schoolhouse, and kept an eye on it. When Aunt Harriet died, among her treasures was a bundle of cards very carefully wrapped up. One or two of them would indeed be treasures now, for they were of silk and from the front line of the Great War. The bulk of the cards so carefully preserved, however, were from our Miss to tell Aunt Harriet when the family proposed to return. Alas, no pictures of romantic places. For four years in succession, Miss had sent the same identical card — a picture of the Three Counties' Lunatic Asylum at Arlesey.

Somehow, I cannot bring myself to feel any shame that I did not make any connection between a picture of Jesus in his bedgown making extraordinary statements on the Mount of Olives and what I knew as geography.

Manchester had a whiff of reality because we had some relations there, and every year Aunt Eva and a cousin or two came from Sheffield. Joyce went to Long Melford, in Suffolk, for her holidays. I envied her such knowledge of the world. In my tenth year, Miss and her family went to Yarmouth for a fortnight, and took me with them. But my little shell was about to be broken open in any case. Somebody showed me a relief map of the British Isles that had been there, in school, all the time: Miss (I cannot now imagine in what context) quoted Elizabeth Barratt Browning on the subject:

As if God's finger touched, but did not
   press
In making England.

That went home. I began to understand. In that year, too, Dad indulged his own love of books by buying all three of us a set worth having. Gerald got *Harmsworth's Popular Science*, Lois a whole set of Dickens, and I got Arthur Mee's *Children's Encyclopedia* (ten volumes). Never have books been more appreciated. It would be difficult to say which of us pored longer over our mines of information, Gerald or I. Lois did not live with hers as we did (though of course, Dad supplemented his own reading with those he had not met before, and I in turn used them when I was studying English later on. They are still in existence, and the set is still intact, though Lois herself has gone. She loved music more than reading.)
   That year, too, brought my entrance to the

Grammar School, and a new life opened for me; but I have not nearly finished with my elementary school yet, and the wonders of what I did learn there.

We did drawing once a week, with a sharply-pointed HB pencil and a drawing-book of expensive cartridge paper. It had no relation to art. We did no science as such, but we did do Nature Study. Being pretty well-versed in practical knowledge of wild flowers and grasses by gathering them by the armful, we advanced to botany's terminology, which delighted me if it perplexed a good many of my peers. I knew and could identify sepals and pistils and stamens and calyxes, monocotyledons and bi-cotyledons, radicles and tubers and bulbs and corms, the thoraxes of six-legged insects and how many legs an arachnid had. We learned (in our case quite unnecessarily) that corn was not wheat, barley, oats, or rye, but included all of them. We even had a lesson on how to tell one crop from another — most of us with barley-awns sticking through our garments and a pocketful of not-quite-ready-to-cut wheat to chew. If you chewed it long enough without swallowing, it became a good substitute for chewing gum.

The boys did handwork — a cane bowl or a raffia mat that as far as I remember never did get finished — while the girls did needlework. I'm afraid I did not find hemming a duster or practising a run-and-fell seam under Granny's instruction very inspiring. I had actually graduated to making myself a pair of calico drawers (long outdated in my case) when to my relief I left them unfinished to go to the Grammar School; but Miss herself taught me things for which I have ever since been grateful — how to do different sorts of darns, how to apply patches of different shapes and materials, and how to make buttonholes with the correct number of stitches in the bar at one end, and the eye at the other.

We knitted from the infant class upward. I made my own first wearable jumper aged eight, and scandalised my parents by turning up to our late Sunday School Superintendant's funeral in it. They thought I was safely in school, but apparently all other chapel children but me had been briefed to go suitably dressed so as to be let out of school to attend the funeral. When Miss announced that it was time for all those who attended the chapel Sunday School to leave, I got up and went with the rest, though I had no inkling where we were going and why. When Mam and Dad, in their best black, joined the rest of the black-clad congregation, there was one terribly jarring note of crude, bright emerald green sitting right up front — me, in my first hand-knitted jumper, all dropped stitches and holes, as well as being without shape, let alone fit. It was Mam who had the fit.

We graduated to four needles when we went into the big room, and were supposed to know how to turn the heel of a sock before we left school. All very satisfying and long-lasting accomplishments.

I am amused at the thought of what we quite correctly called drill — because that is exactly what it was, army-fashion. We performed it in the playgrounds (boys and girls separately — that goes without saying) if at all possible; if not standing behind our desks. The Great War had come to an end, but not our barrack-square antics. Miss, sergeant major-fashion, stood before us and shouted 'Ten-shun! Stand at . . . ease! Form . . . fours! Right . . . dress! Quick . . . march!' We hadn't the faintest idea what it was meant to do for us, and I can't think that Miss had, either. In school, we did arms forward stretch — arms upward stretch — arms bend etc., etc., with rapid changes to catch the sleepy-headed out. How laughable it must have been — peaceful little country bumpkins being, apparently, trained for the front line! What *would* the investigative journalists of today's media have made of it?

We learned country dancing — pure delight to me. Then there was Empire Day (24th May) when first of all we sang the National Anthem and a few national songs — not folk songs, but one song to represent all the countries in the United Kingdom. 'The Ash Grove', 'Men of Harlech', 'Annie Laurie' and 'The Harp that Once'.

After that the girls, crowned with daisy chains, went out into the playground and performed set maypole dances — the Barber's Pole, the Spider's Web, and the Mill Wheel, amongst others I can't call to mind. The Mill Wheel was accompanied by song, the words of which I was never quite sure of as we were never taught them. We were expected to pick them up from the others. It was much the same for the

National Songs, and the folk songs (Cecil Sharpe's book was very much in vogue then). I think I must have known the words of every single song in that book, and there is yet another thing learned young that has stood me in very good stead all my life — especially for singing babies to sleep, and for getting classes of primary children to sing, happily and spontaneously, while clearing up after a dirty paint or clay session, or while sitting patiently waiting for our hot dinners to arrive cold, when school dinners at last reached the rural fastness of my tiny village school in Cambridgeshire.

We were the last of seven villages on the itinerary from the central kitchen, so the van went on a long and wandering journey round six other schools before it got to us. What we got, when we did get it, was hardly *haute cuisine*. I often felt that a large, well scrubbed spud roasted on the top of our old Tortoise stove would have been much more appetising for the children. I took it as a great compliment when one day an eleven-year-old girl, server for that day, lifted the lid from the thermos container before her and announced to the rest: 'Oh! We've got that great, grey-green, greasy Limpopo gravy again!'

What the container held was an already congealing mess of white mutton stew. It surely proved that I was enthusing others with my own love of the sound of words.

Back to my own elementary school experiences. Songs there were reserved for music lessons — each of which, for me, began with ten minutes or so of plain torture.

I could not, and never did, catch on to what tonic sol-fa was all about. I still haven't — though as the voice which, though not musical, was at least able to sing in tune has departed this life ahead of the rest of me, it doesn't matter much now that I could not produce a musical interval on command to save myself from extinction. But this is the one thing that all my life has eluded me, and defeated me. Even my Stretton blood fails me. Here is my Achilles heel. I am convinced that, had Miss decreed we should learn Urdu and Serbo-Croat for a Christmas concert, I should have had little trouble, and taken it in my stride. But that mumbo-jumbo of modulator, pointer, strange, witchlike and bewildering hand-signals, while all the children around me either growled on low note, or leapt about vocally like parched peas in a colander, or 'chaffy grain beneath the thresher's flail' making neither melody nor rhythm of it. What on earth was the purpose of it?

Nobody ever explained it — though it seemed that everybody else knew and understood. And when at last I did ask my cousin Elsie and her extremely musical husband, their astounded reaction to my ignorance was one of such ludicrous disbelief that they laughed till the chance for a bit of instruction was snatched from me by the equivalent of 'the person from Porlock' — somebody at the door.

The arithmetical block eventually moved: the tonic sol-fa block is as solid as ever.

Now if only Miss had but once informed me what her queer monosyllables and extraordinary gestures meant. But she didn't. I could not guess, so this was 'a door to which I found no key'. I hated not being able to do things well. I suffered more in the ten minutes of tonic sol-fa than in any other event of my whole educational life.

After the torture, we sang, and that was good. I loved it, especially when we learned a new song, so that I was with it right from the start. For most of the national or folk-songs it was expected that the younger pupils would pick up the words and the tune from the older ones as they sang. Best of all was when Miss went a bit up-market, and taught us a new song such as *My Mother Bids me Bind my Hair* (Schubert) or *Where e'er You Walk*. We had more satisfying music there than ever my Grammar School offered — which is an accolade Miss Lawrence well deserved.

On the question of poetry, I must bring my friends in. There were several of us gathered round my table quite recently.

Bill (Bedford) was born six months after me, down Harper's Drove. It was in Bill's grand-mother's arms that I was held at the landing window to watch Grandmother being taken for her 'bloody j'yride'.

I have sometimes thought how much we resemble a bundle of celery, such as used to be grown down the fen. Each of us represents a stick in the same bundle, all alike, and all with the black soil still clinging round our roots. And just as the heads of celery were tied with string to make a bundle, so we are all tied together by the threads of kinship.

One Sunday, just as my guests were about to leave, I turned to ask Russ a question. John (another Edwards) was standing by, ready to go, and so were Bill and Geoff. Russ is my exact contemporary; Bill six months younger; John younger than Bill and Geoff younger by more than a decade: but age has little to do with our kinship of spirit. Under such circumstances, leave taking is regretful, and always a long-drawn-out affair. Just as the last goodbye has been said, and half the visiting party is already outside the back door, somebody remembers something that he wants to say 'while he thinks on it' — and back inside they all troop.

It was at just such a point of departure that I remembered what I wanted to ask Russ.

'Russ,' I said. 'Do you remember any of the poetry we learned down the Heights School?'

Russ's face was a study of delighted remembrance.

'Ah, Sybil!' he said 'Now you are talking my subject. I used to love the poetry lessons above everything else. Now let's see. Well, first of all, there was *The Monk Felix*'.

'So there was', I said, and began to quote:

One morning, all alone
Out of his convent of grey stone . . .

and on we went . . .

('Cor!' interjected Tib. 'Ain't you tew got good memories!')

But Russ and I had got well going, and couldn't be stopped. We fished up and recited several other poems, each trying to cap the other. The rest stood silently by.

I said *Home Thoughts from Abroad* — but before I could go on John spoke.

'O, *to be in England, now that April's there*' he said, and we in turn stood quiet till he reached '*That first fine careless rapture!*'

I wonder where else in England you could find another group of men, either retired or nearing retirement age, who left school at fourteen and have worked on the land ever since, nor had the benefit of any education other than that of their village school, so tuned in to real poetry?

We had been subjected to it from a very early age, it is true; but I think also that it was in our blood. We just took to it, like ducks to water.

Russ and I have since tried to put together a list of those we both remember. I left that school at the age of ten: Russ stayed on there till he left school.

The following list contains many we can both still say. There are in it some that Russ does not recall, but I am absolutely certain that it was there that I learned those starred with an asterisk. Because I had my *Children's Encyclopedia*, with its very full poetry section, in my tenth year, I cannot be absolutely certain that I did not absorb the others from poring over them in print. There is no question but that I knew them all before I ever set foot in the Grammar School.

*The Monk Felix (Browning?)
*Home Thoughts from Abroad (Browning)

365

*Paul Revere
*The Slave's Dream
The Wreck of the Hesperus (Longfellow)
The Battle of Hohenlinden (Campbell)
Sir Patrick Spens
Lord Ullins Daughter (Trad. ballads)
*Ulysses (Tennyson)
*The Inchcape Rock
*King Bruce and the Spider?
*The Loss of the Royal George
*The Nightingale and the Glowworm
   (Cowper)
*Young Lochinvar (Scott)
*The Battle of Blenheim (Southey)
*The Destruction of Sennacherib (Byron)
*Abou Ben Adhem (Leigh Hunt)
*The Daffodils (Wordsworth)

It amazes me that my list includes such difficult blank verse as Tennyson's 'Ullyses', though of course the class I was in had an age range of nine to fourteen. I didn't find it difficult, because I had read the Greek legend in its simplified, broken-syllabled form already. I have always loved it, and still do. When anything happens to remind me how fast the years are speeding by, I comfort myself with it. The lights may begin to twinkle on the rocks here and there, but like Ulysses, I can still say

Come, my friends! 'Tis not too late to seek
A newer world

We learned that poetry by heart, not by rote. We

learned our multiplication tables, weights and measures and all the rest by rote. There is a difference, which John surely proved by reciting *Home Thoughts from Abroad* at the drop of a hat standing by my tea-table.

It may be that in this respect at least we had an advantage over our more urban counterparts, for we were all part of the same tribe, and the magic of words seemed to be part of our inheritance as much as the thick arms and thighs of the womenfolk.

There were several old folk when we were children who turned spontaneously to extempore verse to emphasise a cogent point: take Old Woodward, for example. He was sitting on the front of a cart one day when passing the Ram Inn, and from his vantage point of height he could see into the stye in which the landlord kept his backyard pig. It was not well-kept.

Old Woodward stopped the cart, got down and marched into the taproom, where he declaimed on the spur of the moment:

As I was a-passing just now I did spy
A dear little pig in a filthy pig stye.
It had plenty to eat, yes, plenty to gnaw
But O! how it wanted a pottle of straw!

Some local poets took their creations more seriously — like Mrs Carter for instance, who herself wrote the poems she used to recite at village concerts or socials. Bill (and the rest) always mimic the way she stood on the stage, and arranged her feet in the fourth ballet position, before starting.

And, of course, there was Dad, and consequently all three of us, though Gerald's efforts were mainly to be found on the walls of bedroom or barn. Dad wrote doggerel, and was well aware of it. He never took anything he composed at all seriously, though it flowed humorously from his pen as easily as prose did.

After we left home, he always couched his letters to us in his easy doggerel, and naturally, we had to reciprocate likewise.

Sometimes, though, behind all Dad's fun, one could detect that element of feeling that can make the most ordinary words memorable, and turned his verse into poetry — for what is poetry but a kind of emotional shorthand?

Such was the letter I received on the morning of my twentieth birthday, in 1933 — the first birthday ever spent away from home. Dad himself was at his very lowest ebb, because he had suddenly been crippled with gout, and ruined by the agricultural depression. I give the letter as he wrote it, just as it flowed, unpolished, from his gouty hand that had difficulty in grasping a pen. I have no need to be reminded to 'count my blessings' when I unfold that long strip of yellowing paper.

From Dad to Sybil.

My dear little Miss
I am sending you this
A real birthday X
For health, wealth and bliss.
It comes from my heart

As straight as a dart,
I know you'll be glad
Because it's from Dad.
I wish I could place
It right on your face
I send it to greet
You from head to feet.
If I'd wealth untold,
A necklace of gold
A gold watch and chain
I'd send you by train.
But for reasons well-known
We must leave gold alone.

Kind words I must try
For they never die
So, best wishes sincere
For the next coming year,
And a blessing I give
For as long as you live
You realise what it means,
You've gone out of your teens
And it seems rather queer
You're in your 21st year
Your Mam, she will write
Some time tonight
And you may depend
A small present she'll send
May this birthday bring
You just everything
That you may require,
And your heart's desire.
Now this is the end,
And you'll comprehend

Here's the same love from Dad
That you've always had.

Dad used to say that if the love he left behind him was not enough to keep him in remembrance, a gravestone was no good.
He needn't have worried.

10

Grammar School Days

The time had come. I had a new bike, a new satchel, a new tennis racquet, and a new uniform. After Easter, 1924, I became a pupil at the Grammar School. I was proud of myself for being so, though I had no right to be, because I had not, as Jess, her brother and her sister had, won my way there on a scholarship. Of the eight youngsters from our side of the bridge attending at that time, two were lordly male fifth-formers who did not deign to notice girls below their own age. There were three of Jess's family, and Joyce's elder sister: and there were the two rookies, Joyce and me. We split into groups for the journey, according to age. Joyce, Jess and I became a trio.

It was approximately four miles from our gate to the school. It never occurred to anyone, least of all to us, that there was any hardship involved in us facing such a journey every weekday.

I wonder how the transport-pampered children of these days would view such a prospect? Probably with unquestioning pleasure; it would be their outraged parents who would be suing the local education authority for cruelty to children. But then, I also wonder how it is that such rational, logical, practical creatures as most children are manage to grow up into so many fractious, whining, disgruntled, miserable and above all irrational adults, always on the look-out for something to complain and grizzle about.

Of the eight of us who were privileged to do the journey in 1924, it so happened that I stayed on at school the longest. Eight miles each day, five days a week, forty weeks a year for eight-and-a-half years means that I pedalled thirteen-and-a-half thousand miles for my secondary education. The few extended absences, such as that caused by the bronchitis I suffered from skating too long in the moonlight, would have been well balanced by the Saturday attendances for hockey matches and/or the occasional evening functions at the school, rehearsals and suchlike.

There were two ways we could go, and three we could come back. Mostly we went 'St Mary's Way' — up the Ugg Mere Court Road as far as the church, then along the road by the side of the river for about one-and-a-half miles, till the river swerved off to the left, and we went straight ahead into Ramsey town. In summer we could if we wished cut a corner off by following an unmade drove through New Fen; and coming home, we sometimes went 'Upwood way', because that gave us a chance of free-wheeling down two hills — well, inclines — Kingsland Hill and Upwood Hill. We also chose this route occasionally because it offered a change of companionship until we dropped off the contingents from Warboys and Upwood. Now cycling (or plain biking, as we should have said) is one thing; doing it in fenland conditions *faute de mieux* is something else. All our roads were narrow and mostly straight, still made up only with granite lumps, though as the years went by the Council did concede a steam-roller to flatten them a bit. There was still very little motorised traffic — so few private cars that we could recognise 'the regulars' a mile away — the doctor, one affluent farmer (who always greeted us with a wave of his hand as he passed, nice man), and towards the end of my school-life, the parson, who had acquired a high, red-and-gold chariot that would now be worth more than the stipend he had earned in his whole life.

When we turned right at the church, we rode high on the narrow, granited road with deep water on both sides of us.

Between us and the river on our left there was nothing but a few yards of grass sloping very steeply downwards. The same steep slope was on our right, though at the bottom of this there was only a drain.

In case you are not aware what 'only a drain' means, it was a man-made cut about ten feet wide and twelve feet deep, with sheer vertical sides kept roded like that in order that the water could flow freely to 'the Red Engine' — the New Fen pumping engine which my Dad ran both as miller and as Internal Drainage Officer. Almost opposite to the Red Engine, 'Pingy-Pang's Engine' performed the same function for the land on the other side of the river.

We did not consider ourselves in any danger, because we were so used to it; but not all mornings were sunny and calm, even in summer, and not all evenings fine and moonlit. It was dark when we got home in winter, unless we left school like a bullet from a gun when we were released, and pedalled like maniacs till we reached our own gates one by one. There were many mornings when it was so foggy that we could not see the edge of the grass verge along by the river, and the white mist came rolling up towards and over us like froth on the top of boiling jam. If it was foggy as we left school at the end of the day, we either decided to walk, pushing our bikes, for the mile-and-a-half that the road bordered the river, or we went home Upwood way and risked rushing through the fog at what we considered a dangerous pace down the slight hills. Sometimes it rained — not just gentle heavenly rain such as our fathers were praying for, but the heavy, slanting, driving silver arrows of rain that stung our unprotected faces and ran into our eyes and down our necks. This sort of rain was swept towards us by shufts of wind that blew our coats backwards and exposed our gym-slips from the waist downward, so that they clung to our sodden black-woollen-stockinged legs and made pedalling much more difficult. One never seemed to know from which direction the next shuft would come, so they often caught us unawares and turned our front wheels dangerously close to each other. When it snowed, we had to give in, and walk to the station to catch a train; but this meant that we were forced to reach school late and leave school early, and was consequently frowned on. I don't wonder, because it did us no service, actually. We had to walk a mile each end, and we might just as well have walked the other two miles as well.

Wind was our worst enemy, especially that wild, ferocious east wind carrying frost on its tongue, which raced in fury across our fens unimpeded from its den in the Ural Mountains. Black-frost winds we called them. No amount of clothing could keep out the bitter cold they brought as they screamed like banshees round our numbed hands and faces; but the effort of fighting against a black-frost wind was so great that it generated energy enough to keep us sweating inside our fleecy-lined bloomers and quilted liberty-bodices, whatever happened to our extremities.

If such a wind was blowing across the road, we dared not run the risk of being blown into the river, and usually got off our bikes and walked. If it was blowing straight into our faces, we had no option because a shuft catching us fair and square just stopped us in our tracks until we either got off or fell off our bikes. If ever (very rarely) we had the luck to have a strong wind behind us when going home Upwood way, we took our feet off the pedals, held our legs wide and sailed down the hills at what we thought a desperately adventurous, breakneck speed. Most days in winter, though, there was no such fun. I have memories of several evenings when I turned in at our farmyard gate too exhausted to make the journey from Gerald's place to the back door without having to sit down somewhere to gather enough strength to lift my satchel full of books, unstrap my attaché case full of gear from the carrier, and pick up the hockey stick that had fallen from my hands as soon as I had lifted them from the handlebars.

We enjoyed — or at least I did — the days in summer when we could go New Fen way. It afforded a different sort of thrill and skill to negotiate the narrow wheel of a bike through the deep, dust-filled ruts of an unmade drove not much used by other traffic such as carts, to flatten it. For part of the way, the pad we rode along ran close to the dyke sides. They were delightful strips of colourful wild flowers — camomile, St John's wort, tansy, toadflax, jonquils, ironheads (purple loose strife), ragged robin, willow herb, forget-me-not — and many more, as well as all the lovely grasses: clouds of Yorkshire fog, clumps of 'totty-grass', and the spikes of couch grass that we pulled to play 'hen or cockerel?' with. We simply challenged each other to guess, just like tossing a coin, whether stripping the grass between thumb and finger would produce a flat bunch or one with a cock's tail sticking up.

In the dykes themselves there would be patches of yellow iris (flags) and sometimes the sweet-smelling yellow water-lilies.

A main drain had no such decoration, because it had to be kept clear of all vegetation. There might have been some danger to us if any of us had ever scuttered off the pad as we crossed over it and fallen into it, because in spite of us living surrounded by water, none of us could swim. In summer, of course, the water was low anyway, and we didn't take the New Fen route in winter because the mud on the drove would have been too soft to get through.

The main drain through New Fen has several special, if inconsequential memories for me. Apart from everything else, I am always intrigued to consider why it is that some absolutely unimportant things refuse to be forgotten, while other events of much greater significance can only be recalled with effort, if at all; and then only in a misty, wraithlike outline with no details to colour them.

As Internal Drainage Officer (as well as being a Drainage Commissioner), Dad was responsible for seeing that that drain was kept clear. When it had to be dug out (every few years), it was an expensive job, and a team of men would be got together to do it. They had to be paid every Friday in cash, and somehow Dad had to have the cash to pay them with. He was, of course, a very busy man, and though he was paid for his services to the Internal Drainage Board, his remuneration hardly included leaving his own work, changing his clothes, and biking to Ramsey every Friday morning to fetch the money needed. So one Friday — I guess about 1926, when I would be coming into thirteen, I was instructed to meet Dad outside Barclay's Bank during my dinner hour. He took me in, and we were shown into the Holy of Holies, the Manager's office. Here Dad explained the situation, and requested that thereafter I be allowed to cash the cheque on Friday lunchtimes and carry the money home in my satchel. I think the Manager must have bent the rules a bit to agree, but he did. The cheque varied between £150 and £200, mostly, and the money was handed to me in a blue bag a bit like a sugar-bag, except that it had some holes punched through it so that one could see what was inside. I put it into one of the sidepockets of my satchel, and once back at school, hung it on my peg in the cloakroom till home time, when it was carried home on my back. There was no danger to me or the money, in those innocent times.

I have always been grateful for that bit of experience thrust upon me. I never had the fear and embarrassment that so many of my peers endured later in dealing with banks; and I was matured, I believe, by the trust placed in me.

The Grammar School at Ramsey was an ancient foundation, which is not all that surprising, seeing that Ramsey had been a seat of learning since the early middle ages, and the Abbot of Ramsey once the wealthiest prelate in all the realm. The school had less than a hundred pupils, drawn from Ramsey itself and the villages around. There were five teachers on the staff, including the headmaster, plus a visiting music teacher, and possibly, though I am not certain about this, a woodwork teacher. All that we learned, we learned from them. What they could teach us, they did. It was up to us whether we made any use of their efforts.

The school would hardly be regarded as much of an educational institution by modern standards, but as the old saying goes 'valuable stuff often comes in small parcels'. What we lacked in numbers and amenities, we certainly did not lack in *amour-propre*. If we could but

378

have seen ourselves as others would now see us, I doubt if we should have worn the uniform without rebellion. The boys got away with grey trousers, white shirts, a school tie and a cap with the school badge on it, though in summer a few did sport the school blazer. We girls wore navy gym-slips, by regulation just to our kneecaps in length, white blouses, school ties, black woollen stockings and flat black lace-up shoes. We then also sported the school blazer — and the school hat.

Well — nothing so very much out of the ordinary in that, is there? Not until you saw the blazers! And the hats!

The blazers were nothing if not outstanding. The material for them was of flannel woven and dyed especially for us. It had to be, because our colours were purple and gold, and the material was striped in those colours, alternate stripes slightly more than an inch wide. The whole garment (tailor-made for such as could afford it) was piped with gold braid, and the breast pocket bore the badge of which we were so (justifiably) proud — a ram rampant or on a field purpure, the escutcheon within a circle or on a field sable with the motto *Aucto splendore resurgam*.

We certainly rose in splendour in our blazers while they were new: but flannel is not the best of materials when it comes to being soaked through by a sudden driving squall of rain, and hung on a cloak-room peg to dry, without even a hanger to help it keep its shape. They shrank, the stripes became distorted, they no longer fitted. They were far too expensive to be easily replaced, so they got passed down families gradually wearing thinner in some places and matted in others. In summer, they were regulation wear, though a great many children, I think, never owned one. Curiously, those of us who did were still proud to be seen in them — at least, while still young: it is only in retrospect that I remember what sartorial disasters they were.

On the other hand, we detested our school hats with virulence amounting to pure hate. I am not at all sure that I have enough skill in words to describe them. In some respects they resembled a Dutch bonnet. In others, a forage cap worn from ear-to-ear instead of front-to-back on the head. You must visualise a forage cap with a turn-up of about two to three inches, worn close down over the eyebrows. Naturally, it would stick out over the ears, but this, in our case, was part of the design. Where the turn-up protruded, it was caught so that back and front were pinned together, forming lugs. Now imagine it in bright purple, piped wherever possible in gold, with the badge on the front, resting more or less on the bridge of the nose. The stuff was thick and heavy, and they were, of course, lined. When new, they had, at least, the virtue of being distinctive. As we were absolutely forbidden to leave the school gates without them, the privilege of wearing them became a dubious one. Perhaps not too irksome for the first week when they were brand new.

But wait! How long could it possibly be, in our fenland conditions, before they were soaked through and through by a squall of rain as we pushed our bikes to and from school? Then, like our blazers, they shrank, and lost any shape the designer had intended. The thick double band of heavy material would no longer fit snugly round the head. It just wouldn't go on — so one either wore it, as per regulation, pulled shapelessly down over the forehead (God only knows what it must have looked like from the back!) or perched it where it would sit 'like a pimple on a round of beef' as one of my non-Grammar-School friends commented. Worse still was the fact that once it had been thoroughly wet, the side peaks opened, held by the button into two rounded pots.

Whichever way one decided to make the best of it, the result was that it looked like a purple chamber-pot upside down, with two smaller gold-edged chamber-pots the right way up for lugs. In summer, those who could possibly squeeze one out of their impoverished parents wore a panama with a purple and gold band. Such of us as had older sisters in the school were lucky. Lois's panama had been of the cartwheel variety with an enormous brim: and as it had suffered a few immersions in the Ouse while she had been out punting, I was spared it, and got one of my own.

This chapter ought, I know, to deal with my education; but I wonder how many children have ever remembered being educated? They remember odd incidents that took place in the context of education. I had no concept at all that I was being educated, nor what it was all in aid of. I went to school, and things happened there to me as they did to everyone else. I understand now, because of the results of those years, that I must have absorbed everything that was poured over me as a plant absorbs moisture and light, but I was no more conscious of doing so than the plant is.

I suppose I began my secondary education under a misapprehension — that as far as 'cleverness' went, I was a second-class citizen compared with those like Jess and all her family, as well as the new friends I met there, who had all won their way in on scholarships. I hadn't. Don't ask me why — I never even sat the scholarship examination. I can only guess that Joyce's family had been advised that she stood little chance of getting a free place, and as there was no shortage of money there, her parents had decided to start her as a fee-paying pupil in the term after her eleventh birthday. I was still only ten, but perhaps Dad thought I ought not to be parted from my best friend, or that Mam saw some sort of cachet in my being a fee-payer. Unfortunately, most of the fee-payers were thick, and in class a drag on the brighter ones. It did not take me long to work that out — though it did not apply to Joyce and me. Joyce was (and is) one of the most happy, merry, mercurial characters ever born, full of mischief and never without a smile. She was, I think, already too fond of living every minute as it went by to bother about lessons. I was amenable to education, and accepted it; but I can't say I was concerned about it, or my place on the internal examination lists, until much later.

My first real hurdle was that, because I had no

basic understanding of arithmetic, I met algebra and geometry as I might have done Urdu or Chinese. Luckily, I was interested in them, and because I started them from the beginning, I understood both better than I ever understood their arithmetical base. My consequent difficulties with mathematics examinations that included all three branches (plus some trigonometry) all boiled down to the fact that my mathematical edifice had no foundation. I am sure that our head teacher, Jock, or 'Jocko', only found this out when he looked in horror over my shoulder at the nonsense I had written on my first School Certificate arithmetic paper. It took about two half-hour sessions with him to make me see the light, but by then it was a bit late. My desire to be able to do algebra helped considerably, though I had a lot of misunderstanding to get rid of before the penny finally dropped.

The only thing I really remember about my first term is that, as we joined a class who had already been doing French for two terms, we were set to learn a French poem. That was of no difficulty whatsoever to me, except for its subject matter:

Papillon, beau papillon
Vole vite, beau papillon.

If anything could have put me off French forever, it would have been its first association — with a butterfly.

After one term, we moved up into the third

form. A whole year, with only two memories.

The first is that wearing my new uniform, I stood with my peers to line the street at 'Old Lord dee's' funeral. It made me sad, on two counts. I remembered the occasion when, after the end of the Great War, I had stood with Mam to see the blind old man helped up the steps to a platform erected close to 'The Dummy' in the Great Whyte, and had heard him speak. I did not understand what he said, being only five, but I had understood Mam's tears when she explained to me that he had lost both his own sons. He had been both revered and loved, and the famed beauty of his wife was still a legend. He was always referred to as 'Lord dee', rarely as Lord de Ramsey. I had liked the look of the poor old man, and felt privileged to form part of the guard of honour as his coffin passed the spot where I stood. My second feeling of sadness was for the boy walking immediately behind the coffin, the heir and the new 'Lord dee'. I was not more than eleven, but there was something about that fifteen-year-old figure that went straight to my heart; and stayed there. It was as if I understood in a flash of extraordinary insight, that to inherit a barony and all that went with it was not just the romantic glory story books made of it. I was filled with a sort of momentary anguish, not for the blind old man in the coffin, but for the lonely, burdened young heart following; and I was glad to be just me.

The other memory is an absurd one of the

variety I seem blessed to be able to carry with me forever, and laugh at in the endless hours of the night, for example when strapped to a hospital bed after an operation.

Because we had only five teachers to cover the whole curriculum, the permutations would not always work out. Thus it happened that there was a period of our third form timetable marked English, but the only teacher free to take it was the new science master.

His way of coping with a problem he had, I am sure, never anticipated, was exactly the same as Miss had employed in teaching us the Scriptures. He chose a long poem, apportioned stanzas round the class, and sat on his high stool behind the teacher's desk while we committed them to memory. We read them aloud round the class, first — and thus I heard for the first time Macaulay's rolling, unforgettable description of Horatius keeping the bridge. Once we began to have to recite it, I could have prompted anybody who stuck. (We later did large chunks of *The Lay of the Last Minstrel* and *Marmion* in the same fashion.)

But I believe it was due more to my whole family's sense of the ridiculous than Macaulay's wonderful poem that the experience has remained forever fresh to me.

There was the none-too-bright girl, who, scanning the stanzas she had been allotted, raised her hand and said in a puzzled voice 'Sir, I don't understand this. What does it mean? And sick men born in litters?'

(And sick men borne in litters
High on the necks of slaves)

Then we had what was called a group inspection, which meant that three HMIs were in the school for a week. The English Inspector (deliberately looking for a weak spot, or just obeying Sod's law?) chose to visit us in the third form during our 'Horatius' period.

Sir was decidedly nervous and flustered, and showed it because his usually fair skin was so suffused with blood that he looked like an over-ripe plum. His anxiety communicated itself to us as we were called upon to demonstrate our knowledge of English literature by saying our recitation piece.

I have to say for Sir that he had showed some perspicacity in allotting the stanzas, so that I, for example, had those describing the gathering of Lars Porsena's army from romantic sounding but unpronounceable places, while the less English-minded boys got the exciting bits. It was, therefore, a boy of thirteen who was picked on to declaim the fight between Astur and Horatius.

I was thrilling to it, inspector or no inspector, as always.

But hark! the cry is Astur,
And lo! the ranks divide,
And the great Lord of Luna
Comes with his stately stride.
Upon his ample shoulders
Clangs loud the four-fold shield

And in his hand he shakes the brand
Which none but he can wield.
He smiled on those bold Romans,
A smile serene and high;
He eyed the flinching Tuscans,
And scorn was in his eye.
Quoth he 'The she-wolf's litter
Stands savagely at bay:
But will ye dare to follow
If Astur clears the way?'
Then whirling up his broadsword
With both hands to the height,
He rushed upon Horatius
And smote with all his might.
With shield and blade Horatius
Right deftly turned the blow.
The blow, though turned, came yet too nigh;
It missed his helm, but gashed his thigh:
The Tuscans raised a joyful cry
To see the red blood flow.
He reeled, and on Herminius
He leaned one breathing space;
Then, like a wild-cat mad with wounds
Sprang right at Astur's face
Through teeth, and skull and helmet
So fierce a thrust he sped,
The good blade stood a hand-breadth out
Behind the Tuscan's head.

How unbelievably breathtaking it is! Can it be
wondered at that I can recall every word of it
after sixty years packed full of different
experiences, including miles of other poetry? Will
there be anybody in the year A.D.2055 who will

be able to recite even a few lines of the unrhymed, unrhythmical sort of stuff by poets of today that is dished out in schools now?

At this point, the narration passed to another boy named Charlie — a clever, intelligent boy, but a sensitive one who had picked up Sir's nervous tension. He rose, and began:

And the great Lord of Luna
Fell at that deadly stroke
As falls on Mount Averna
A thunder-stricken oak.
Far o'er the crashing forest
The giant arms lie spread
And the pale augurs, muttering low
Gaze on that blasted head.
ON ASTUR'S HEEL HORATIUS
RIGHT FIRMLY PRESSED HIS THROAT . . .

The scene the words visualised being too much for me, I gasped, sniggered, giggled, choked back the giggles, and clung to the sides of my chair in a great effort to control myself. I nearly succeeded, too — but I had undone poor Charlie, and poor Sir. There was a moment's awful silence, while everybody started at me — Sir brick-coloured, HMI po-faced, and all the rest of the class who had heard nothing amiss in incomprehending bewilderment. The bell for the end of the period released us all, and I escaped to let my stifled laughter free. I hope I did Sir no lasting damage, for I owe him more than he ever knew, or I realised at the time.

As for this tiny, so vividly remembered

incident — well, as our irascible horsekeeper used to call out to me every time he passed as I sat among the buttercups in the grassfield making daisy chains

I would prefer to re-word his sarcastic comment into 'Little things please minds ready and willing to be pleased.'

The next year, in the fourth form, is almost as blank, but not quite. Once again, the permutations of staff and subjects meant that for a period marked English on the timetable, the English teacher was not available. The last period on Monday mornings was the Cinderella this time, and the stand-in, the headmaster. He was equally at home with arts or sciences, and had not the same inhibitions as Sir in the third form.

He introduced us to *Selected English Essays*. A born teacher who loved the subject he was teaching, he had me hooked from the moment that we began on Francis Bacon's essays on 'Gardens' and 'Revenge'. The essay has remained my favourite form of literature ever since, and there is no doubt in my own mind that it was those Monday morning lessons that first set my feet on the road to Cambridge University, even though it took me the next thirty-six years to get there.

It was Jock, too, who first made me appreciate the short story as an art-form. If a games period had to be cancelled because of bad weather, he made certain that we neither skived off early nor spent the time flicking ink-pellets at each other. He gathered us together and read short stories to us — H.G. Wells, Conan Doyle, Brett Harte,

Conrad. I loved them all.

It would not be true to say that Monday mornings are the only thing I remember about my fourth form year. It was a rule of the school that nobody carried matches, but a rule constantly broken, especially by the boys. One day when our proper English teacher was holding forth about Wordsworth's sonnet *Upon Westminster Bridge*, a boy called Harry fiddled with the box of matches in his trouser pocket, undid the box and managed to rub two match-heads together, instantly igniting the whole boxfull. Harry was a rather large specimen, wedged into a desk too small for him which in turn was too close to the desk each side. His subsequent antics, and those of the unfortunates in the same row, hardly need to be described. It was a lively few minutes, against which the somewhat timid English mistress and Wordsworth came off decidedly second best. Harry was only one of several of my classmates who went to serve in 1939, and never returned.

At the age of fourteen, I entered the Lower Fifth form. This was, in effect, the top form, because those who took the Oxford School Certificate Examination stayed in the same room as the Upper Fifth and if (a big if) anybody stayed on after that to take The Higher School Certificate, he or she became a one-pupil Sixth Form, but had nowhere else to go, so remained at his desk in the fifth form room most of the time.

In the fifth, therefore, we caught up with others older than ourselves. I started that academic year while still only thirteen, Jess being the only other quite so young (Jess and I were born within three days of each other). Most of the others were a year older.

Being in the same room, perforce we did the same lessons as the Upper Fifth; and it was understood that whatever play of Shakespeare was set (or chosen) as the examination text for the Upper Fifth School Certificate English Literature paper, that same play would be performed by the Lower Fifth on Speech Day. I have to say it was a bold undertaking on everybody's part, sustained more by faith and hope than confidence, because we had a minimum of drama or dramatic experience before aiming as high as Shakespeare. The year I went into the Lower Fifth, the play was *Julius Caesar*. Books were dished out, one between two, and we began to read.

Why is it that memory graves so deep sometimes? I can hear every overtone and undertone of the voice of one of two brothers — the one we called 'Jelly' — as he read in his (embarrassed) Ramsey voice:

Wot noos, theow knaave, theow naughty knaave, wot noos?

(Jelly and his brother both died of thirst in the desert, after their separate planes had crashed.)

So began our rehearsals for the exam (for some), and the great performance for the rest of us, when I found myself playing Trebonius on the stage at The Abbey Rooms.

We had no histrionic talent at all, and it was very difficult to cast the play. Joyce the mercurial, for example, played Casca! There was no boy among our form equal to the task of playing Antony, but at the crucial moment of final casting, fate sent a new girl into our midst. She had spent most of her life abroad, and was very dark, very handsome, very well-spoken in contrast to our shrill fen voices and our flat vowels, besides being the possessor of a most enthralling deep musical contralto. She also claimed to have had some previous experience in treading the boards. There was no jealousy or resentment when we were told that she would play Mark Antony.

That left Caesar. Well, as Caesar is bumped off quite early in the action, he was not going to have to give up a great deal of time to rehearsing, so it was agreed that the one-man-sixth-form could be borrowed — my best Grammar School friend — Chris's brother, and her only surviving one, a brilliant boy of whom Jock expected great things. As his study-load was very heavy, he could attend only very few of our scrappy, ragged rehearsals, but we had no worry on that score. Our worst difficulty was that we only had one rehearsal, the dress rehearsal, on the actual stage at the Abbey Rooms where we should perform the next day. All in all, no blame can possibly be attached to anybody for what happened.

Caesar had been clobbered, and 'Et tu Brute?' — ing tragically, had fallen obliquely across the centre stage. Brutus (one of our lot and normally a bit nondescript) was playing up marvellously, and, as directed, turned his back to the audience to throw out his left arm in a pointing sort of gesture to the entrance back-stage right, declaiming:

'But here comes Antony!'

We conspirators, as we had been directed and had rehearsed, all half-turned to follow his pointing finger — and our star turn, the practised actress with the plum part, walked on back stage left, and therefore behind us all. I was told off severely by Mrs Allen next day for grinning broadly as we all shuffled hastily round to face Antony — apparently the only conspirator/ murderer to be struck by the ludicrous element of it.

But worse was to follow. Antony having come in from the wrong side, the carefully worked out placement of actors on a too-small stage was shattered. In order to make the great oration, Antony must somehow get to centre stage. But Caesar lay dead in her path. Would she orate from where she was squeezed into a back corner, behind him? Should we risk shuffling ourselves to make way for her round behind us? Poor Brutus, apparently mesmerised, still stood with back to the audience, one gangling arm outstretched. For one horrified moment, I thought Antony was about to hitch up her toga and step boldly over mighty Caesar lying so low — and indeed, I believe that must have been the outcome, but for the fallen Emperor. When the pause in the action had become unbearable, he settled the matter. The corpse of Caesar obligingly drew up its knees, and allowed Antony to pass.

Julius Caesar remains one of my favourite Shakespeares, and I still know much of it by heart; but the scene of Caesar's death can never again be anything but tragi-comedy for me — except, that is for the real tragedy that followed. Within three years, our Caesar followed his brothers to the grave, dying, like them, of TB. He was twenty-one.

In his family all the males were doomed. Chris is still alive and well, sturdy and rosy as ever in her eighth decade with her golden wedding a year or two behind her; a near enough neighbour for us to meet once or twice a year. She, incidentally, played the soothsayer.

In the next academic year, we became the Upper Fifth, and it was our turn to take the School Certificate Examination. Jess and I were still only in our fifteenth year, though all the others were in their sixteenth.

This placed Jock in something of a dilemma. The external examination we sat was the School Certificate set by the Oxford Examinations Board. There was no choice at all about what subjects one took. To gain the certificate, one had to pass in eight subjects made up of selections from different groups. The compulsory subjects were English Language, English Literature and Mathematics; to which had to be added one language, RE, one science subject, history, geography — and one other, in which a little bit of flexibility was allowed in principle. In our case, it was not. To cover eventualities on the science side, Jock decreed that we all (girls as well as boys) took chemistry, physics and agricultural science. So in fact we took nine subjects, out of which we had to pass eight to be awarded the Oxford School Certificate.

Fees were charged for every pupil sitting the examination; but if a whole class was entered, the county paid up. Naturally, for his own reputation, Jock could not afford to risk too many abject failures — but he was quite well aware that some scholarship children came from homes that could not raise the required fee. So he usually gambled, and bunged the whole Upper Fifth in (though I guess there was a bit of juggling about who was, and who was not, so classified).

It was no surprise to me whatsoever that Jess passed with flying colours — indeed with honours, and that I did not. I was still absolutely lackadaisical about my own progress, and I hadn't expected to match Jess or Chris, in any case. Jock was disappointed, because apparently my other marks were very good indeed — even the science ones — but I had failed the mathematics, and without a pass in maths, no certificate was given. I had not been helped by fate in that particular paper. We each had our desk set at the regulation four feet from the next to prevent copying, and each of us had to leave on it each afternoon those things we would need for the examination that started at 9.00 a.m. next morning. For maths, a wooden ruler was part of the equipment, and I had placed mine down across the rounded wooden groove made to hold pens and pencils. My desk was directly under a window, and when, at 8.55 a.m. I sat down to check my equipment, I picked up the ruler. Snug in the groove beneath it was a winged insect, which, of course, rose into my face at once. It was, in fact, a large red-under-wing moth, but I had not had time to register that before my heart stopped and the awful nausea threatened to make me throw up all over the arithmetic paper lying face down on the desk, ready to be turned over. Perhaps if the wretched insect had taken refuge under anybody else's ruler than mine, I might have scraped through, and got my School Certificate at fourteen. Not that it made any difference in the long run. The next year, Jess got higher honours, and indeed I passed with third-class honours, having scraped through the maths paper somehow.

The summer of this year left another memory with me, unconnected with my education direct, but leaving me forever after with a sense of gratitude never properly expressed. As the years go by me, there are a good many people I would like to have back from wherever they are on the other side of death long enough to let them know how much I appreciated their many little unremembered acts of kindness and of love; the sort of things even adults in full maturity take for granted until too late, and young people accept without thinking.

I wish I could tell 'Old Puss' (Miss Mary

Passmore, Jocko's chief assistant teacher) how many times I have thought of what she did, and how much I appreciated it even then, though I guess all I said was a brief, embarrassed thank you.

There was that summer a total eclipse of the sun, visible in England, but between 4.00 a.m. and 5.00 a.m. Jock the Scientist was determined that we should not only understand the phenomenon, but should view it in his company, so that he could explain to us, stage by stage, exactly what was happening. Having done a bit of prospecting, he decided that our best vantage point would be the churchyard at Bury, which was on what we called a hill about a mile from the school. Jock could not force attendance at 4.30 a.m. from anybody, even those pupils who lived in Ramsey and Bury; but all of us were invited in a manner that left no doubt we were expected to be there.

We had to give in our names a week before the event, and during the intervening week Jock himself or the science master supervised the smoking of a suitable piece of glass for each of us, through which to view the corona.

Miss Passmore was our history, French, religious knowledge and needlework teacher, as well as being generally in charge of the health and hygiene of the girls. We considered her the original Ancient of Days, though I doubt if she was much over fifty. She was short and stout, and wore thick pebble lenses through which her green eyes occasionally glinted in a curiously disconcerting way. This was probably why she

397

was called 'Puss', though I never thought of it then — I had known about 'Old Puss' from Lois long before I ever set eyes on her. She wore her hair still in an Edwardian pompadour style, and did not enhance her own general appearance by never wearing anything but sturdy, flat, rubber-soled lace-up shoes. Like most of us, she had her little ways. She was inclined to waddle as she walked, silently because of her soft soles, down the corridor of the school; and as she walked she would suddenly double her pudgy right hand into a fist, strike herself a blow on her right bosom, and say aloud 'Ah, well. Hum-m-m-m-m-m-m,' the hum being a sort of mosquito-like, high-pitched whine.

It was only to be expected that as soon as every girl's bosom was big enough to hit, she joined the throng of impersonators. I, being like the rest of my family too-well endowed above the waist, could not have escaped if I had wanted to.

Puss also had a slight speech impediment that prevented her from enunciating the letter 'l' clearly, so what she actually said as she struck herself sounded like 'Ah, we-w'. We talked to each other in 'Puss' language, thinking ourselves great wits. 'Now, in the middew ages, men often used battew-axes to settew their quarrews' . . . and so on.

A rumour persisted that Puss was the only daughter of a wealthy London merchant, and would one day be an incredibly well-off woman. It was most probably a myth, but that I don't know. I can't imagine, if it were true, why she stayed on year after year slogging along with such unpromising material as we must have been.

School dinners had never been heard of then, so those of us who couldn't get home at mid-day took packed lunches, which we ate sitting at tables for six in an old army hut situated at the bottom of the boys' playground. It was among Puss's less than pleasant duties to supervise us as we crammed our mouths over full in order to get away first and stand some chance of getting a warm-up by the measly cloakroom fire. Some of us needed it badly — if our woollen stockings had been soaked on our way to school, they were still sticking damply to our legs at lunch time.

Puss had announced to us that as, on the morning of the eclipse, we should have to leave home by 4.30 a.m. at the latest, she would arrange for hot drinks to be served in the hut for those who could not go home to breakfast.

The eclipse itself was a great success — still the best I have ever seen. Then we trooped back to school around 7.30 a.m., and those who could went home to breakfast. We sauntered down to the hut for our promised cup of cocoa. Puss was there, striking herself and humming louder than usual as she watched our astonished faces when we opened the door and went in.

Every table was covered with a white damask cloth; silver-plated cutlery marked every place: a tiny flower-arrangement graced the centre surrounded by such comestibles as none of us had ever seen before, and only such avid readers as I had ever even heard of. There was ham, beef, tongue, smoked salmon, chicken in aspic; there were pies, galantines and patés, and plates piled high with crusty bread rolls, and mounds of golden butter.

By the side of each table stood other hampers from Fortnum and Mason, from which came honey, strawberry conserve and a bewildering array of different marmalades. We did more than justice to such a feast, but it was not yet finished.

From still other hampers came gateaux and patisserie — choux buns and éclairs and everything else all laden with chocolate and swimming in cream: and, for the first time in my life, *real* coffee.

All of it, of course, the brain-child and the gift of Miss Passmore, who had not only organised the treat but paid for it, every penny, from her own pocket. From the kindness of her heart, and from her genuine affection for a bunch of such nasty little horrors as we were, who mocked her and made fun of her every day of our lives.

I hope I expressed my thanks that morning as sincerely and as graciously as any of the thirty-plus of us who were there; but oh Puss! Oh, dear, dear old Puss, how I want you at this minute back from the Shades just long enough to let you know that one of your pupils, at least, has never forgotten that morning's breakfast, which stands like the star on the top of the tree of everything else that you did for us, day after day and year after year.

My education had not yet finished, and I was at the Grammar School for three more years; but school was not the whole of my life, so I had better catch up on other things before continuing.

11

The Beginning of the End

Civilisation only began to catch up with us after the end of the Great War, but even then the pace of change was very slow. I foresee that historians born after the end of World War II may have great difficulty in apprehending the decisive nature of the years 1914–1946 as a watershed — not of change, which they will surely comprehend easily — but of the pace of change. Until 1920, people in rural areas as isolated as our fen did not have to contend with any startling changes in thought or outlook. News from the outer world reached us days, weeks, or even months after the event. Fashions, innovations, and modes of thought lagged behind urban areas in the same way. Those born into the postwar world of technology are accustomed to news, views, ideas and so on reaching everywhere simultaneously. In considering pre-Great War history, they, the historians for the future, will have to make deliberate compensation for the fact that rural England lagged at least a decade behind the times in most aspects of life.

This had a curious effect on us of the fens, in our extra isolation. For one thing it created a gap, larger than the ordinary generation gap, between those born before the Great War, and those whose formative years were during or after it. In 1914, everything stopped short, and was in effect, put into mothballs for the duration; but because of the time-lag, our fen had not yet got out of the Victorian age when this happened. Consequently, the gap stretched from c.1900 to 1920, with no true Edwardian bridge across it.

This gap was very evident in my immediate family. Gerald was born in 1903, Lois in 1905, and I in 1913. The other two were on the Victorian side of the gap. I struggled out of it into the twentieth century.

As years passed and I caught Lois up, so to speak, when I began to leave childhood behind me, no two sisters could have been more alike, more devoted to each other, or better companions. We loved to be together, to the end of Lois's life, and preferred each other's company to that of most other people: and yet — she, like Gerald, was still basically Victorian in outlook, and much as they loved me, they could not approve of my independent and, to them, unconventional way of life.

Gerald's heart was not in farming. He had been bitten by the science bug, and in particular that concerning the internal combustion engine. Dad could not come to terms with his desire to become an engineer, especially as he had bought his mother's farm for Gerald to take over in due course. So Gerald himself was a victim of the time-slip. In mind, he had jumped the gap into the age of technology; in heart and in spirit, he was still Victorian. He bowed to convention, and stayed on the land. Lois, at thirteen, had won a scholarship to the Grammar School, and it was this that in due course led all the family into a wider world, and drew us into the twentieth century. She made friends who were not of our immediate neighbourhood, clan or tribe, and they, in turn, introduced us to new ideas.

It was our good fortune that Mam was ahead of most fenland women of her time, and let us free to enjoy what pleasure came our way. Dad, if he didn't exactly welcome or approve of the things post-Great War youth got up to, was broadminded enough not to try to prevent us 'getting in the swim'.

Our 'goings-on' scandalised our close relations, and caused much censure from our still Victorian neighbours — especially our constant and easy relationship with members of the opposite sex. We were the 'fast' trend-setters of our particular fen.

Take, for example, the question of music. We had been brought up with music always in the background and in our home, even if it was centred round hymns. But as Lois grew up, her gift as a pianist could not and would not be restricted to music connected with chapel (as that of at least two of our cousins was). It was the age of syncopation, and in syncopated jazz she found her true métier. Though she continued to have piano lessons till she was eighteen, and could sight-read anything put before her: though she was a most accomplished accompanist, and earned much praise in this way almost to the end of her life, it was syncopated rhythms that inspired her fingers; and it was those same rhythms that set my feet dancing, and continued to give me exquisite pleasure all my life — well, until a cancer and an arthritic hip put an end to dancing. I refuse to have any inhibitions about my low-brow taste for listening still to Charlie Kunz or Ambrose; it doesn't mean I can't, or don't enjoy other music too, any more than it stopped Lois from practising Chopin or Beethoven. I cannot but think that such musical snobs as frown upon me must lack the ability to move their bodies exactly, in ecstasy, to rhythm; so perhaps they are to be pitied. Maybe they don't know what they are missing.

By the time I had recovered wholly from my trip to the Valley of the Shadow of Death, Lois was seventeen. The nature of our musical evenings had certainly changed. Instead of being put to bed early to further my recovery after my tonsillectomy, I sat, night after night on the floor in our front room between the end of the couch and the door to the front porch, quiet as a mouse and hoping to remain unnoticed while Lois practised, or played for her own pleasure. When there were just the two of us there, I did not bother to hide my presence, but from my chosen spot would call out my requests to her for my favourite pieces: Brahms waltzes: Cons' 'Scandinavian Dances': 'Demande et Réponse from Taylor Coleridge's 'Petite Suite de Concert: 'Valse Triste': Henry Gheel's 'For you Alone', and Chopin, especially 'Trois Valses Brilliantes'; but once into Chopin, it was not long before Lois's agile fingers strayed into Billy Mayerl's latest composition, and from there into the latest popular songs. Then Gerald would open the door and slide in, sitting down in the chair at the side of the piano so as to be able to rest his teeth on the arm of it, because his deafness was largely a matter of conduction, and he heard music better this way. Then the rhythm would 'get' him, and he would fetch any sort of domestic or culinary articles from which he could construct a percussion set, and join in.

Gerald always had difficulty in holding hordes of girls at bay, and it was he who first brought home a girlfriend whose beautiful voice had been properly trained. Finding in Lois an almost perfect accompanist, they became inseparable friends and remained so, long after Gerald had lost interest. 'Mu' as we always called her, was not a local girl, though now living near. Her excellent all-round education had included a high-class specialisation in music, and she was as catholic in her taste for songs as Lois for playing or I for reading. Ballads were still very much in vogue, and Mu gave voice to a Victorian ballad as happily as to Schubert or Jerome Kern.

So there I would sit, hidden in my corner, my presence forgotten by everybody else, and let the tears trickle down my face as Mu's pure voice hit a top A, or came down to a mellow contralto to sing what were to me the magic phrases of 'Nirvana'

I have come from the silent forest,
My beautiful lotus flower . . .

(Better than 'Horrocks's Calico' or 'Capital Redemption' had ever been!)

There was more, and better, still to come. The daughter of one of our neighbours had married an army bandsman, and once he discovered our modern musical proclivities, he would join us (much to his wife's vexation, because her parents were of Grandmother's persuasion and forbade her to accompany her erring husband into such a den of vice). So clarinet and/or saxophone was added to Mu's ability with a ukelele, and she sang pop songs such as 'Charmaine' or 'More than you know' instead of ballads. (I am aware that my memory has telescoped many years together, and that the songs I have quoted may not have been written till much later, when the musical ensemble had turned itself into a dance-band with Mu as the vocalist.)

In the sequence of events, however, the peak of my delight was reached when from somewhere or other came 'Mr Appleby' and his violin. I don't know where he came from, or what he was doing for a period of months only in our midst, but to me he was the ninth wonder of the world. I cannot remember him ever saying a word to me, or even noticing that there was a child in the room; but the evenings when he was there were those in which I cried non-stop, because the sound his violin made touched some spot deep inside me that even the indescribable beauty of my kittens had never reached before.

More than anything else in the world, I wanted to be able to play a violin. I made my desire known, and had been promised a violin for my next birthday, my tenth. One autumn evening, when I was still only nine, Mrs Banker

Bill called to see Mam, bringing with her a child of my own age — some distant relative who was staying with her. We were sent out into the garden to play, though dusk was already falling. Dad had set me up with swings and a see-saw remarkable for the length of its plank, because it was firmly and ingeniously fixed to the remains of an old butter-churn, and was therefore heavily based and quite safe. Safe, that is, except for the unimaginable. The other child was a townee who — surely it must be so? — had never ridden on a see-saw before. When her end was on the ground, and I some six feet or more high in the air, she stepped off, and gravity did the rest. My left arm was broken, and has remained bow-shaped ever since, with the elbow locking at an angle of about fifty degrees. I wonder what my future might have been, but for that silly accident. I never even learned the child's name, and never saw her again.

My ambition to play a violin thus being snatched out of reach for ever, I was sent to have piano lessons instead (not as a consolation — there was none). In the first place Mam and Dad took it for granted that because Lois seemed born to the piano, I should be the same, but it didn't work that way at all. In the second, I knew from the start that I could never compete with Lois: and thirdly, I did have bad luck with my teachers. I was sent first to our Miss at school, who had been Lois's first piano teacher too, and who found me a disappointing pupil both in comparison with my sister and with myself in other subjects. At the age of twelve, I

407

was transferred to my first male teacher, and by fifteen my third male teacher had driven me to rebellion against another piano lesson, ever. The first expected me to concentrate on the keys while he mauled my top-half and laid his head on my shoulder; the second made sexy remarks that I half-understood, and which caused me to break out into a sweat and turned me beetroot-colour with embarrassment; the third occupied a duet-stool with me, constantly attempting to push his big ugly hands up my navy-blue school uniform bloomers. It is a measure of the age gap between us, or perhaps even more of the difference in our pre-war/post-war *mores*, that this was one thing I could not bring myself to tell Lois about. So nobody at home ever knew the real reason why I did not progress with my music as well as I did with the rest of my education. I wonder how many of my Grammar School friends had the same experience? I would have endured torture rather than speak of such a thing to Mam! The eight-and-a-half years between Lois and me had never seemed greater than it did just then. So I gave up lessons, and have, musically, been a second-class citizen ever since.

I was growing up, though, and quite suddenly it seemed that I had caught Lois (and Mu) up, so that I was included in their grown-up pursuits — but I don't want to leave my early years behind me just yet.

At the time of my broken arm accident, we got our first district nurse — and were we lucky! She was a Londoner, but one who fell into our community with ease, understanding, and sympathy. She fell in love with the fens (and eventually, with one of Banker Bill's household). She, too, was musical, though her forte was singing folk-songs, including Cockney ones. She had ideas, and they took root in the fertile ground of our socially-deprived lives. She instituted a concert party called 'The Swallows' — about twelve of us in all. Custom and courtesy demanded that our school Miss should be the official accompanist though she refused to wear the black-and-white Pierrot-type costumes Lois and Mu designed and made. Mu, of course, was chief vocalist: Lois was the soubrette and also played her mandoline. (She was sitting cross-legged on the stage playing and singing:

Poor old Uncle Sambo!
Sings he softly and low,
Spare me do, a penny or two . . .

at one performance, when the audience began to throw coins as requested, and she had to retire after several encores with a black eye and a split lip.) She also accompanied Mu's solos, Miss gracefully conceding that Mu should have her own accompanist. Nurse was everywhere, keeping the whole show moving, while I (still only ten), and my friend Joyce acted as the troupe's mascots. Dressed like the others (I in a top-hat like the other men) we had our spot in the programme, sitting together in a round wicker chair made to look like a bird's nest, and singing a duet.

Joyce If I should marry you, little love-bird
What would my pin-money be?
Me I'd settle up all the bills you incurred
And never discuss £.s.dee.
. . . in our little nest on the tree-top.

Lois, remember was in her early twenties by now, and her favourite boy-friend was a public-school boy who was that extremely rare being in those days, an electrician. He was as fascinated by radio as Gerald by motors, and was constantly improving on the radio receiver sets he made for himself. He knew what he wanted to build, but he lacked the means to buy the necessary parts. In the end (c.1924), Dad agreed to fund the project, and it went ahead successfully. In 1926 (I think) we became only the fourth household in the entire county of Huntingdonshire to apply for a radio receiving licence.

Everybody, of course, was interested in Will'en's new 'whim-wham' (any object whose purpose was not immediately obvious, or necessary, was referred to as a whim-wham for a duck's arse). Most of them had heard something about 'wireless', though they showed signs of doubting the truth of what they heard. Even when sets — crystal sets — began to proliferate, many older folk like Uncle John still regarded them with suspicion, and showed that even the word wireless meant little to them. Such a set was usually called 'th'ole wulless'.

Dad was interrogated about it wherever he went. One of his farmer neighbours who had a high squeaky voice, and could always be relied on for an amusing quote waylaid Dad to enquire about it. Dad explained, as far as he could, its nature and its purpose including the licence fee.

Al	'Is it on at night, like, when you get 'um fum wuk?'
Dad	'Yes — news, and music, and such like.'
Al	'Well, I shou'n't want one o' them bloody things blarin' music out when I wanted to go to bed!'
Dad	'You don't have to have it when you don't want it. You turn some knobs, and shut it off.'
Al	(after some thought). 'I should ha' thought yew'd a'had more sense, Will'En. Wha's the good o' payin' good money to keep somink as yew 'ev ter shut off to git rid o' the row it makes?'

In those very early days of broadcasting, 2LO only came on the air for a couple of hours in the morning, a short period in the afternoon, and then from about 6.00 p.m. till 11.00 p.m. — maybe midnight, but I have forgotten the exact details. The point is that broadcasting was not continuous all day.

This caused us some difficulty, and even distress. Though, like Al, they might turn up their noses at it, and have some doubts about Dad's sanity (though he was known to be 'a bit of a cure'), they all secretly longed to be able to

411

say they had seen it and heard it, so Mam had a good many visitors, mainly female, who just dropped in with feeble excuses, hoping to be given a demonstration of 'the wulless'. When, as often happened, 2LO was not operating, all she could do was to turn on the four valves (separately), and produce banshee-like howls and squeaks. Some went away convinced that the Will'En family had at last 'whully gone' — (round the bend, that is). Others were sure that Mam wanted to keep her treasure to herself and would not allow them to hear it, going away deeply offended.

One morning, Mam answered the door to our erstwhile neighbour in Lotting Fen, the epileptic, Jimmy. His speech was always difficult to interpret, but Mam understood that he had come to see and hear 'the wulless'. She asked him in, sat him down in Dad's chair, and tried to explain to him that he had come at the wrong time, when there was no broadcasting. It was beyond his powers of understanding, and he chose to think he was being denied. He became very agitated, shouting and yelling to the accompaniment of howls and screams from the set as Mam frantically cranked the valve knobs in desperate hope. Lois was with her, luckily, and they both watched with rising fear as he began to foam at the mouth and tried to get up, it appeared with the intention of smashing the set. Instead, he fell in a fit on to the hearthrug. Neither Mam nor Lois did anything to help him — they rushed into the pantry and shut the door. Then Mam's conscience smote her, especially as she thought of the blame that would fall on her if Jimmy died in his fit, and she was about to order Lois to run and find Dad, when Dad opened the door. *Deus ex machina* — he seemed blessed with a gift of always being near at hand when needed. Jimmy was no worse for that fit than he had been for many others, and by the time he had come round completely, there was the announcer's voice saying '2LO calling, 2LO calling', so poor Jimmy went away satisfied after all.

We may also have been one of the first households to be the victim of radio thieves. Because of the hasty division of the farmhouse into two, neither house was well designed. Each had a narrow pair of stairs on the outside wall, which turned steeply at the bottom to a door which led directly into the house-place. This door was at right-angles to the back door which led out on to the concrete doorway. A large window in the same wall, looking down the garden, had standing beneath it another of Mam's antique finds — a lyre-legged bamboo table with a chequer board inlaid in its polished top. It was on this chequer board top that our new wireless was placed, so that aerials, etc. could go out at the window.

Dad always got up at 5.00 a.m., summer and winter alike, and went straight out into the yard to do the milking and any yardwork other than the horses, which was the horsekeeper's job. Then he came in for breakfast. One beautiful summer morning just after we had acquired our wireless, he came downstairs as usual only to find that nohow could he get out of the stairs door. He was a big man, six feet tall and well built (although his long thin neck and clean-cut face always gave the impression that he was thin), and in the end he had to use force to open the door. To his amazement, he found that the cause of the obstruction was a kitchen chair wedged under the door-knob — it had collapsed in pieces under his strength. The back door stood wide open, and so did the window. The precious 'wireless' had been unshipped from its aerial wires, and was balanced precariously half in and half out of the window, across the sill.

So somebody had attempted to steal it. Somebody who knew that our back door was rarely locked. It all pointed to one of our friends or neighbours, yet none of them would have been so minded even if they had had any idea what to do with it, or how to get rid of it. Dad, in his usual philosophical way, said that all we had lost was an old kitchen chair, so why make any fuss about it? Perhaps we had better lock our back door in future. He didn't want it thought that he could possibly cast aspersions on anybody.

Mam was not so easily assuaged. She made a good deal of song and dance about the incident to anybody who would listen. Aunt Harriet made it fairly plain that we had got our just deserts for having anything to do with such works of the devil.

Now Uncle Jim, Aunt Loll's husband, was a signalman-porter at our little branch-line station, and had been on duty when the early morning train left for Holme, Yaxley, Peterborough and, by changing at Holme, with the main line to King's Cross. He had, that very morning, observed a man in cap and raincoat who had got on the train — a man, he said, whose face was vaguely familiar. Uncle Jim was an extremely truthful and very conscientious man, and it occurred to him where he *might* have seen the chap before: accompanying Aunt Lizzie on her trips to see us, when Uncle Jim had inspected his railway pass and had known perfectly well that Aunt Lizzie was not the man's wife.

He had, of course, kept quiet about this irregularity rather than have the family tainted with such scandalous goings on. He felt, though, that in the case of the attempted theft of our wireless set, he ought to tell Dad of his suspicion. The trouble was that it had been a very busy morning when he had been supervising farmers 'putting on' potatoes, allocating trucks etc. as well as working the signals and issuing or inspecting tickets for passenger trains, and his only complete recall of the incident was of his own surprise that a complete stranger should be getting on the train at our station at that time of the morning. He hadn't bought a ticket, so Uncle Jim had assumed he had a return. Uncle Jim stressed, over and over again, that he could not be sure the stranger was Aunt Lizzie's lodger — he just had an uncomfortable feeling that that was why the chap looked familiar.

And therein lay the real reason for the coolness that developed between us and Aunt

Lizzie. Our detestation of the lodger was such that we wanted him to be blackened as our burglar and it was quite beyond Mam to keep the secret to herself when next she saw her sister. Aunt Lizzie, of course, was deeply offended, and in her turn deeply offended Mam by her passionate defence of George.

Dad tried hard to reason it out, and wean the rest of us from our conviction that we need look no further for the intruder. Dad asked sensible questions, such as how had George got to us from Peterborough in the middle of the night without coming by train the night before, when either Uncle Jim or the one other railwayman must have seen him? Nobody had seen him walking from the station, or back to the station. Moreover, he must have known quite well that Dad got up at 5.00 a.m. — and if he had been there, how, in the Lord's blessing, asked Dad, had he expected to carry away a thing the size of our wireless set (12 inches × 15 inches × 24 inches), trailing wires, getting it a mile up the road and on to a train without being observed?

Dad was probably right, of course, and George entirely innocent. A much more likely explanation is that the would-be thief was one of Lois's many boy-friends — that is, one of the group to which the electrician belonged, or one of Gerald's many acquaintances from Ramsey or even further afield. Some of these had access to a car, and were as familiar with our household's ways as ever George was. Poor Aunt Lizzie! How much more we should have loved her and wanted her if she would have jettisoned George;

the other down-and-outs of her entourage we were quite able to accept, but George was anathema. At any rate, Uncle Jim saved us from George's visits thereafter, though he lived in Aunt Lizzie's house where she and Uncle Bill cared for him night and day through a dreadful protracted fatal illness till his death from skin cancer, many years later.

There were so few cars around our district at that time that no one seems to have considered a car to be involved with the attempted theft. We had, of course, seen cars coming down our road, even during the Great War years, but ordinary folk did not possess such things. Moreover, they were accepted as replacements to the horse only with great reluctance. It was conceded that for use (as in the case of the doctor) they might have some relevance to us, but everybody was 'agin' the use of these monstrosities for pleasure. The phase didn't last long — youngsters like Gerald soon made sure of that.

While it did last, cars were *events*. If we children saw one raising the dust in the distance, we yelled to each other to come quick and see it go by. When we were assembled, we kneeled down in a line along the very edge of the sloping grass verge of the road, and put our ears to the ground to listen to the increasing vibration as its narrow tyres coped with the huge lumps of granite on the road.

'Stop your bloody Monte Carlo' shouted an irate farmer to an intrepid motorist outside our house one day, 'Cayn't yer see as my 'oss is frit?'

There was no telephone on our side of the

bridge until about 1928, when our tiny sub-post office was connected. All the same, we were moving gradually into the twentieth century. For one thing, a private bus company included Ugg Mere Court Road in its itinerary, and the main bus service connected us with Ramsey two or three times a week, as well as with Peterborough on Saturdays. These service buses were bright scarlet in colour, so you could see them coming a long way off. This was quite useful, because Mam was always less than punctual for anything, and Dad invariably found something that had to be done at the last minute before he put on his collar and tie, and changed his shoes. So whenever either or both were going anywhere by bus, I was sent out to watch for it and give them warning. If they were not yet dressed, I had to hold up my hand to stop it, and explain to the conductor, who then obligingly waited till the traveller(s) appeared. The pace of life throughout the twenties was still slow and peaceful. The buses did make a difference to our lives, though, especially as the proprietors began to hire out their buses for day trips, for bodies such as the Women's Institute and the Farmer's Union. The latter arranged a day-trip to Southampton to see over a great ocean liner. Bill Bedford's grandfather stood at his gate and watched the bus filled with neighbouring farmers pass by.

'T'aring fools!' he ejaculated. 'T'aring fools!'

Dad was among the tearing fools, and gave us great anxiety that night as the hours went by and no bus returned. When, at last, he walked in, well towards morning, he looked as sheepish as I ever saw him. It seems that he, with A1 (the one who didn't want a 'bloody wulless') in tow, had wandered away from the party being shown round, and gone exploring on his own. He did not anticipate the long corridors all looking exactly alike, and got hopelessly lost in the bowels of the ship. The full bus waited and waited, and still there was no sign of Will'En and A1. When the leader of the expedition realised that the gang-plank was about to be raised, and the ship to sail, he made it known that there were two prospective stowaways aboard, and two very relieved fen tigers were rescued and set ashore.

Dad said afterwards that he wouldn't have minded a voyage to the USA — but not with A1 to look after. It would be about the same time that a terrible scandal (or a bout of highly outraged feelings) was caused by a family new to the fen. When somebody in the family died, it was decided that he should be taken, like Grandmother, for 'a bloody j'y ride' to Ramsey cemetery. Relations came from far and wide, and it was rumoured that it was going to be 'a big fun'ral', so all the blinds were drawn in houses along the route, and every woman stood behind her drawn blinds to peep at the grand cortège as it passed. And there was the hearse — a *motor-hearse* — followed by one huge, high, brilliantly scarlet bus!

Towards the end of the twenties, Gerald bought his first car. The distance between us and the rest of the world was shortening with every day that passed; but we were still largely dependent for anything in the way of entertainment upon ourselves.

We had no sports facilities of any kind, except that nature provided us often in winter with a skating rink *par excellence*. I remember 1929 in particular. I was sixteen, and in love. My sweetheart was a boy still at school though about to leave, and skating provided us with a wonderful chance to be together all day — day after day, week after week, all over Christmas and into the New Year. In early February, there was a full moon. Lois and Gerald were out skating under the full moon all night, so why shouldn't I be, as well? Reluctantly, Mam gave in. It was a lot colder than I had expected it to be, and I never was the skilled, practised skater that my sister and brother were. They could keep themselves warm. Perhaps, with my sweetheart at my side, I didn't give enough attention to the actual skating. Whatever the reason, I took ill, and had a very severe attack of bronchitis (during which time my faithless swain turned his attentions elsewhere). The point of my anecdote is that during my long time in bed, Mam moved me into the second bed in the front bedroom, where I could have a fire. Once I began to sit up and take notice, she moved the bed so that I could see out of the front window, and as I sat there one morning waiting for my breakfast, a figure appeared on the road outside. It was Gerald, striking out on his Norwegian skates, leaning forward with arms swinging — skating down the High Road. There had been a slight thaw, the waters had come down with a rush and flooded us above the level of the road, and then the frost had set in again.

The road had been frozen over before — I suppose many times, though I can only vouch for one other such occasion, when one of Mam's friends died and was taken to Ramsey for burial. Dad was against Mam setting out for the funeral, and for once she heeded his advice. She was glad she hadn't gone, for somewhere along the way one of the horses slipped and fell, and overturned the hearse, spilling the coffin out onto the road.

I don't suppose the road was ever actually under ice again after 1929, because by 1934 the new pump had been put in at St Germans, and flood water thereafter was kept more in control.

One of the reasons we had few sports facilities was the shortage of grass. Fen land was too fertile to waste on grass, hedges or trees. Every inch of it, as close to the dykesides as was possible, was cropped. However, farmers had to have somewhere to graze their horses, and the few cows or bullocks that they kept. Bullocks were mostly 'joisters' (agisters), kept in the yards to provide manure; looked after by the farmer but belonging to somebody else. Cows did well enough wandering along the grass verges all summer, provided they had 'an ol' bor' (or 'gal') in attendance. We were lucky again. At the back of our farmyard lay an eight-acre grassfield, where our three cart horses and Mam's pony grazed along with our small herd of milking cows. As it was not only the largest grassfield, but also happened to lie almost opposite to the school, it was used exclusively for any outdoor celebration such as the Peace Celebration, Coronations, Jubilees and/or anything else. (So was our piano — standing on one of our trolleys, and covered with a stack-cloth in case of rain.)

It was Uncle Jim who came up with the idea that we ought to have a tennis club. It still puzzles me why he happened to know all about tennis, but there it is, he did. He canvassed for support among the young folks, and found many willing to turn their hands towards making a court. Where? Well, there was only one possible location — in our grassfield. Uncle Jim and Dad (the ever-willing) went surveying, and decided that the levellest patch of the eight acres was plump in the middle. So work on it began.

Peat, unadulterated peat, is no foundation for a flat, level surface. Roll as the boys might, with a huge heavy roller, it swelled into bumps and sank into hollows after every drop of rain, or in hot dry weather cracked from side to side with fissures wide enough to lose a golf-ball in. The posts set up to hold the net at the correct height yielded to the tension on the wire, and gradually leaned inwards till the sagging net caused the handle to be turned once too often, and the posts collapsed towards each other. Around the outside of the court, a chicken-wire screen about twelve feet high was erected to contain the balls. There was no money to buy anything with, so improvisation was the order of its erection. (Mam lost both her specially made clothes-props, and was far from pleased.) Some of the boys cut poles from the silver birch that grew down the fen — anything but straight, but they held up the wire, for a short time. They were too short and too pliable to be of much use, and as they were only just stuck straight down into the soft peaty earth, they swayed drunkenly in every breeze and very soon worked themselves loose. Besides, as the purpose of having a grassfield at all was to graze animals, there was nothing to stop a hefty cart horse from using one of them as a scratching-post, or an inquisitive cow from hooking a horn through the wire-netting, and then backing off taking a whole section of fence with it. If the nature of this improvised screen lowered its efficiency, it certainly added variety to our tennis, because it always sagged low enough somewhere or other to allow balls to escape.

The uneven peat of the court itself meant that one could never be sure how a ball would bounce, so at least we became very alert players, prepared for anything; and when a ball hit a bump, or a hollow, one took a wild swipe at it that sent it soaring over the sagging chicken-wire, where it inevitably landed plop into the middle of a newly-dropped cowpat. Then the game stopped while it was recovered and cleaned; and perhaps one of the set made use of the pause to rush home and start baiting one of his horses, or if a girl, to put on supper for younger members of the family.

In spite of these unusual conditions, some of us became quite keen tennis fans, and reasonably good players. We played matches against the few other villages who had the use of a court and could raise a team. I have to say that some of us, of course, also played tennis at school, under different conditions and a modicum of coaching. Most village clubs had two or three Grammar School pupils, past or present, at the core of their match team.

Ramsey itself had a flourishing tennis club, but we understood that it was only for the élite, and we would not have suggested playing them; but other large villages were not so snooty, so we played Yaxley and Sawtry and Holme. We also went to Yaxley and Sawtry for whole day tournaments if we could make the journey, and as individuals we entered tournaments at Ramsey and at St Ives on Regatta day.

The fun came when our opponents came to us for a return match. We had only one court, so a match went on for hours and hours and hours, but at least we stood some chance of winning, because we knew our own peculiar court, and they didn't.

Uncle Jim was still the doyen of the successful club he had set up, though he did not play himself except for an occasional knock-up. When we played matches, however, he acted as umpire, turning out in a pair of white flannels and blazer. Miss, as the club's secretary, arranged the order of the matches and wrote them on a board hung on the wire-netting gate. A village schoolteacher was expected to be in on everything, and take the lead. Beside her own job of teaching us, our Miss was church organist, president of the WI, accompanist to the concert party, secretary of the tennis club, pianist for village socials, etc. etc.

etc. She did not play tennis, but like Uncle Jim, came suitably dressed to lend some dignity to our home-made set up.

When all was ready, Uncle Jim would mount a pair of ordinary household steps by the side of one of the net posts, between it and the outer fence. His perch was, to say the least, insecure, and we watched with amused anticipation for the moment when his weight caused the legs of the steps to sink into the peaty ground. Then, without warning, the umpire would suddenly disappear from view as the steps lost the battle and the centre of his equilibrium fell outside his base, tipping him backward against the wobbly wire of the fence, or forward on to the court, tangled up with the collapsed net and its supports.

What a boost for us all our apology for a tennis-court became! It was the 'open sesame' to a wider social life for me and my contemporaries, because the boys from our mixed Grammer School cycled out at weekends to play tennis with us. Our visits to other villages — Yaxley, for example — were made possible when Gerald and Miss acquired cars. Gerald's was only what would now be called an old banger, a two-seater with a 'dickey', but as many of us as possibly could hang on anywhere were transported in it. It was a bit hard on Gerald himself, because to the end of his life he despised organised games, taking his own pleasure in such solitary ones as shooting and fishing. Besides, he always had far too many other hobbies — painting pictures, building boats, perfecting inventions, etc. to want a place in our tennis team; but willy-nilly, he had to have one, because we needed his transport. As his heart was never in the game, he did his best to make sure we lost as soon as possible, so that we got home earlier to release him to his other hobbies or his entourage of would-be girlfriends. Like dear Mu, most of them came to the family as Gerald's girl, and stayed on as friends. On one occasion Mam found herself getting tea for no less than nine of his cast-off girlfriends on the same afternoon.

When Gerald finally rebelled, we were out on our own. Lois was between boyfriends, the electrician having been given the push (reluctantly) after eight years because his prospects of marriage at thirty-four were no better than they had been at twenty-six, when he had first fallen in love with my sixteen-year-old schoolgirl sister. She was now twenty-four, and I sixteen. We were tennis mad, and were not going to let lack of transport stop us. After all, we had our bikes. Mu, like the bold spirit she has always been, somehow acquired a motor bike, so sometimes she and Lois went off without me, Lois riding pillion with her lap full of equipment and her arms round Mu's waist. On such days I sat at home and sulked (or cried), as the afternoon hours dragged by till the butcher's son had completed his round, togged himself up, and came with his brand new motor cycle combination to collect me to go dancing with him.

(Sich forrard wayses! Whatever was Bill thinking of, to allow such behaviour!)

However, Mu was not having a very happy

426

time, and could not always escape to take Lois. Then Lois and I went together — as far as I was concerned, the happiest outcome of all, because I preferred her company to that of any of my friends, male or female. Besides, with her as chaperone, I was allowed much more freedom than I might otherwise have had.

So — where there's a will, there's a way. We had our bikes, and when we wanted to enter a tournament at Sawtry or St Ives, we had no option but to use them. With suitcases strapped to our carriers, balls in a net and a pair of tennis shoes tied to the head of our rackets, we cycled the ten miles or so to our destination. Once there we put on our tennis outfits, and played vigourously all the afternoon; stopped for a cup of tea and a lettuce sandwich, and went on playing again throughout the early evening. At 7.30 p.m. approximately, the winner was declared and we retired to the lavatories (sometimes, a ladies cloakroom) for a swill with cold water, a brush up, and a crude make up. Out came our dance-dresses from the suitcases, and our evening sandals. At 8.30 p.m. or so, we rejoined the rest of the afternoon's competitors on the dance floor of the local village hall (read hut) or school. We danced till midnight, hastily changed back to the clothes we'd left home in, and pedalled the ten miles home again — unaccompanied, unafraid, and even then, unwearied.

I must be getting old. I allow what is called sport nowadays to irritate me. There seems nothing but constant demand for better facilities for the poor, deprived young, though all they do when they get the facilities is to vandalise them. Sport nationally is commercially based and tazzled up with politics: football is a religion demanding frequent human sacrifices. Tennis and snooker make heroes of unsocial boors on the grounds of which of the pack can make the most millions in a season. Even dart-players, complete with their beerguts, are held up as examples of 'sportsmen', and are decorated at Buckingham Palace.

Our half-crown's worth of physical effort gave us no opportunities for fame or fortune, but the pleasure it gave us could never be valued in such terms.

We were entering 'the dancing years', and of all pleasures, to me dancing was the apogee. To many young folks, the dance floor has always been the stage for romance, for a meeting of the sexes, legitimised because it took place in full view. Besides, every girl did her best to look pretty, and every boy to be clean and neat. To most of my friends, this was the greatest attraction of the dance — and so it was to me, to some extent, but only minimally so. I can find no words to describe the sensation that moving to the rhythm of the dance sent pulsing through me; of being able, effortlessly, to anticipate whatever complicated footwork my partner required of me in a quick-step: the precise balance needed for a slow-foxtrot: the thrill of stepping exactly on the beat in waltz-time, and never losing it while expertly reversing: or, best of all, leaning away from an equally expert partner at shoulder level, while feet were placed as close as possible to create the spinning-top shape necessary to execute a fast and furious Viennese waltz without stumbling. The glory of it! The glory of it, so sweet in remembrance that I have only to lay aside my crutches, lie back in my recliner chair, switch on a cassette and close my eyes to relive it all again. The music throbs through me from head to toe, through wrists to fingertips, just as it always did. I often find that my back and leg muscles are actually still moving to the rhythm — and there's no sadness of nostalgia about it. Half a loaf is better than no bread at all!

So my partners were not prospective sweethearts, let alone potential husbands. They chose me for the same reason that I accepted their courteous 'May I have the pleasure?' — they knew that I could dance, and I knew that they could. Once on the floor, I could lose myself completely in the dance.

I owed it a lot to Lois that I was able to dance so much, and so often. Apart from her chaperonage, it was she who made my dresses. She was an expert needlewoman, and having a new dance dress for herself often depended upon her bargain with Mam (who controlled all our purse-strings still) that if she could have the material for another dress herself, she made me one as well. Not that she ever needed any persuading, because she loved dressmaking and she loved me as much as I adored her. Up to that time, though our house was full to overflowing with youngsters of both sexes, nobody had had occasion to call 'I spy strangers'.

We should all have had enough sense to know it could not last forever. Sorrow and sadness, as well as financial difficulties, were waiting in the wings.

It may be that Lois and Gerald were already aware of straitened circumstances, difficulties, and a souring of our so-far happy home atmosphere, but I was not. I was, after all, only fifteen, when Lois was twenty-four and Gerald twenty-five. And for me, life was still pretty good — composed of all that I liked doing best.

I had two rival swains — one a farmer's son and the other a butcher's son. Neither was my ideal of manhood: one kept up a constant supply of chocolates, and the other of new books. One had a car, the other a combination motor-bike and sidecar. Maybe that one, educated and courteous, could have been taken a bit more seriously than he was but for Mam's predilection for him, against which I rebelled. So I made use of both, especially for transport, and never got involved beyond accepting the gifts — especially the books!

There never had been any prohibition on my having boy-friends, and I wanted them as chauffeurs and dancing partners. I was not in the least concerned with any more adult relationships, in spite of the fact that our household was more emancipated in this than most. We must even have been a decade or so in advance of the average working class of the nation, let alone the still-Victorian mores that prevailed all around us.

I was just as happy curled up reading as I had

ever been, except that there didn't seem quite so much time for it, with school on the one hand, and dancing and tennis on the other. I suppose I must have attended to my homework with fair conscientiousness, or the results would have been different, but once I had got that School Certificate, I never let my school life interfere with my growing up. All my friends had decided on their future careers. I hadn't a clue, except for one thing. Most of them were heading for the teaching profession. I was not. The one thing I had decided was that I did not want to be a teacher.

After the summer vacation of 1929, I went back to school, still only in my sixteenth year.

It came upon me as a great shock to discover that Jock and his staff regarded me as potential University material. Me? The duffer of the pack who couldn't do arithmetic to save her life? I was utterly astounded, and so incredulous that I didn't take them seriously. Jock explained to me that in order to get exemption from the London Matriculation, I had to have 'credit' in six subjects in the School Certificate, which credits must include maths. I already had more than six credits, but only a pass in maths. I should therefore have to take the School Certificate again (and as it happened, again and again) till the magic credit appeared on the mark list.

I still thought the whole thing a lot of bunkum. For one thing, if I was going to a University, it was going to be Cambridge — and a fat lot of chance I stood of getting in there, because I had done no word of Latin, and I knew I couldn't get in without it. As I didn't know what else to do, anyway, and Dad seemed happy to go on paying the fees, I went along with the school's plans for me.

I joined the group destined to take the School Certificate the next June, making one special friend among them, Ellen. Everything was a bit vague. I just let things happen to me — and happen to me they did.

One thing really 'got my goat'. I was, of course, still required to wear the school uniform. I was very large, particularly round the bust, and a gym-slip didn't do much for my ego. Nor did that terrible school hat! Being of a responsible age, I was entrusted with all sorts of commissions for family and neighbours which entailed walking the streets of Ramsey in my lunch-hour. What was I to do when I came face to face with a young farmer from St Ives who only twelve hours before had been whispering endearments to 'his Indian Princess' as he wrapped around me (Lois's) long-fringed silk shawl over my sleeveless, backless dance-dress of black satin embroidered all over with rosebuds? Who tried to arrange another dancing date with me as I waited for Lois to emerge with the rest of the band, clutching my gold, strappy, six-inch heeled sandals and my gold-beaded evening bag?

There I was, gym-slipped, black-wool-stockinged, boat-flat-laced-shoe shod and crowned with that ridiculous hat! He didn't recognise me, thank God!

My blazer had had it. It was no longer big enough. I made a fuss, and insisted that if I was going to stay on at school, I had to have a new blazer.

It occasioned a lot of worry at home, and for the first time I understood that things were not as rosy in the world of farming, and that money was not as free as it had been. From that time, I lived three lives — one the schoolgirl, following a predestined pattern as immutable as the laws of the Medes and Persians, a sort of background life to which I gave little thought or attention. Then there was the one who enjoyed life to the full whether I was under an apple-tree reading, or playing Rosalind for a WI drama competition, or (above all else) out dancing till the early hours, energy never flagging. To these two was added a third — a nearly adult who now had a constant thread of anxiety about all sorts of straws in the wind at home. Things were not what they had been. My new blazer was ordered from Ramsey's bespoke tailor. Its price was such that Mam explained I should have to have it for my sixteenth birthday present. I agreed, and put it on for the first time on my birthday. Joyce was still at school with me, but my memory is vague about the others. I know Joyce was there, because of what happened.

It was our laboratory day, and after morning break we gathered for chemistry, with 'Sir' of the Horatius episode in charge. The experiment we were to carry out involved the use of concentrated nitric acid, a small quantity of which Sir held up in a beaker for our inspection, as he stood behind the raised teacher's bench — warning us over and over again of its dangerous properties and enjoining us to be more than usually careful. I remember remarking to somebody that it looked just like golden-syrup.

We split into groups, and prepared the equipment for our experiment. I had not taken off my beautiful new blazer, because it was very cold in the lab, and a lot of others were wearing theirs, too.

We needed a clamp. They were kept in a cupboard under the teacher's bench which had doors in the front that opened outwards, towards the class. I opened the cupboard and foraged about with my head inside it to find the best clamp I could. Sir had no idea that I was there as he handed to a girl from another group a beaker half-full of the sticky golden nitric acid. I had found what I wanted, and backed out. As I stood up, the top of my head came into contact with the arm of the girl just accepting the beaker of acid from Sir's hand. She let go, and I looked up. The acid rained down on me in big, viscous globules, mostly on my face, neck and shoulders.

I have said before, while accounting Sir's discomfiture as a poetry-teacher, how much I had to be grateful to him for. In icy calm, he asked me 'IS THAT ACID?' I nodded. 'AMMONIA' he yelled — and the next moment I had been taken by the scruff of the neck and literally shoved under a cold tap. One of the more intelligent boys had leapt to find a bottle of ammonia, and still holding the back of my neck in a grip of iron, Sir slashed ammonia into my face, commanding me to keep my eyes firmly closed. The water, and the ammonia, ran down my neck, and over my arms. Sir was by now mopping off the ammonia with cotton wool.

One teardrop of acid had landed on my right eye-lid, just under the eyebrow. I had closed my eyes instinctively just in time. Another had missed the same eye by a whisker and landed on my nose. These two, Sir dared not neutralise properly because the ammonia would have been as deadly to my sight as the acid. Both had pitted already before Sir was able, with infinite care, to wipe them with a diluted solution of ammonia. I bear the scars to this day, though both now have to be looked for.

Sir's calm, prompt action had saved the worst effects. I was taken to the staff-room to be treated for shock, as face, throat, arms and hands began to swell and were swathed in bandages. Sitting in Miss Passmore's chair while this was being done, I complained that only my right foot was really hurting me. Nobody had bothered much about anything but my face. I looked down at my foot, surprised to find that my black stocking was now striped with brownish yellow. Off came the stocking (in spite of Jock's presence!) and it was discovered that a drop of acid had descended on to the top of my foot, and had been burning its way in for some minutes by then. This has been the only one to cause me any lasting damage — the pit healed slowly, but the scar is exactly where the vamp of any smart shoe rests. It is still painful when a tight shoe rubs on it.

It was decided that I should be sent home

— on my bike, bandaged as I was, and only able to squint out of my left eye. That is how I know that Joyce was still at school with me. She was sent for, not having been in the chemistry class, and told to ride home by my side, going on ahead when we neared my home to warn the family of my wounded-soldier appearance.

It so happened (Sods' law again!) that one of our friends who was a journalist was there when we went in, and as he worked on a local paper, he naturally reported the accident. Jock was furious, and gave the whole school a lecture about keeping their mouths shut about anything that happened in school. Such a disgraceful bit of unwanted publicity was never to happen again!

(No wonder! Just think what damages Dad could have claimed on my behalf if the accident had happened yesterday, instead of sixty years ago.) It is quite probable that he could have got something then if he had tried — if it was only the cost of my new blazer. I had asked for it when ready to start for home, and it had been handed to me — a soggy mass of material hanging dejectedly in brown-edged purple and gold strips. My gymslip, stockings and shoes were also complete write-offs — but I wasn't. In the days that followed, my face healed well except for the two scars so near to my eye, though the skin came off my arms and neck in long, horrid strips. There is no doubt at all that Sir's prompt, cool reaction saved not only my looks, but probably my sight. As Mam would have said 'It don't bear thinking about!'

I got back for a few days in January before my skating-induced bronchitis caused another long-ish absence, and I can only guess that it was at this period that Joyce left. I found myself taking the School Certificate examination again, this time with Ellen's year. I had A grades for everything else but the maths, which I passed, but without the necessary credit. It was at this juncture that I somehow became a sort of twelfth-man to any group of other examinees. First there was Ellen: she needed her School Certificate because she wanted to be a teacher — uncertificated — but she had tripped up somewhere along the line of subjects, and as her father could afford the necessary fees, it was decided she should sit the examination again the following Christmas (1930). I was also entered, 'to keep Ellen company'. I was bored by being in 'the fifth' and plodding along the same old path year after year with a new set of classmates. That I was a House Captain and Head Prefect was only a sop to my pride — a bit like offering a hungry donkey a strawberry. Until that year, I had been so exemplary a pupil, behaviour-wise, that my name had hardly ever been read out at the Friday-morning assembly for having received a detention for some specified crime during the week.

Now it was such a regular feature that the members of my house anticipated it with glee: I could hardly round on them for losing us house-points when I was doing it so constantly myself.

With a pained expression on his crumpled

face, Jock would look up from the ledger-like detention book lying before him, search for me standing in my accustomed place at the combined school assembly, stare reproachfully at me before enunciating slowly and with elaborate distinctness 'Sybil Edwards: for reading *Bulldog Drummond* in the history lesson' or 'for reading *The Broad Highway* during a scripture test': or (most often) for Zane Grey, Baroness Orczy or Jeffery Farnol in geography, the lesson I cared for least of all and which was taken by the one member of staff not so far mentioned, an ageing, shrunken bachelor we called 'Old Nap' because of his irritating habit of sniffing loudly while napping his eyes. We did not know he was ill, and desperately trying to cling to his job long enough to make his pension big enough to support him in retirement.

Anyway, it was a new teacher's suggestion that when I was informed that I was to run alongside Ellen in the Christmas examination stakes, we were also told that we had been entered for a paper no one had ever sat before, called 'General Literature'. Here was the challenge I needed. Ellen got her certificate and I, wonder of wonders, at last achieved the credit in maths, as well as a distinction in English.

But now a pace-maker was needed for someone else — a girl a year my senior who was making a bid for a Higher School Certificate. As with the School Certificate itself, this higher qualification could not be obtained piecemeal. It was necessary to achieve passes in two main and two subsidiary subjects all at the same time

— sitting ten or eleven three-hour papers in all.

The other girl had been working towards it for a year and one term already, so I had no choice but to join her in her chosen subjects — English and Divinity as main, French and History as subsidiaries.

Nobody expected me to pass, but it was considered good practice for me for my own attempt at this higher hurdle next year; but there must have been a good deal of earnest discussion amongst my teachers. My running mate had chosen seventeenth-century literature for her special period paper — something I had never studied. Nor could I be expected to know much about Divinity, on the strength of what we had had to do for the ordinary RE in the School Certificate. (My teachers could not be expected to know of my long-standing, close acquaintance with the Bible and all its works, even unto the obscure prophets of Hosea and Amos, which the examiners that year had selected for special study.) Even without knowing about that, Jock, Puss and Miss Oddy thought I might stand a one-in-a-million chance, even though I only had two terms to prepare myself.

Jock took me aside for a long, serious talk. He did not make the mistake of giving me hope, but he spelled out the possibilities of chance. My French and History were quite up to the standard required as subsidiaries. I could be absolutely relied upon to do well in the English essay, and in the English language papers. The Shakespeare paper consisted of the study of three plays, two of which I already knew in depth. Only *Coriolanus* was new to me. That left the Divinity papers and the seventeenth-century literature paper. I could spend my two terms concentrating on *Paradise Lost*, Fuller and Lord Clarendon, with a bit of Dryden thrown in, and *Coriolanus*. He trusted to my ability with words to make a little knowledge go a long way, he said — especially as there really would be no time to tackle Divinity properly. BUT — I was still only seventeen — and there was a regulation that any who succeeded in this examination before reaching the age of eighteen could automatically claim a State Scholarship for a University place.

When the results were published, I was neither surprised nor disappointed, but Jock was as bitterly angry as his high intelligence and passionate care for his pupils could make him.

Of the eleven papers I had attempted, my marks on ten of them were remarkable — even the Divinity, for reasons well known. But among the list of very high marks was one incredibly low one — for the Shakespeare paper. Without that, one could not pass English as a whole, and I had consequently failed on my one sure subject. Without English, there could be no Higher School Certificate at seventeen, and therefore no State Scholarship.

Jock stormed and railed. As he had done the invigilating of the examination himself, and as he had only two candidates, he had had plenty of time to stand behind each of us and observe how were were tackling the questions. Moreover, when time was up and we handed our completed papers in to him, he had (of course) taken a quick look through them before parcelling them up for dispatch to the Board for marking. So he knew perfectly well that I had written an excellent Shakespeare paper. Caution thrown to the winds, he declared to me, 'You couldn't fail an English paper, especially a Shakespeare paper, if you tried!'

The marks had been rigged to fail me, and he knew it. He protested: he demanded that my paper be marked by other examiners; he suggested I should be allowed to sit it again. 'Said the gnat to the elephant, 'Who are you pushing?' ' He was banging his head against a brick wall of offical bureaucrats, who that year must have had more potential State Scholars on their hands than they were prepared to support.

It was sadder for me than Jock understood. In 1931, the Agricultural Depression had begun to bite deep in the fens, with us as much as with everybody else. I was worried about the cracks appearing in our family solidarity as well. I had not hoped for the chance of a University place before it had been so tantalisingly dangled before me, because I knew Dad could not contribute towards it. A State Scholarship would have made it just within the bounds of possibility.

I accepted my failure with a sort of dogged fatalism — as Mam would have said, 'setting a hard heart against hard sorrow'.

What was the good of staying on at school yet another year, to try again, on my own behalf instead of as pace-maker to another, when I knew that even if my results at eighteen were good enough to gain me a place and a

441

scholarship, I could not take it up? I should have to go out to work somewhere, at some job, to keep myself and even, perhaps, to help keep the farm from bankruptcy.

It was many, many years later that Mam, in conversation with Jock's wife, let slip the truth of why I had so disappointed them. It seems incredible that they had had no inkling of the financial straits we were in, and had sought in vain to explain to themselves my incomprehensible decision not to go forward and through the pearly gates to Cambridge. Had they but known, they said, the necessary funds would have been forthcoming from somewhere, if it had had to be a loan from their own pocket. It was that stubborn old fen pride that had stood in my way, and in the end I have not been sorry, except for one thing.

In that last term, trying to make sure I understood what it was I was throwing away, Mrs Allen had said to me 'You know, Sybil, you must look further ahead than the next year or two. One of the great advantages of going to a University is that you would probably meet a husband there. Where else are you likely to meet one compatible with you?'

Well, certainly, it was a point that I had not considered — but how right she was. Compatibility, not only with us but with our close-knit family, was going to be vital to us all. At the time, it was a prospect too far away to set against the other, more immediate pressures.

I'm glad to be able to report that Mrs Allen — though not Jock — lived long enough to ask

442

me to tea when I could legitimately put MA (Cantab) behind my name, and present her with a signed copy of my first book in print. As I left, she put into my hands one of her own treasured possessions, taken on the spur of the moment from a table-top. A photograph of Jock. They had no children of their own.

The house in which they lived has now been demolished, and where it stood is a little patch of grass and shrubs, kept neat and inviting by the Ramsey Council. It is next to the library, and there are seats on which the old (and young) can rest. Above is a tasteful notice informing anyone who does not know that this tiny patch of ground is really a memorial. It simply says Allen's Piece. I hope there are a few others that it means as much to as it does to me.

But I did go back to school for another year. If I had fatalistically given up hope, my teachers had not. Since I had set my heart on Cambridge, there was one great obstacle — I knew no Latin. There was still one whole school year before the examination, and I was a quick learner with a love of words. Both Jock and Miss Oddy would give up all their free periods to teaching me Latin. Puss had a hand in it, too, because I can remember her spitting on me as she made me repeat

Put the ablative with *de*
Cum and *coram*, *ab* and *e*
Sine, *tenus*, *pro* and *pre*

One bit, at least, that I haven't forgotten! It rattles about in my memory-box along with

Henry VIII's wives and the formula for solving quadratic equations:

$$x = -b \pm \frac{\sqrt{b^2 + 4ac}}{2a}$$

I think it was Thomas Fuller who observed that people who dwelt in houses of learning were often found to have little of any value in their top-loft — or words to that effect!

Poor Old Nap had not quite made it to his retirement. He died suddenly in his last year of teaching, and we had a new, young geography master. That wicked fairy who at my awakening had robbed me of any sense of direction had left me with a mental map upside down, and a built in mistrust of anything to do with maps thereafter. I was no great shakes at geography, and I can but suppose that I was hampered rather than helped by all those outdated facts memorised at the Heights School a decade earlier. But the young master who came to take Nap's place wanted his finger in the pie of giving me a chance to make up for the cruel fate of the previous year's examination. He, too, would give up all his free periods to what amounted to private tuition in geography. I was, consequently, entered for English and history as main subjects, with geography, French and Latin as subsidiaries. Is it really necessary for me to report that my examinations results were all that my teachers had hoped for? The only person not delighted and excited by them was me. I had been aware from the start that whatever they were, I could not follow them up.

It was a strange, extraordinary year, that last one of mine at school. With the advantage of hindsight, I know now that my almost frenetic pursuit of enjoyment outside home and school was the result of my understanding that what had always been so special about our home life was under threat from all sides. My teachers, aware of my double life, did their best to warn me that I could not have the best of both worlds.

'Ah! Take the cash, and let the credit go!'

The music of the distant drum of academic success was not so brave in my ears as in theirs. It stood no chance against the pulsating rhythm of the dance bands, and the hypnotism of the dance floor, the only place where I could truly and wholly forget the nagging of unhappiness in my family circle.

Besides, I could not (I believe that to be truer than that I would not) accept their reasoning that I could not have the best of both worlds. Why not? I had to get rid of my overplus of vitality somehow.

So I 'recked my own rede', and danced whenever and wherever an opportunity arose. There was a dance I wanted to go to in the very week I sat the last few of my Higher School Certificate examinations. The history course had three, if not four, three-hour papers. One, devoted to the British Empire, I had dealt with between 2 p.m. and 5 p.m. in the afternoon. I cycled home, had a meal, washed, dressed and went with Joyce to a dance. It was 3 a. m. when I crept up the stairs again at home, and as I took off my sandals I realised that in six hours' time I had to be back at Ramsey to take another paper on European history, about which I felt (at 3 a. m.) that I did not know enough even to waffle on for three minutes. So instead of going to bed, I washed, put on my school clothes, lit my candle and began to read. Buoyed up by the dancing and the music, my brain was clearer than it had ever been about European history before. Facts registered, and stuck: sketch maps of changed boundaries, campaigns and battles photographed themselves in my mind. I was still as fresh as the proverbial daisy when I opened the examination paper and realised that my difficulty would be in selecting the three questions I could do best, not finding those I could do at all. I could have answered every one. I was not tired, I was exalted, every faculty sharpened and polished by the euphoric exertion of the evening before. (I would not recommend an evening in the pub, smoking pot, or watching a blue video as a substitute for the physical pleasures of the dance.)

I passed the examination (in toto) with honours. I was informed, officially, that as I had exemption from the London Matriculation and such high results in the Higher School Certificate, I could, if I wished to settle for London University, regard myself as having

acquired already the Intermediate BA

But as I knew, I wasn't going anywhere, except to work. There was only one thing I could do — apply for a job as an uncertificated teacher in a primary school. As it happened, it turned out well.

12

But not the End...

It was less than two decades since I had sat up in my cradle and known so clearly that I was me, who was also part of a family.

We had come a very long way in those decades. Not only had the whole fen been connected with the outside world; we had remained uniquely ourselves, though as our circumstances had changed, so, to some extent, had we. Mam and Dad appeared to be in their prime. Two out of the three of us were grown-up in every sense, and though I was still at school, I was of an age when several of my fenland contemporaries were already wives and mothers.

The whole fen had lifted itself up by its own boot-straps, and was no longer isolated from the rest of the world. It was looking upwards and outwards towards a brighter future, when along came the Great Depression, to clobber everybody.

It is often said that we never learn the lessons that history could teach us if we would but listen. I do not think it is our fault. By the time events have become history in the accepted sense of the word, only the dry bones of the facts remain — sifted and sorted and processed and dessicated till they no longer savour of the historical event any more than a packet of dried soup can be reconstituted into a kitchen garden.

Imagination is the only additive that will bring any of the flavour back, and without small, specific details, even imagination fails. Ask anybody who lived through the second world war. All the history books that have been written about it since cannot bring a shred of the emotion of that time back — but the strains of *We'll Meet Again*, or the sound of Winston Churchill's voice declaring 'We will fight them on the beaches . . . ' can and does. They roll the years back in an instant, so that you see a room, a dancing partner, a dress, a cat that was sitting on the rug beneath the wireless set, and you feel the tug on the heartstring and the thrill of fear or of joy for a second, exactly as you felt it then.

What effect does the Wall Street Crash have upon the students who now have to study it, cold, so to speak? Not, I know, what the sound of *Brother, can you spare a dime?* does to me.

The agricultural depression which was affecting us was but a pimple on the skin of the world-wide recession, but it was that which affected us personally. The great cities had found that old Isaiah's exhortation to go buy 'without money and without price' could not be taken at face value. And if they couldn't buy, we couldn't sell.

It took exactly four years to turn Dad back from a well-to-do, prosperous farmer to a man on the verge of ruin; and as each of those years passed, the strain put on us as individuals changed our outlook, our personalities, even, and our relationships with each other.

All around us, our friends and neighbours were in the same boat and everybody knew the straits that everybody else was in. Being tough old fen folk who had so often before faced ruin from flood or a fen-blow in May, they made little complaint, especially to each other. Pride forbade it. But a new catch-phrase was soon abroad — the usual cynical brand of humour, turned upon themselves, making communication where 'grizzling' would have failed. You heard the catchphrase everywhere, as people met on foot or cycle or high on the front of carts.

'Do yer 'old 'em?'

Now I do wonder what future historians and/or sociologists would deduce or invent to account for such a catchphrase as 'Do you hold them?' if somebody or other such as I could not elucidate. What could it be that they were so ironically enquiring about? THE DEEDS OF THEIR PLOTS OF LAND AND/OR THEIR DWELLINGS. The most difficult years were the last three that I was at school, and those immediately after I left.

Though I was the youngest, I was the first to leave home. We were still a close and united family, but the years of stress had not passed over us without making changes. They began to show in our attitudes towards our somewhat idiosyncratic home life.

Dad, whose rock-solid character and philosophy had been our anchorage for so long, began to show the Celtic strain Cato had remarked, of being 'despondent in defeat'. He began to lose heart, and it was he, not Mam, who grizzled or 'maunch-gutted' when sugar-beet returns were not up to expectation, or when bills came in that he could not pay. He had never had much entrepreneurial spirit; nothing to match Mam's, for instance, and he did not make much effort to meet new challenges. Gerald had been restless for some time. He had never really wanted the farm, and he was irked that he felt tied to it for Dad's sake, when his whole heart was with machines, especially the internal combustion engine. He had been agitating for Dad to buy him a tractor and/or a lorry, with which to set up a business of his own, reducing the amount of his hand labour on our land but making up for it by doing with his mechanical aids what Dad needed doing very cheaply if not for nothing. Dad would not take the risk, especially after the depression began to bite. So Gerald stayed on, longing for independence. He was, after all, in his late twenties, and his deafness was gradually getting worse. He had lost his best friend and constant companion, and though he never lacked friends of either sex, it was from this time that he began to take up solitary pastimes, as his deafness made him even more shy than he had always been.

Lois, also in her mid-twenties, was perhaps the most restless and unhappy of us all, though she did not often show it. She had most cause, too, for wanting to escape from Mam's increasing domination over us all. We had, somewhat naturally, all taken it for granted that she would marry our electrician, who, though ten years her senior, had fallen in love with her when she was only sixteen. But while he was waiting for her to reach marriageable age, fate had removed his father, and all his hopes of being able to support a wife as well as an impoverished, demanding mother and an unmarried sister. The courtship had been going on for almost a decade, during which he had been constantly in and out of our home, and we all loved him dearly. He was that most rare thing in our society, a natural gentleman as well as one brought up in and shaped by the code of the public school at which he had been educated. He had high standards of personal honour, and made no promises to Lois that he could not keep. So when the time came, and Mam felt it necessary for him to declare his intentions, he withdrew his suit, and came to our house no more. If he had been killed in an accident, we could not have felt more bereaved. We never could decide whether Mam had done right, or a great wrong, in forcing the issue; but at the time Lois felt relief as well as sadness. I know, because by this time I was almost grown-up, and was closer to her then than ever before or after.

One of her problems was that the electrician (and Gerald's friend Blazes) had set standards of behaviour that it was impossible for other, more local suitors to match. Suitors there were in plenty — they came singly or in braces, coveys and gaggles, but alas, not in charms or exultations. One, the squire of a village ten miles or so away, might have satisfied Mam by reason of his position, his supposed wealth, and the beautiful old house he had inherited; but Lois said she would rather marry one of his prize Tamworth pigs, which to tell the truth, he somewhat resembled. He was a non-starter, with a vengeance.

It was, I am sure, in a fit of desperate frustration and rebellion that Lois got herself engaged to be married to a stranger who had appeared by chance in our midst — a glove-salesman from London. To put the matter crudely, I believe Lois cared less for him than any of the rest of us, if indeed that could have been possible. At any rate, it was often she who led the hoots of laughter and derision that we regularly engaged in when, plus-foured, helmeted and goggled, he finally bestrode his Norton motorcycle combination and headed back to London after a weekend visit to his affianced bride and her family.

But there, the sight of Mam mimicking him would have made the cat laugh. Somehow managing to shrink her sixteen-stone odd into a finicky fuss-pot with a vague eighteenth-century foppish air, she took an imaginary pipe from her mouth, pursed her lips, and enquired in a voice of pseudo-philosophical inquiry, 'In what way?'

We all agreed that of all his irritating habits, the one that made even Lois want to brain him with a flat-iron was his inability ever to answer a question directly. If one simply asked 'Have you seen today's paper?' he would cock his curly head to one side, try to look like Einstein inventing the theory of relativity, remove his overlarge pipe and say with grave impressiveness, 'In what way?'

Poor man! There never was a suitor so absolutely a fish out of water as he was in our circle. There were many times when Lois could hardly bring herself to be civil to him. One would not have expected so incompatible an engagement to have lasted more than a month, but in fact it staggered on for a year and a half, before suddenly fizzling out with barely a spark or a crackle. No tears were shed for him by anybody.

During those years while we were still grieving inwardly for our lost electrician, we were also bereaved of another visitor so constant and so compatible that he, too, was accepted as an extra member of the family. The greatest loss this time, was to Gerald, in whose life nobody ever replaced Blazes as a friend. Blazes, as we all called him, was another public school boy who had come one day on a visit from Peterborough with Aunt Lizzie, when he was thirteen and Gerald fourteen. The boys had 'clicked' from the moment they set eyes on each other, and Blazes seemed to have decided that New Fen was only just short of heaven. He cycled from Peterborough to be with Gerald at every possible opportunity, spending all his long summer holidays working on the farm at Gerald's side and adding his knowledge to Gerald's inventiveness in winter as they thought up together yet more ways of experimenting with perpetual motion, or more outrageous pranks with gunpowder.

When Blazes left school at eighteen, he became a journalist on a local weekly paper, and the friendship went on as both boys matured into men; but Blazes, too, was the victim of a strong-willed ambitious mother. She wanted better things for him than to be a hack journalist on a local rag, and persuaded him to take a post on *The Straits Times*. When he sailed for Singapore, it was as if Gerald had lost a fraternal twin. He had other mates galore, but there was only one Blazes.

Mam was not made of the stuff to sit down and weep, or advertise our changing fortunes to the world. As money grew tighter, she became more and more extravagant, flaunting her hospitality and even getting herself into debt secretly rather than lower her standard an inch. She rounded on Dad unmercifully for his constant fits of 'maunch-gutting'. If he couldn't manage our finances better than he was doing, why didn't he let her? She was full of wild ideas for restoring our fallen fortunes — wild because in the prevailing economic climate, they were so utterly impossible. It would have been really funny, if it had not been so tragic as well: Dad should sell up at once. (Who on earth did she think could, or would have bought the farm?) With the proceeds, he should set her up with what she had always wanted — a boarding-house at Yarmouth. Not that it made any difference where, because nobody could afford holidays, even if Mam had had the least notion of how to run such an establishment.

By 1930, Dad was sixty. The worse things got

for him, the more he turned for solace to his love of reading. Mam had always resented his ability to withdraw himself in this way, but had had too much sense to try to stop him. Now, because she was beginning to lose her own bounce, she chuntered at him incessantly for 'always having his nose in a book', neglecting her, and sitting maunch-gutting about his bank balance instead of doing anything about it. Even she was losing her faith in the future. Molehills become mountains when there is no strength left to go on climbing.

Poor old Dad. In the middle of all this other misery, he lost his pipe-tooth, and could no longer enjoy a bit of pleasure from his pipe. Now Mam had always liked him to smoke a pipe. She thought it manly, and though she had been his wife for thirty years, she still had an eye for him as a good-looking male. She was right, too, because there is no denying that when washed and dressed and relaxed at his ease with his pipe in his mouth, there were few stars of the (still new) cinema screen to match him for looks.

But when he had to lay aside his pipe, he took to smoking cigarettes. How are the mighty fallen! He was a careless, dirty smoker. He stuck the 'fag' in his mouth, started reading, and forgot it. The ash fell off down his waistcoat, burnt holes in his trousers and scattered over the rug. He sometimes dropped off to sleep till it fell out of his mouth or burned his handsome moustache.

Then, just about the time I left school in 1932, Dad began to suffer from sore ears. Nothing to worry about, surely, a pair of scaly, tender ear-lobes? Probably because they looked rather horrid, Mam chivvied him into going to see the young doctor who had taken over our old one's practice.

When Dad came back from the visit, he was in a mood of unwonted disgruntlement, and said little.

'Well?' said Mam, turning up her expensive ear-phone (as she always called it) to its loudest, oscillating worst. 'What did he say?'

'Numbskull!' exploded Dad. 'Took one look at my ears and said there was nothing he could do, it was gout. 'Gout' I said, 'What do you mean, gout? Me? I'm never had as much as a bottle o' whisky all put together in my whole life!' I never heard such a lot o' fool's talk from a doctor afore, as I know on. So I put my cap on, an' walked out. An' to think as I shall get a bill for such a dollop o' foolery. I reckon as it were him as had been on the bottle. Gout! In my ears!'

However, the doctor's diagnosis proved correct. It was not long before Dad's ankles and wrists became so swollen, painful and stiff that he could not stand without support, or hold a cup of tea or his book. But the darkest days of all were still to come, when, after Christmas 1932, I left home to take up my first job. In spite of all my resolutions against it, I had been forced to seek a post as an uncertificated teacher. After several half-hearted applications, I was appointed to a primary school in Essex — untrained, unqualified, and completely lacking any shred of experience. It turned out well; that is all that I need to record here.

The school to which I had been appointed was in a temporary wooden building hastily erected to cater for those refugees from London's East End who had fled from the terrible conditions of the depression to shacks on the Essex marshes: in this particular instance, the marshes bordering the river Crouch. The temporary school still stands, and was still in use only a year or two ago. Indeed, it may still be in use, for all I know, though it now stands in the middle of that large new town called South Woodham Ferrers.

I suppose one is always at one's most selfish and thoughtless between the ages of eighteen and twenty-one. I know I was, I had been disappointed in my hopes for better things, but I was fatalistically hedonistic about it. I can understand now why both Gerald and Lois were somewhat bitter and jealous that a way of escape had opened for me though I was so much younger than they. I remember one day when Dad was 'mourning' about the coming separation, as the first of his brood prepared to leave the nest. He was hoping, aloud, that I should be all right.

'You needn't worry about Sybil,' Lois snapped. 'There'll always be some fool of a man at her beck and call — like there always has been.' And the glare she gave Dad made us all laugh, including her. Maybe just at that time I was Dad's favourite, but apart from that Lois sometimes showed her frustration by being awkward and sharp-tongued even with him.

So though half of me looked forward, half of me hung back. I knew only too well, what my

458

going would mean to Mam, and even more to Dad. Apart from missing me, and apart from worrying that I would cope and be happy, they also felt guilty that though they could not help it, they had failed me.

We made the most of that last Christmas at home, in spite of the gloom. Though another of Lois's suitors and Gerald's poor, neglected, patient, stand-by girlfriend were there with us, they were only extras. Much as time had changed us, we were still the same family bound firmly together by love and laughter that I had opened my eyes to on the day of my Awakening.

It had been arranged that on the second Sunday in January (1933) my previously rejected farmer suitor, who now had a new Austin 7, should take me to my new lodgings in Essex. Lois and her fiancé were to accompany me, and see me settled in. Mam, making a great physical effort, took out her feelings by planning the best valedictory luncheon she could devise. Gerald's gun had provided a splendid brace of pheasants. Mam turned them into a meal fit for a king, adding all the refinements that 'Ol' Eve', Gerald's girlfriend, called etceteraments (she shared our particular brand of humour). There were our own snowy potatoes: sprouts from another of our fields, just right after the first touch of frost on them: stuffing made of herbs from the garden, and bread sauce: apple pie from our own trees, with Mam's feather-light pastry and bowls of yellow Jersey cream, thick enough to cut with a knife, fresh that very morning from our special pedigree cow, Golden Fairy. That lunch was Mam's farewell offering, and I was aware that I should have to eat it even if it choked me, as I was afraid it might.

We were all trying to pretend it was just a normal Sunday morning, though we knew different. Before lunch my chauffeur and Lois's escort arrived. The morning seemed very long.

Dad sat in his chair with a book on his knee. I went and sat on the hearthrug at his feet, and ordered my tabby cat, Tigger, to roll over. I looked up to see if Dad was noticing Tigger's obedience, and saw the tears slipping silently down his handsome nose from under his Woolworth's spectacles. I hid my own tears by laying my face on Tigger's stripey belly, and drying them on his fur.

Lois set the table while the three men packed the car. We took our accustomed places, and Mam triumphantly bore in the dish containing the pheasants, surrounded by small, brown roast potatoes. She carved, as she always did, serving the visitors first. Lois dished out the vegetables and the etcerteraments.

'Do start' said Mam. 'I hate to see a good dinner get cold.' The visitors attacked their full plates at once. None of the five of us felt like eating a mouthful. Dad made the first attempt.

'Where's the gravy, Mam?' he asked.

Mam's face was a study. She had forgotten to make any. She jumped up, swollen knees and hands alike forgotten. 'It won't take me a jiffy' she said — and sure enough she was back with a brimming, steaming gravyboat in what seemed no time at all. The visitors ate stolidly on while we waited, and they refused the gravy when it was offered. So Mam passed on behind us, pouring liberally from the gravy boat onto each plate as she did so. We waited still till she sat down, and took her own first mouthful.

Then pandemonium broke loose as we all followed her example, spitting out, retching, 'cagging' and choking.

She had reached to the shelf above her head for the salt, but blinded by the tears she had been holding back all the morning, had taken down the wrong packet. Our rich dark gravy had been well salted with Persil soap-powder.

Well, it prevented us from having to try to swallow the food nobody wanted; and it was exactly the sort of silly incident that always caught us on the funny bone. Somebody began to giggle, and we laughed till we cried, with the two outsiders still stolidly eating and wondering what on earth we found to laugh at in a good dinner being spoilt. The sight of their puzzled but unsmiling faces only made us worse; luckily, neither of them was aware when the tears of laughter turned into those we had all been restraining all the morning. Gerald pushed his chair back and went out into the yard. I understood. 'Ol Eve' kissed me, and followed him. So that when the moment for me to leave came, there were only Mam and Dad to say goodbye to. They came to the front gate, and as the car drew away, they stood with their arms round each other, and Dad's tall head bent so that his cheek lay on the top of Mam's snow-white but still beautiful head.

And that, surely is the place for me to stop, suspended, as it were, between one life and another.

★   ★   ★

But I had not left the fens for good. I was home again to live four years later, to changed circumstances. Dad had agreed reluctantly to sell the farm (though not the house) in order to set up my brother and my brother-in-law in partnership in a highland farm. He was better in health, and so was Mam, but they were not as happy as they deserved to be. As one of Dad's friends had warned him 'a family partnership is no ship to set sail in.' ('Co-ship is no-ship' was the phrase used.)

Then the clouds of war began to gather, and burst over our heads, quite literally, at midnight between the 6th and 7th June 1940, when a lone Nazi airman opened his bomb doors above our patch of fenland, and gave us the distinction of receiving one of the very first salvoes of HE to be dropped in that war on English soil. As we had been welcomed into New Fen by a bomb from a Zeppelin, so those bombs were ultimately to be the cause of us all leaving there forever. Though not quite yet . . .

But when the blast of war blows in our
    ears . . .
Stiffen the sinews, summon up the blood,
And imitate the action of the tiger . . .

Mam and Dad had stiffened their sinews, in every way. Like every other region of Great Britain, our fen had summoned up its blood in the face of a new enemy, as it had always done in the past against the elements; and tough, red, fighting blood it was. As for imitating the action of the tiger, Shakespeare's injunction in our case was not really necessary. We could hardly imitate ourselves. Were we not 'tigers' already?

We do hope that you have enjoyed reading this large print book.

Did you know that all of our titles are available for purchase?

We publish a wide range of high quality large print books including:
**Romances, Mysteries, Classics
General Fiction
Non Fiction and Westerns**

Special interest titles available in large print are:
**The Little Oxford Dictionary
Music Book
Song Book
Hymn Book
Service Book**

Also available from us courtesy of Oxford University Press:
**Young Readers' Dictionary
(large print edition)
Young Readers' Thesaurus
(large print edition)**

For further information or a free brochure, please contact us at:
**Ulverscroft Large Print Books Ltd.,
The Green, Bradgate Road, Anstey,
Leicester, LE7 7FU, England.
Tel:** (00 44) 0116 236 4325
Fax: (00 44) 0116 234 0205

GRAND AFFAIR

Charlotte Bingham

Unaware of the misery that surrounded her birth, for the first four years of her life all Ottilie Cartaret knows is love. And when her mother, Ma O'Flaherty, moves her family to St Elcombe in Cornwall, their fortunes seem set fair. However, Ma tragically dies and Ottilie is adopted by the Cartarets, who run the Grand Hotel. The little girl grows up pampered and spoilt, not only by her adoptive parents but by all the visitors — with the exception of their mysterious annual guest, nicknamed 'Blue Lady'. But as times change and the regular vistors die off, only Ottilie can save the now-decaying hotel.

THE DEATH ZONE

Matt Dickinson

Ten expeditions were high on Everest, preparing for their summit push. They set out in perfect conditions on 10 May 1996. But twenty-four hours later, eight climbers were dead and a further three were to die, victims of one of the most devastating storms ever to hit the mountain. On the North Face, a British expedition found itself in the thick of the drama. Against all the odds, film-maker Matt Dickinson and professional climber Alan Hinkes managed to battle through hurricane-force winds to reach the summit. This is Matt Dickinson's extraordinary story of human triumph, folly and disaster.

STILL WATER

John Harvey

The naked body of a young woman is found floating in an inner-city canal. Not the first, nor the last. When another woman disappears, following a seminar on women and violence, everyone fears for her safety — especially those who know about her husband's controlling character. Is this a one-off domestic crime or part of a wider series of murders? What else has been simmering beneath this couple's apparently normal middle-class life? As Resnick explores deeper, he finds disturbing parallels between the couple he's investigating and his own evolving relationship with Hannah Campbell.

AN APRIL SHROUD

Reginald Hill

After seeing Inspector Pascoe off on his honeymoon, Superintendent Andy Dalziel runs into trouble on his own holiday. He accompanies his rescuers back to their rundown mansion, where he discovers that Lake House's owner, Bonnie Fielding, seems less troubled by her husband's tragic death than by the problem of completing the Banqueting Hall. Prompted not only by a professional curiosity — why would anyone want to keep a dead rat in a freezer? — but also by Mrs Fielding's ample charms, Dalziel stays on. By the time Pascoe reappears, there have been several more deaths . . .

TREVOR McDONALD FAVOURITE POEMS

Trevor McDonald

Trevor McDonald, popular newscaster and also Chairman of the Campaign for Better Use of the English Language, has now compiled an anthology of his favourite poetry from across the ages. The collection is based on material published in his regular Anthology column in the *Daily Telegraph*. It is a comprehensive introduction to the poetry of the English language, from Milton to Ted Hughes, from Britain and abroad. He has included both perennial favourites and less familiar but accessible poetry. Each poet is introduced with a concise history of their work and there is something to suit all tastes and moods.

E